FROM EDEN TO GOLGOTHA
Essays in Biblical Theology

SOUTH FLORIDA STUDIES IN THE HISTORY OF JUDAISM

Edited by
Jacob Neusner
William Scott Green, James Strange
Darrell J. Fasching, Sara Mandell

Number 52
From Eden to Golgotha
Essays in Biblical Theology

by
R. W. L. Moberly

FROM EDEN TO GOLGOTHA
Essays in Biblical Theology

by
R. W. L. Moberly

Scholars Press
Atlanta, Georgia

FROM EDEN TO GOLGOTHA
Essays in Biblical Theology

©1992
University of South Florida

Publication of this book was made possible by a grant from the Tisch Family Foundation, New York City. The University of South Florida acknowledges with thanks this important support for its scholarly projects.

Library of Congress Cataloging in Publication Data

Moberly, R. W. L.
    From Eden to Golgotha : essays in biblical theology / by R.W.L. Moberly.
    p. cm. — (South Florida studies in the history of Judaism ; no. 52)
    ISBN 1-55540-749-8 (alk. paper)
    1. Bible—Theology. I. Title. II. Series: South Florida studies in the history of Judaism ; 52.
BS543.M575 1992
230—dc20   92-32008
                                         CIP

Printed in the United States of America
on acid-free paper

To David

Friend, and companion at *The Seven Stars*

TABLE OF CONTENTS

REFERENCES

These essays, with the exception of the final one, have all appeared previously, in the following publications:

"Did the Serpent Get it Right?", *Journal of Theological Studies* 39 (1988), pp.1-27.

"Abraham's righteousness (Genesis 15:6)", J.A. Emerton (ed.), *Studies in the Pentateuch* (*Supplements to Vetus Testamentum* 41; Brill: Leiden, 1990), pp.103-130.

"The Earliest Commentary on the Akedah", *Vetus Testamentum* 38 (1988), pp.302-23.

"'Yahweh is One': The Translation of the Shema", in J.A. Emerton (ed.), *Studies in the Pentateuch* (*Supplements to Vetus Testamentum* 41; Brill: Leiden, 1990), pp.209-215.

"Proclaiming Christ Crucified: Some Reflections on the Use and Abuse of the Gospels", *Anvil* 5 (1988), pp.31-52.

"Story in the Old Testament", *Themelios* 11 (1986), pp.77-82.

"Political Wellbeing in a Biblical Perspective", *Studies in Christian Ethics* 3 (1990), pp.14-29.

"'Old Testament' and 'New Testament': The Propriety of the Terms for Christian Theology", *Theology* 95 (1992), pp.26-32.

All these essays have been reused with permission. They have also all been slightly modified.

INTRODUCTION

These essays have been brought together with a number of purposes in mind, within the context of a basic concern to explore something of the depth and vitality of the Jewish scriptures and of the Jewish and Christian religious traditions that have grown out of them.

My stance in writing is explicitly that of a Christian theologian, and I am aware that a number of objections may be raised to such a stance. One is the general point that a Christian hermeneutical stance may make one a bad exegete, unable to discern or do justice to the subtle nuances of meaning present in the biblical text. In the first five essays I have tried to show that this need not be so. Another more specific point is that the Christian interpreter may not do justice to Jewish perspectives, both in the text itself and in the history of interpretation. I have sought to show that this too need not be so, primarily in ch.2 but also in ch.3 where the interpretation of Abraham's obedience at Moriah is, I think, as congenial to a Jewish perspective as I believe it to be to a Christian perspective.

One frequently exasperating aspect of contemporary biblical study is the common polarization between "liberals" and "conservatives" (not to mention "fundamentalists"). One of the fundamental issues at stake, it seems to me, is the question of what constitutes truth in a narrative text. A recurrent assumption among conservative scholars is that a narrative text must be historically accurate as a necessary condition of its truth. The value of including two essays addressing this issue was suggested to me by a recent reading of the overview of the Bible from the perspective of an (avowedly atheist) ancient historian, Robin Lane Fox's, *The Unauthorized Version: Truth and Fiction in the Bible* (Viking: 1991). For here a narrow understanding of narrative truth in terms of historicity is more or less consistently applied. With a splendid begging of the questions of precise literary genre and of the nature of truth Lane Fox writes:

> "They [the Gospels] are historical works, in intention, because they aim to give the true actions and sayings of a historical person during phases of his biography; they are distinct from historical romance, because their authors believe that they are telling the truth. They have a religious aim (the fourth is written 'so that we may believe and have eternal life'), but their status as 'good news' Gospels does not override their historical aspiration: if Jesus does not do what they describe, meet the people whom they mention or do the basic actions which they interpret, then they are false" (p.203).

One is hardly surprised, then, when the Chronicler is dismissed as a "splendid liar" (p.196), the opening chapters of Genesis are "totally untrue" (p.26), or when the hermeneutics of inner-biblical interpretation is described as "constructive abuse" of the text (p.24). For the most part, the only truth which the biblical stories contain is the truth that their authors believed certain (mistaken) things about God. Such an approach is not only sadly retrograde in itself, but is liable to provoke responses from conservative Christians couched in the same categories of argument as Lane Fox himself has used. In chs.5 and 6 I have tried to address such conservative Christians and suggest that there may be a better way ahead.

Finally, I have discussed basic questions of method and purpose in biblical theology in chs.7-9, which represent preliminary attempts to reformulate the nature of the enterprise. I am conscious of having done little more than sketch a few outlines, but I hope they may nonetheless contribute to the debate as to what constitutes a responsible Christian appropriation of the Bible as scripture in a modern Western context.

I am deeply grateful to Prof. J. Neusner for his encouragement with regard to these essays and for the opportunity to publish them together in book form in a series that he edits.

DID THE SERPENT GET IT RIGHT?

No story from the Old Testament has had a greater impact upon the theology of the Christian Church and the art and literature of Western civilization than the story of "man's first disobedience" in Genesis 3. The modern interpreter of this story, therefore, cannot but be aware of the great interpreters who have gone before, and may well wonder whether there is anything worth saying that has not already been said. Nonetheless the fact is that the story continues to excite interest in a wide variety of ways, be it in popular debates about science and the Bible, the perennial debate about the origins and nature of evil, new approaches in the light of feminist or ecological perspectives, or simply the intrinsic fascination of the story in itself. Indeed, such is the profound and suggestive nature of the story that it would be in principle impossible for any one definitive interpretation to be produced. Some interpretations, however, are better than others, and it is my conviction that certain important aspects of the story have been neglected in many modern studies that has prompted me to produce my own attempt to shed fresh light upon the ancient text.[1]

I

Before starting, three preliminary points. First, I do not propose to discuss the classification of the story as myth, saga, folktale, or whatever. This is partly because these terms have been used in such a diversity of ways that they lack precise content unless carefully explained, and partly because I do not think that the Genesis material lends itself to any precise classification. Rather, I believe it will be more helpful simply to establish a correct general perspective on the story. This means recognizing that while the story is set in the context of the beginnings of human history, it is not actually told from that perspective but from the perspective of Hebrew life in the historical context of ancient Israel. This emerges most clearly through reflection upon the fact that the story is told in the mature language of classical Hebrew and embodies the developed concepts of classical Hebrew theology. Language is a social and cultural phenomenon which cannot exist in isolation, nor can there be reflective theological thinking without an appropriate language to express it. Classical

---

[1] I am grateful to my friends and colleagues, D. Day, A. Gelston, C. T. R. Hayward, and G. J. Wenham for their helpful comments on a draft of this paper. The approach in this paper is in terms of a conventional historically orientated literary criticism. Those who are interested in how Gen. 2-3 might be understood in terms of structuralist perspectives should refer to *Semeia* xviii (1980), all of whose articles are devoted to this topic.

Hebrew language and theology therefore presuppose developed Hebrew culture. Such culture could not have existed in the story's own context, which is far removed from the Hebrew world of ancient Israel in both space and time.[2] This has at least two implications. First, the story will of necessity illuminate essentially the cultural context within which it was written, rather than the primeval context in which it is set. Secondly, it will mean that it is appropriate to interpret the story in the light of a discriminating use of the rest of the Old Testament, as at least some of the rest of the Old Testament is presupposed by the story.

Secondly, my concern is to read the text as far as possible as a coherent literary unity, in the belief that the meaning of most great stories can be grasped much more through close attention to the text as it is, than through possible reconstructions of how, when, and where the text came to be. This is, however, no easy undertaking with a text such as Gen. 3 which gives the impression of standing at the end point of a long and diverse history of reflection upon the issues and motifs that are central to it, and which may in certain respects only be explicable in the light of educated guesses as to what this history may have involved. Most obviously, for example, the tree of life, which is referred to in the introduction and conclusion (Gen. 2:9, 3:22,24) but is entirely absent in the main action of the story, gives the impression of being an interpretation of what is entailed by human obedience and disobedience to God that has been joined to the tradition yet not fully integrated into it.[3] Moreover, the reference to the naming of Eve (3:20) gives the impression of sitting a little awkwardly in its present context.[4] This means that any literary reading can explain only some and not all features of the text. Nonetheless, while such difficulties must be recognized, I believe it is important to maintain the principle that any great work of literary art, such as Gen. 3, has its own integrity and meaning, which must be respected; and that the integrity of the whole will transform and transcend the meaning of the possibly once-independent elements that have been incorporated into it.

---

[2] Before the advent of a critical historical awareness, it was naturally assumed by many that Hebrew was the original language of mankind. This was based on the combination of Gen. 2:23 (Adam making a play on the Hebrew words for man and woman) and Gen. 11:1 (only one language before Babel). See, for example, Rashi's comments on these verses (A. M. Silbermann [ed.], *Pentateuch with Rashi's Commentary* [Silbermann/ Routledge & Kegan Paul: Jerusalem, 1973], pp. 12, 14). For a similar Christian understanding in ancient and medieval times, see, for example, J. N. D. Kelly, *Jerome* (Duckworth: London, 1975), p. 154 and n. 7; B. Smalley, *The Study of the Bible in the Middle Ages* (University of Notre Dame Press: Indiana, 1952, 1964), p. 362.
[3] This is more fully discussed below, n.39.
[4] For further possible indications of the internal history of the narrative, see G. von Rad, *Genesis* (London: SCM, 1972: ET from German), pp. 98f; C. Westermann, *Genesis 1-11* (Minneapolis & London: Augsburg/SPCK, 1984: ET from German), pp. 186-96.

Thirdly, the primary object of this exercise is to read the story as a piece of ancient Hebrew literature in its ancient Hebrew context, which will require the exercise of both historical knowledge and historical imagination. However, the reason I am interested in the story is not simply the fact that it is a famous piece of ancient literature, but because I reverence it as part of holy scripture. This has at least three implications. First, it means that I, like many other commentators, interpret the story with at least half an eye on the hermeneutical question of its value and meaning for the believer today. This adds to the interest of the study - but it also carries the danger of reading into the story what one wants to read out from it. Secondly, it means that I regard it as important to escape from the notion that a story such as Gen. 3 has only one meaning. Meaning is determined by context, and the meaning of the story will naturally vary according as it is read within its ancient Hebrew context or within a Christian or Jewish context, and each of these three contexts is itself complex and variegated. All valid interpretations should surely in some way stand in continuity with the likely original meaning of the text, but their validity is determined by the way they genuinely utilize and illuminate aspects of the text in the light of their own general theological framework, rather than by any straightforward correspondence to the supposed original meaning. Thirdly, I consider it important to take seriously the history of interpretation of the story within both Christian and Jewish contexts where it has always been read as scripture. For a modern Western Christian this means that one cannot avoid some engagement with the question of whether the classic interpretation of the story in terms of "The Fall" is a valid reading of the text, even though in an essay such as this one can only deal with the larger issues in the briefest of ways.

II

The story of Gen. 3 must first be set within its immediate context of the narrative from Gen. 2:4 onwards. YHWH God creates a man and puts him in a garden in Eden, a garden whose trees are of particular significance (2:9). It is instructions with regard to these trees in 2:15-17 that set the scene for chap. 3, and so it is here that the detailed study must begin.

God gives the man a position of responsibility in the garden (v.15; a role not dissimilar to that specified more generally in Gen. 1:26-8). Within this setting the man is given a command (v.16) and a prohibition (v.17). There are several points of significance in this. First, the command, which although grammatically a command ("You shall eat") should no doubt be rendered permissively ("You may eat"), is remarkable for the freedom it gives; an emphatic verbal form is used (RSV "You may freely eat": Heb. *'akol to'kel*), and the range of options given is as wide as it could be ("every tree", "all the trees": *mikkol 'es*). Secondly, within this wide-ranging permission, there is one prohibition, expressed in the emphatic form (*lo'* rather than *'al*) as in the Decalogue. What exactly is meant by the "knowledge of good and evil" which is prohibited is not made explicit in the text, and need not, I suggest, be an issue at this point.[5] In the context of the story it is the fact of prohibition, rather than the content of what is prohibited, that assumes central importance. Thirdly, the penalty for doing what is prohibited is death. The emphatic verbal form used ("You shall surely die": *mot tamut*) is similar to the standard idiom for the death penalty in a legal context,[6] and the identical expression is used elsewhere in a variety of contexts, usually with the imminent demise of the addressee in view.[7] God's words therefore naturally mean an imminent termination of the man's life if the prohibition is disobeyed. Fourthly, it is important to note that no reason is given by God either for his command or for his prohibition. There is no attempt at justification, such as "It will be good/bad for you" (unlike the immediately following creation of woman which is introduced by "It is not good for the man to be alone"). Nonetheless, the story clearly assumes and implies that both the command and the prohibition are for the man's good. YHWH God who has made the man and the garden knows what is best for them, so that obedience to his words is entirely natural and proper. Fifthly, it is also important to note that the command and the prohibition are the *first* words of God to the man,[8] and so presumably are of fundamental importance for the relationship between them.

In the light of these detailed points one can see that the situation in 2:15-17 is surely an exact depiction of the general Old Testament understanding of humanity, especially Hebrew humanity,[9] in the world. Humankind is given the dignity of a responsible role to fulfil, and it is to be fulfilled through obedience

---

[5] For discussion, see below. p.21.

[6] E.g. Exod. 21:15-17, Lev. 20:9-16, cf. Gen. 26:11, Exod. 19:12. In these legal contexts the verb is invariably Hophal, *mot yumat*, with the literal sense "be put to death".

[7] E.g. Gen. 20:7, 1 Sam. 14:39,44, 22:16, 1 Kgs. 2:37,42, 2 Kgs. 1:4,6,16, Jer. 26:8. In all these instances the verb is Qal. On the difference between the Qal and the Hophal, F. Delitzsch comments, "Hence it is said *tamut* [Qal], not *tumat* [Hophal] - death will not be a judicial execution, but a consequence involved in the nature of the transgression" (*A New Commentary on Genesis* i [Edinburgh: T. & T. Clark, 1888: ET from German], p. 139).

[8] If one reads Gen. 2-3 independently of Gen.1, then the words of 2:16-17 have the same sort of significance as 1:26-8 as a general commission of God to humanity. If one reads Gen. 2-3 in its canonical position, then 2:16-17 is the first direct, personal address by God to humanity, in contrast to the blessing of 1:28 which is generalized and lacks the more intimate and specific setting of Gen. 2-3.

[9] It is likely that the distinctive situation of Israel should be seen as the presupposition underlying Gen. 2-3 as a whole; cf. K. Barth, *Church Dogmatics* III:1 (Edinburgh: T. & T. Clark, 1958. ET from German), pp. 240,267f,273.

to God's torah, his laws given for the guidance of life.[10] Obedience is not automatic, for the possibility of life or death confronts people, and they must choose obedience if they are to live and avoid death. However, obedience is not seen as repressive or restrictive. Rather it lies at the very heart of Hebrew religion that freedom necessarily recognizes limits, limits which are specified in Torah, and which are good for humanity because they are God-given. It is this context of certain basic principles of Hebrew theology and ethics which, I suggest, sets the scene for chap. 3.

Before we come to the main narrative there is the intervening paragraph concerning the creation of animals and of woman. At present we may simply note that this is integrated into the story as a whole, as it is one of the animals here created together with the woman who take centre stage as the story continues, and the concluding note about the nakedness of the man and the woman likewise sets the scene for what follows.

The story continues with the introduction of the serpent, who is said to be cunning to an exceptional degree and is one of the creatures made by God. The significance of this characterization we will return to later. At present it will be appropriate to pass on swiftly with the narrator to the content of the serpent's words to the woman.

First, it is unclear whether the serpent's words are a statement ("God has forbidden") or a question ("Has God forbidden?"). As the Hebrew stands it is more naturally a statement, but the rendering as a question is more subtle and does no violence to Hebrew idiom,[11] and is, moreover, widely supported by the ancient versions and by the great majority of commentators both ancient and modern.[12] The rendering as a question is therefore preferable, although either way the general import of the serpent's words is not greatly affected. Secondly, the serpent's words are introduced by the idiomatic phrase *'ap ki* which is a common Hebrew expression of emphasis even though there is no exact parallel

---

[10] There might possibly be significance in the writer's choice of the verb *şiwwah* in 2:16. Cassuto comments, "This is the first time that the verb to *command* appears in the Torah...serving as a symbol of, and introduction to, similar injunctions that were to be given to Israel in the future" (*Commentary on Genesis* i [Jerusalem: Magnes Press, 1961. ET from Hebrew], p. 124).

Likewise, there might possibly be significance in the fact that both the command and the prohibition concern food. This could be taken as suggestive of Israel's dietary laws, observance of which is a mark of Israel's unique relationship with YHWH (cf. Lev. 11:43-5, 20:22-6).

[11] It would be unnecessary to adopt the suggestion in *BHS* that an initial interrogative particle *(h)* has been lost, presumably through haplography with the end of the previous word *ha'iššah*; cf. *GK* 150a.

[12] For a denial that 3:1 is a question, see E. A. Speiser, *Genesis* (Garden City, New York: Doubleday, 1964), p. 23; J. Walsh, "Genesis 2: 4b-3: 24: A Synchronic Approach", *JBL* xcvi (1977), p. 164.

to its introductory usage here. It is important to maintain the emphasis by a rendering such as "Has God really said?" or "Is it true that God has said?".

Next, we see that the serpent neatly reverses what God had previously said. God's words had emphasized freedom - the man could eat of every tree with only one prohibited. The serpent makes the prohibition universal. Instead of "You may certainly eat from every tree of the garden" we have "You shall not eat from any tree of the garden" attributed to God. Why should the serpent say something which, as the woman duly points out, is clearly not the case? Apart from the fact that the serpent thereby engages the woman in debate, the main point lies presumably in the *implication* of the serpent's words. What matters is not that the serpent's words are obviously false, but that they imply that a total prohibition is the sort of unreasonable prohibition that one might expect from God, who is to be seen as more interested in restriction than in freedom. Such an innuendo is not dismissed simply by pointing out the obvious inaccuracy of the serpent's words.

Finally, it may be significant that the serpent uses the bare term "God" (*'elohim*) rather than "YHWH God" as is universally used in the surrounding narrative (with the sole exception of the woman's response, which adopts the serpent's wording, and the serpent's further words in verse 5). The use of the personal name of God, YHWH, could be seen as implying something of God's caring relationship to his people. If the serpent is implying that God is uncaring, the omission of God's personal name is a natural corollary.

The woman's response to the serpent reaffirms God's permission to the humans to eat, but is worded differently. The verb, simply "we may eat" (*no'kel*), lacks the emphatic form of God's original permission (*'akol to'kel*), there is no reference to "every" (*kol*) tree, and the death sentence, "in the day that you eat of it you shall surely die", becomes simply "lest you die". Apart from this consistent weakening of God's words, the woman also increases the scope of God's prohibition by adding "nor touch it". It is difficult to decide how much significance is to be attributed to such variations. They could be simply a stylistic variation of purely literary significance.[13] Traditional Jewish commentators, however, have usually seen significance in terms of the principle of Deut. 4:2, Prov. 30:6 of neither adding to nor subtracting from God's word,[14] and I would judge that such an intuition is probably correct. It is not difficult to see the woman's answer as showing some uncertainty and lack of confidence in what God had said - hence her saying both less and more - and to connect this

---

[13] Some of the ancient versions tend to assimilate the woman's wording in 3:2 to the wording of God's command in 2:16 (see *BHS*), which suggests that the translators were not aware of any particular significance here.

[14] See *Bereishis: Genesis/ A New Translation with a Commentary Anthologized from Talmudic, Midrashic and Rabbinic Sources,* vol. 1, Artscroll Tanach Series (Mesorah Publications: New York, 1977), pp. 116 f.

with the negative suggestion about God's character in the serpent's opening words.

The serpent now replies and comes straight to the point. First, he flatly denies the explicit warning of God. God had said they would die, the serpent says they would not die.[15] Secondly, the serpent says that the result of eating will be positive, not negative: (a) their eyes will be opened, an expression which elsewhere in the Old Testament has positive connotations of a new God-given quality of perception (e.g. Gen. 21:19, 2 Kgs. 6:17,20); (b) they will be like God[16] who knows good and evil,[17] and this too picks up one of the positive fundamentals of Old Testament faith, that human nature finds its fulfilment in the imitation of God (so e.g. Gen. 1:26-8, Lev. 19:2).[18] So the serpent is offering a prospect that is in principle entirely good and desirable.

Thirdly, the serpent implicitly attributes a base motive to God for making the prohibition in the first place. The clear implication is that God acted out of fear and envy. Thus the silence about the motivation of the prohibition in 2:17, which in that context was presumed to be for the man's good, is given an entirely different slant by the serpent - repression, not benefit, was the reason. It will naturally follow from this that if an unworthy motive underlies the prohibition, then there will be little wrong in disobeying it. It is noteworthy that the serpent never tells the woman to transgress God's prohibition. He simply calls into question both God's truthfulness (by denying his warning) and God's trustworthiness (by impugning his motives) and leaves the woman to draw her own conclusions.

The woman does draw her own conclusions. She looks at the forbidden tree and can only see that it looks good. It appeals to her physical senses ("good to eat", "delight to the eyes"), and, moreover, it appears to promise positive enhancement of life ("to be desired to make one wise"). She can see nothing wrong, only something attractive and promising. So she takes and eats its fruit and her husband does likewise. Thus they disobey God's prohibition.

And what is the result of this disobedience? In the light of God's original warning of death the reader would naturally expect punishment to come in one

---

[15] The unusual syntax of the serpent's words, *lo' mot temutun* rather than *mot lo' temutun* is probably to be explained by the explicit recollection of the earlier words of God; cf. *GK* 113v.

[16] The term *'elohim* could also mean "gods", i.e. divine beings such as the members of YHWH's heavenly court (cf. Gen. 3:22; 1 Kgs. 22:19-23; Job 1:6, 2:1), but in context a challenge to God himself seems more likely.

[17] The phrase "knowing good and evil" could be in grammatical agreement with "you", i.e. the man and the woman, as well as with "God", but the difference is only a matter of emphasis .

[18] For a fascinating exposition of this important aspect of traditional Jewish theology, see M. Buber, "Imitatio Dei" in his *Mamre: Essays in Religion* (Melbourne & London: Melbourne University Press, 1946), pp. 32-43.

of two ways. Either the tree would be deadly in itself and have a poisonous effect, or some penalty such as fire from heaven or the earth swallowing them up would be inflicted. In fact neither of these happens. The divine death sentence is not - apparently - executed. On the contrary, things turn out as the serpent said they would. Not only do the man and woman not die, as he said, but also their eyes are indeed opened, as he said. And later in the story God confirms that the man has indeed become godlike, knowing good and evil (3:22), as the serpent said. Everything happens exactly as the serpent had said.

Nor, moreover, is there anything obviously bad in the new kind of vision that the man and woman now possess. Clearly the fact of their nakedness, which their eyes had looked on before (cf. 2:25), is now perceived in a new way, but their making loincloths for themselves need not be read as an action of sudden shame and confusion in any negative sense. We do not have to find here the fear subsequently engendered by the approach of God (3:10). The Hebrews had a deep instinctive dislike of nakedness.[19] The writer needed to add "they were not ashamed" in 2:25 to make clear that the nakedness of the man and woman was not something negative as the reader would naturally interpret it. Since the dislike of nakedness is never considered something negative or sinful elsewhere in the Old Testament,[20] the natural Hebrew assessment of 3:7 would surely be to regard the making of loincloths as something positive. As soon as the man and woman consciously realized their nakedness, they met the first situation of need they were confronted with in a constructive way. Their life does indeed appear to have been enriched.

III

Before going any further in the story, we must pause to reflect on what we have just read. The whole story thus far has revolved around God's prohibition and the serpent's enticement to transgress it. God had said categorically that the

---

[19] Public exposure, particularly of one's private parts, was a matter of deep shame and distress (Gen. 9:21-3; Exod. 20:26; 2 Sam. 6:20; Ezek. 16:37; Lam. 1:8), and the practice of stripping one's defeated enemy was a vivid symbol of his total humiliation (Isa. 20:2-4, 47:2f; 2 Sam. 10:4; 2 Chron. 28: 15; Mic. 1:11). Consequently, nakedness also symbolized poverty and powerlessness (1sa. 58:7; Hos. 2:3 [Heb.5]; Job 1:21, 22:6, 24:7,10) and the provision of clothing symbolized care on the part of the giver and security for the recipient (Ezek. 16:6-14; Hos. 2:9 [Heb.11]; Gen. 3: 21).

One can see a similar outlook in the New Testament also in passages such as Matt. 6:30; 2 Cor. 5:3.

[20] It is notable that even YHWH's heavenly attendants, the seraphim, cover their private parts (Isa. 6:2 - following the customary interpretation of "feet" as a euphemism for genitals, cf. Exod. 4:25; Judg. 3:24; 1 Sam. 24:3 [Heb.4]). Their action is part of a natural and proper reverence in the presence of God, without the slightest implication of guilt or fear.

man and the woman would die,[21] and the serpent had said equally categorically that they would not die. And apparently the serpent was right, since they did not die. Moreover, God had at least implied that fullness of life came from obedience to him. The serpent had explicitly said that disobedience would bring enhancement. And again, apparently the serpent was right. How is one to account for this? Did God subsequently change his mind? Or was he simply wrong? The fact that apparently the serpent and not God spoke the truth is, I suggest, the central issue that the story raises. The crux for the interpreter must surely be the resolution of this remarkable anomaly, and the interpretation of the rest of the story will depend upon the decision made here.

It is precisely here that many modern commentators seem to me unsatisfactory in their treatment. Westermann, for example, says, "One must agree then with H. Gunkel and many others: 'This threat is not fulfilled subsequently: they do not die immediately; this fact is not to be explained away, but simply acknowledged.' Gunkel says that our difficulty with this was not felt so strongly by the ancient narrator, who would reply that God is and remains master of what he says. One must agree."[22] But must one in fact agree? At the very least such a claim about the standards of the ancient writer should be justified and not merely asserted; and while the text certainly should not be explained away, it does still need to be explained, and a recognition of the problem is not an explanation.[23] Westermann himself concludes that the non-fulfilment of God's words is in fact essential to the narrative on the grounds that "it shows that God's dealing with his creatures cannot be pinned down, not even by what God has said previously. And so even God's acts and words are open to misinterpretation and the serpent makes use of this."[24] But to say that God's dealings "cannot be pinned down" and are "open to misinterpretation" in no way meets the problem the text poses of God's words being positively false and misleading.[25] The problem should not be watered down. Rather, it needs to

---

[21] The original prohibition was, of course, addressed to the man alone, but the woman is naturally presumed to be included in it as soon as she joins the man - thus the plural verbs in 3:1-5.

[22] *Genesis*, p.225.

[23] Gunkel himself does no more than cite Gen. 20:3 as a parallel situation in which God threatens Abimelech with death but then mercifully allows him to live (*Genesis* [Göttingen: Vandenhoeck & Ruprecht, 1922], p.10). This is, however, no true parallel, as not only does God insist that Abimelech first make an act of restitution (which would be the equivalent of repentance, though the text recognizes that repentance as such was not called for [20:5,6]), but also God requires that Abraham should pray for Abimelech (20:7). Thus the story is closely conformed to the theological norms that we find elsewhere in the Old Testament, as outlined below.

[24] *Ibid.*, p.225.

[25] This was already an issue in the second century AD when Irenaeus (*Against Heresies,* 5:23) responded to gnostics who concluded that the Creator had been left powerless in the

be faced and assessed in the light of the Old Testament's own standards of divine consistency. Since much depends on whether or not the non-fulfilment of God's words would have been a genuine issue for the ancient writer, it is this that must be examined.

The idea that God could apparently change his mind is not, of course, alien to Hebrew theology. On the contrary, there are many famous instances of God "repenting",[26] and not doing what he had said he would do.[27] It should be noted, however, that God's words have this conditional quality because of their moral and relational nature. What God says is designed to elicit a response of obedience from people, and it is the nature of people's response that determines how God will act towards them. This is the principle which is stated with regard to the individual in Ezek. 33:13-16, and which is classically enunciated in corporate terms in Jeremiah 18:7-10:

> If at any time I declare concerning a nation or a kingdom, that I will pluck up and break down and destroy it, and if that nation, concerning which I have spoken, turns from its evil, I will repent of the evil that I intended to do to it. And if at any time I declare concerning a nation or a kingdom that I will build and plant it, and if it does evil in my sight, not listening to my voice, then I will repent of the good which I had intended to do to it.

This principle is faithfully adhered to in every narrative which speaks of God repenting, with the addition of the other factor that the prayer of the faithful, as well as the repentance of the unfaithful, can move God to modify his actions.[28]

---

face of Wisdom, which spoke through the Serpent. For a discussion of Irenaeus' response and exegetical suggestions, see A. Orbe, "Cinco exegeses ireneanas de Gen. 2, 17b adv. haer. V, 23, 1-2", *Gregorianum,* lxii (1981), pp. 75-113 (conveniently summarized in *OT Abstracts,* 4:3 (1981), p.222).

[26] This traditional rendering is not entirely satisfactory, as "repent" in modern English has moral overtones which are out of place with reference to God. But no alternative word or expression, such as "regret", "relent", or "change one's mind" has the same flexibility of usage in English as "repent", and so for convenience, though with reservations, the traditional term will be retained here.

[27] This important topic has received relatively little attention in modern Old Testament scholarship. For a recent discussion, see T. E. Fretheim, "Divine Foreknowledge, Divine Constancy, and the Rejection of Saul's Kingship", *CBQ* xlvii (1985), pp.595-602. Fretheim also provides a bibliography on the topic, p. 596 n.3.

[28] The one apparent exception, as far as I am aware, is 2 Sam. 24:16 where YHWH "repented of the evil" without being moved by either repentance or prayer. Perhaps the writer/editor is thereby making a point about the unique theological significance of Zion. Even here, however, one must presumably assume that David in v.17 was unaware of the divine decision in v.16. His confession of sin (v.17) is prompted by his seeing the angel

Thus, for example, the sinfulness of humanity (Gen. 6:5-7), the sin of the sons of Eli (I Sam. 2:17,30), and the disobedience of Saul (I Sam. 15:11,23,26) all lead to God bringing disaster instead of the promised blessing. Conversely, the repentance of the men of Nineveh (Jonah 3:7-10), Hezekiah's fear of God and prayer (Jer. 26:18-19), the prayer of Moses (Exod. 32:11-14), and the prayer of Amos (Amos 7:1-3,4-6) all avert the judgement God had pronounced and secure his mercy.

Such frequent language about divine repentance is a natural corollary of the profound Hebrew understanding of God's relationship with humanity as a genuine relationship, which involves and commits God as much as it involves and commits people. Moreover, a relationship between a moral God and varyingly obedient and disobedient humanity will necessarily involve paradoxes which Hebrew theology does not shrink from expressing in bold anthropomorphisms.

The Old Testament does, however, recognize certain important limits upon its language about divine repentance. First, it is notable that usually the word for God repenting (*niḥam*) is not the word used for human repentance (*šub*). This difference is regularly observed, and the words can be explicitly juxtaposed - when people repent (*šub*), God repents (*niḥam*) (Jer. 18:8; Jonah 3:10).[29] The practice of using a different word for God's repentance as opposed to human repentance makes clear that any analogy between them is only partial. Presumably the main point that is being safegbarded is the moral point that God does not need to turn from evil as people do. It is the dynamics of varying human response, not any struggle of his own with evil, that cause God to "repent".

Secondly, there are two passages which deny that God does repent (Num. 23:19; I Sam. 15:29). It is clear that neither of these is denying the point already established about God's doings varying according to people's response, but are rather making the different point that God is never untruthful but always stands by what he has said. For in each passage the statement that God does not repent is parallel to the fact that he does not lie (*lo' 'iš 'el wikazzeb*, Num. 23: 19; *lo'*

---

smiting the people (v.15), not by seeing the angel stay his hand (v.16); and the following narrative (vv. 21,25) links the averting of the plague with David's repentance and sacrifice. Although, therefore, the text lays emphasis upon God's initiative in showing mercy, the overall theology of the passage is not significantly different from that elsewhere.

[29] The distinction between *niḥam* and *šub* is not absolute. For *niḥam* can be used of people, sometimes in the sense of changing one's mind or having compassion (Exod. 13:17; Judg. 21:6,15) and sometimes in the sense of moral repentance (Jer. 8:6, 31:19; Job 42:6), and *šub* can be used of YHWH (Jer. 4:28; Joel 2:14//Jonah 3:9; Ps. 90:13). When, however, *šub* is used of YHWH the sense is never that of moral repentance, but rather of responding flexibly to a situation in the sense indicated by *niḥam*.

yeŝaqqer, I Sam. 15:29), and in each passage the issue is God's faithfulness to his word (see esp. Num. 23:19b), in the one case God's irrevocable blessing upon Israel (Num. 23:20-24), and in the other case his rejection of Saul which is the counterpart to his choice of David (I Sam. 15:28). That is, God's choice of Israel and the house of David are at stake, and it is impossible that in his purposes of redemption God should ever go back on his word.

It is worth noting that this sense of God not repenting in the sense of being false to his word is fundamental to Old Testament faith, and is not called in question by events apparently contradicting his word. God's apparent failure to honour his promises to Israel and the house of David is explicitly addressed in two of the most moving lament psalms (Pss. 44 and 89), neither of which ends with any word of hope or any resolution of the contradiction between what God has promised and what is actually happening. Nonetheless, it is important that neither psalm therefore questions the truth of God's promise; the promise is affirmed, as are the events which go against it, and the psalmist's only solution is to cast himself upon God's steadfast love (*ḥesed,* Ps. 44:26 [Heb.27], 89:49 [Heb.50]). Whatever the anguish of conflict between faith and circumstances, the possibility that God should prove false to his word is not seriously entertained.

It is in the light of this consistent Old Testament understanding of the ways in which God does and does not repent that Gen. 3 must be read. While the Genesis writer would no doubt entirely accept Gunkel's point "that God is and remains master of what he says", we have seen no evidence to suppose that he would draw Gunkel's corollary that God's sovereignty is ultimately arbitrary. On the contrary, the strong likelihood is that he shared with other Old Testament writers the conviction that God's sovereign freedom of action is always accompanied by a fundamental consistency of moral and redemptive purpose. It then becomes clear that human disobedience to God's explicit prohibition, as in Gen. 3, is not the kind of human response that could ever modify a word of judgement or lead God to repent of what he had said, even though some such divine repentance has often been suggested by commentators both medieval and modern.[30] Rather, if God did not execute his death sentence upon the man and the woman, then he would be guilty of repentance in the sense of proving false to his word. Is this conceivable in Gen. 3, when not only is the context set in Gen. 2:15-17 that of some of the basic theological and ethical assumptions of the Old Testament, but also the setting of the story in its context at the beginning

---

[30] So, for example, Ibn Ezra, who significantly postulates that Adam must have repented first (*Bereishis,* p.103). J. H. Hertz comments that "in view of all the circumstances of the temptation, the All-merciful God mercifully modified the penalty, and they did not die on the day of their sin" (*The Pentateuch and Haftorahs I: Genesis* (London: OUP, 1929), p.21; cf. J. Skinner, *Genesis* (Edinburgh: T. & T. Clark, 1912), p.67. It is, however, difficult to see what the mitigating circumstances might be.

of Genesis - these were the first words of God personally addressed to humanity - makes it in some sense normative for the Old Testament as a whole?[31]

Furthermore, there is the question of whether it is conceivable not just that God could be wrong but that the serpent could be right. How is the reader expected to respond to the serpent? It is unnecessary here to explore the symbolic significance of the serpent in the ancient Near East generally, as two simple considerations will suffice for our purposes. First, elsewhere in the Old Testament, with the one notable exception of the brazen serpent made by Moses (Num. 21:4-9), the serpent consistently represents hostility and threat to humanity,[32] so much so that it will be one of the notable marks of a transformed world when this is no longer the case (Isa. 11:8). Secondly, this general Hebrew attitude is shared by the Genesis writer. For even though from the perspective of the story the enmity between mankind and the serpent still lies in the future (3:15), from the perspective of the writer and his readers such enmity is already an established fact. It is inevitable, therefore, that the known fact of enmity should colour the reader's response to the initial appearance of the serpent in the story. When one adds to this the obvious point that the serpent in Gen. 3 is deliberately undermining human obedience to God, there are clearly no grounds for the reader to regard the serpent as anything but a natural enemy. The conclusion that follows from this is that it is surely inconceivable that the Genesis writer could have allowed that in the situation of Gen. 3 the serpent could be right and God could be wrong.

IV

How then are we to understand the text? I suggest that there is only one avenue of interpretation open to us, namely that God's death sentence was indeed carried out, but in some way other than the obvious and straightforward way that his words initially implied. If we look again at the wording of his warning ("In the day that you eat of it you shall surely die") there are two elements which can without difficulty lend themselves to non-literal interpretation - "day" and "die"; and indeed numerous non-literal interpretations of each have often been proposed.

First, day. One ancient approach, for example, has been to appeal to Ps. 90:4 (and 2 Pet. 3:8) and so interpret "day" as a "day of God", that is, 1,000 years, that being the period during which Adam did die (after 930 years, Gen.

---

[31] Admittedly Israel could live with the apparent non-fulfilment of divine promises, as noted above, but that was hardly considered normative; and it is hard to escape the impression that Gen 2-3 is intended as a normative portrayal of God's dealings with humanity.

[32] See, for example, Gen. 49:17, Exod. 4:3, Isa. 14:29, 27:1, Jer. 8:17, Amos 9:3.

5:5).[33] Such a suggestion, however, is not only wholly implausible in context but is also simply unnecessary for b^eyom (lit. "in day") is in fact a common Hebrew idiom for "when".[34] Thus the question whether "day" is literal or not is beside the point.[35] This means that we must focus on "die" as the crucial term, and this anyway is what the text requires, for death was the substance of God's warning, and it was this that was flatly denied by the serpent.

How then should "you will die" be understood? Commentators have sometimes suggested some qualification such as "you will deserve to die" or "you will be doomed to die", but such guesses are unconvincing because they lack clear warrant in the text.[36] Alternatively, commentators have argued that "you will die" means "you will become mortal",[37] an argument which may be supported by appeal to the subsequent loss of the tree of life (3:22). Nonetheless, such a rendering is unsatisfactory for three reasons: (a) It implies that the man in the garden was immortal, which is not even hinted at elsewhere in the text, particularly in the crucial verse about the creation of the man (2:7).[38]

---

[33] See, for example, *Bereishis*, pp. 102 f. This was already one of the options considered by Irenaeus (see n. 25 above).

[34] Cf., for example, Gen. 2:4, 5:1,2; Exod. 32:34; Num. 3:1; 2 Sam. 22:1; Isa. 11:16.

[35] The common usage of b^eyom is for *yom* to be in the construct before an infinitive, as in Gen. 2:17, 3:5. This means that although b^eyom is itself indefinite (lit. "in day"), it may become definite in sense ("in the day") since a suffix attached to the following infinitive makes the whole expression definite (cf. *GK* 127a). Thus the words b^eyom *'akol^eka* can mean "on *the* day of your eating". This meaning, however, is not absolutely required by the Hebrew (cf. *GK* 127e), and if a writer wished unambiguously to ensure the sense "on *the* day", it would be necessary to use the definite article with *yom* and employ a different construction, for example, *bayyom 'aser to'kal*.

[36] A number of such suggestions are given in *Bereishis*, pp. 102 f., and Cassuto, *Genesis*, pp. 124f. See also Speiser, *Genesis*, p.17. The best parallel for some such meaning would be the usage of *mot tamut* in Ezek. 33:8,14. There, however, the context requires such a meaning, which is not the case in Gen. 2:17.

[37] Jerome, for example, glossed Gen. 2:17 with "mortalis eris" (*Liber Hebraicarum Quaestionum in Genesim:* PL. XXIII, 308), and many other Christian commentators followed him. Even those not concerned to uphold this traditional interpretation may still argue for an interpretation in terms of becoming mortal; D. Jobling, for example, comments, "All would be logical if 2:17 were to read 'you shall become mortal'. Such a semantic 'translation' is permissible and indeed necessary. To be transferred from the sphere of immortality to that of mortality is not much different in the semantics of myth from dying on the spot ("The Myth Semantics of Genesis 2:4b-3:24", *Semeia* xviii (1980), p.47).

[38] Traditional Christian exegesis has argued for the original immortality of humanity not so much on the basis of Gen. 2-3 in itself as on the basis of the story when read in the light of the Pauline references to the introduction of death into the world through Adam's sin (Rom. 5:12; 1 Cor. 15:21). Death in these Pauline contexts has been interpreted as

Even the reference to the tree of life does not indicate that the man was immortal, only that he could have become immortal by eating its fruit, which, by implication ("lest he take also"), he had not yet done.[39] (b) It becomes difficult to see what is the relevance of God's encounter and words in 3:8-19 if they are not themselves the primary outworking of the threatened sentence. (c) There is the fact that the Hebrew words *mot tamut*, simply do not mean "you will become mortal", but rather mean "you will die".[40] One must conclude that when God

---

physical death, and the references to its introduction into the world have been taken to imply that there was a time when Adam was not subject to death.

[39] Those who try to integrate the tree of life into the story as a whole have to deduce from the fact that only the tree of the knowledge of good and evil is prohibited that man could, and presumably did, eat from the tree of life; but that the tree only gave eternal life as long as one *continued to* eat from it, which was then made impossible by the expulsion. Such an interpretation is perfectly reasonable in itself, but unfortunately creates new problems.

First, how can one reconcile 3:3 which indicates only one tree, that of the knowledge of good and evil, in the middle of the garden, with 2:9 which indicates that the tree of life was in the midst of the garden? It achieves little to argue that the "middle" may refer to a general area which could have had more than one tree, for whether "middle" is an exact spot or a general area the crucial fact remains that, were there more than one tree, the prohibited tree could not be identified in the way it is in 3:3, solely by reference to its location. One is easily reduced to some rather bizarre speculation about two trees sharing a common trunk (see the discussion in *Bereishis,* p.96).

Secondly, 3:22 clearly implies that the fruit of the tree of life worked in the same way as the fruit of the tree of the knowledge of good and evil; that is, one only had to eat of it once for its effect to be produced. The proposed integration again runs counter to the plain sense of the text.

It might of course be argued that to seek a smooth integration of the tree of life into the story as a whole is to impose an anachronistic standard of literary coherence which is inapplicable to ancient traditional material. There is indeed force in such a consideration. Nonetheless, I find it difficult to escape the impression that a certain overall realism and coherence was intended bv the ancient writer(s), in the sort of way that makes the absence of the tree of life in 3:3 a genuine difficulty. As indicated at the beginning, therefore, it is preferable to see the tree of life as an interpretation of the story (cast in the same narrative form as the story), rather than as an original part of it.

For a sophisticated theological integration of the tree of life into the story as a whole which does not, however, resolve the literary problem, see Barth, *Dogmatics,* III: 1, pp.256f., 276ff.

[40] It is in fact unclear how "you will become mortal" would be expressed in biblical Hebrew, as biblical Hebrew does not have any adjective (or noun) corresponding to "mortal". But it does not follow from this that *mot tamut* would be as good a way as any of expressing it. The nearest the Old Testament comes to the phrase "mortal man" is probably Isa. 51:12, where "mortal" is indeed expressed by *yamut* in the elliptical phrase *'enoš yamut*. But the point in context appears to be the weakness and frailty of humanity

said "you will die", there is no reason to suppose that he did not mean what he said.

It is at this point, when the various ways in which the sentence of death might be qualified all appear unconvincing, that most modern commentators have abandoned the attempt to reconcile what God said with what in fact happened. There remains, however, one way in which the problem might be resolved, and that is to interpret death itself in a non-literal, metaphorical way to signify something other than the termination of physical existence.[41] The justification for such an approach is the fact that "death" and "life" are both terms that in religious and moral contexts are inherently suggestive of meta-phorical senses in which they apply to the *quality* of human life, rather than its mere presence or absence. Such metaphorical, qualitative usage is well attested elsewhere in the Old Testament. In Deuteronomy, for example, life and death are set before Israel (Deut. 30:15,19), and while their meaning no doubt includes the literal sense of existence and non-existence, the primary concern of the text is the quality of life that will characterize Israel's occupation of the land. The fact that "life" is linked with good and blessing, and "death" with evil and curse, makes this clear. A similar usage of "life" and "death" is also common in the ethical instruction of Proverbs.[42]

Given such metaphorical usage elsewhere in the Old Testament, the question then is whether it is reasonable to apply such a sense to Gen. 3. It has

---

in contrast to God, and so *yamut* is simply an expression of human limitation, not of some implied contrast to immortality. Otherwise, since a phrase such as *ben mawet 'attah* would be ambiguous, an unambiguous expression would presumably need to be, say, "Your end will be death" (*qiṣ^eka mawet*), or "You will not live for ever" (*lo' l^e`olam tihyeh*), neither of which, however, would fit well in Gen. 2:17.

In specific criticism of Jobling (see n.37), J. G. Williams notes that the expression *mot tamut* "is close to being a 'performative': the speaking itself is to bring about what is predicated - unless the decree is lifted". He further suggests that "if 2:17b meant 'one doomed to die' it could have read *we'akalta mimennu wemet* [sic. perhaps rather *umet*] *'attah* (see Exod.12:33; Deut.17:6; Gen.44:22). Although this would still be ambiguous, it is in keeping with a formula that is not a performative" ("A Response to Jobling", *Semeia* xviii (1980), p.52).

In general, this difficulty in expressing "you will become mortal" in biblical Hebrew should remind us that the idea of immortality, while not unknown (cf. Gen. 3:22), plays no significant role in classical Hebrew theology, whose concern is almost exclusively with life under God on this side of the grave. A theology which understands this life explicitly within the context of the life to come or eternity only emerges at the end of the Old Testament period, and receives full expression in intertestamental and New Testament literature.

[41] This is no novel suggestion, for it was often made by older commentators. See esp. Calvin's comments on 2:17 (*Genesis* [London: Banner of Truth, 1965], pp.127f).

[42] So, for example, harlotry is a way of death, Prov. 5:5f,20-3, 7:21-7.

already been noted that it is the Hebrew understanding of life under Torah, as classically expressed in Deuteronomy, that has set the context for Gen. 3 in Gen. 2:15-17. There should be no intrinsic objection, therefore, to the proposal that the metaphorical sense of death as a result of disobedience to Torah, such as in Deut. 30:15,19, may also be present in the Genesis narrative. At least it will be appropriate to see what is the result of reading the story in this light.

As the story continues we see that, as soon as God appears, all in the garden is not well. Whereas previously God and the man had worked together closely (2:19,22), now the sound of God inspires fear so that the man hides (3:8,10). Although the man had covered his nakedness (3:7), the approach of God makes that covering apparently worthless (3:10). Whereas previously the man had delighted in the woman as "bone of my bone and flesh of my flesh" (2:23), he now refers to her as "the woman you gave me" and shifts the blame on to her (3:12). What we see is a degree of alienation and fear between the man and God, and the man and his wife, which did not exist previously. Both relationships have been poisoned by the act of disobedience. Thus the ancient writer is surely expressing the truth that evil, like good, brings its own reward. As the true reward of obedience is personal growth, so the true reward of disobedience is personal decay - a kind of dying instantly begins, even though this only becomes apparent in the presence of God.[43]

Furthermore, there follows a series of divine judgements. The serpent will be not just the most cunning (`arum) of creatures but also the most cursed ('arur), its crawling in the dust will become symbolic of this curse, and instead of conversing freely with the woman it will be in perpetual enmity with her and her descendants (3:14f). The woman is to suffer inasmuch as in the two fundamental roles of ancient woman in which she should find her dignity and fulfilment, that is as wife and mother, she will now be subject to pain and domination (3:16). The man likewise, in his fundamental role as farmer and food-producer, is subjected to pain and ceaseless toil; and the final pronouncement on the man who aspired to be like God is "You are dust, and to dust you shall return" (3:17-19). These words of judgement, which inflict penalties within the public life of the world, can be seen as complementary to the decay and death in the personal life of humanity, on the principle that there should be a correspondence between the personal and the public situation of

---

[43] Westermann (*Genesis,* p.252) sees underlying 3:1-7 a primitive and partly magical understanding of the effect of a crime whereby "the crime of its very self was the source of the harmful consequences to the one who perpetrated it", which gives way to the more advanced understanding of a personal and judicial process as in 3:8ff. By contrast, I would argue that it is in 3:8-13 that we have the understanding of the crime as harmful in itself, and that this is not simply primitive or magical. Admittedly such an order of things is not in itself moral, but it is a presupposition for morality. The writer's portrayal shows a remarkably sophisticated grasp of the relationship between morality and integrity.

humanity.[44] There may also be the point that since personal decay and death may be a process of which the person in question can be to a greater or lesser extent unaware, it is appropriate that there should be public consequences of which one cannot but be aware. Then finally the man and the woman are expelled from the garden, which symbolizes removal in some way from God's presence. Since God's presence brings life (in normal circumstances), removal from his presence suggests a process of death. Moreover, the possibility of eternal life which was apparently open to the man in his initial situation in the garden is removed from his grasp. While obedience to God had in some way contained the potential for eternal life, disobedience makes that deep human longing unattainable; death in the literal sense, as well as the metaphorical, will be the human lot.

If this interpretation is on the right lines, how does it affect the assessment of the story as a whole? What we have is a study of how a person is tempted to disobey God's Torah, and what are the consequences of such disobedience. The serpent's words to the woman are a brilliant portrayal of the psychology of temptation. The woman's trust in the goodness of God's prohibition is subtly undermined until the way of life and fulfilment appears to lie in disobedience. The main point then comes in the consequences of such disobedience. For what one would naturally expect would be immediate retribution in the form of physical death. This was the clear implication of God's initial warning, and such retribution is certainly found elsewhere in the Old Testament.[45] But the writer's concern is with the fact that, in general, disobedience to God does *not* meet with any such penalty, and that therefore the relationship between human disobedience and divine judgement is to most appearances ambiguous. This problem was often faced by the prophets,[46] and is indeed inherent in the whole understanding of a God whose way of life for humanity has been expressed in the gift of Torah. The point, therefore, is precisely that it is often the case that apparently God is wrong and the serpent is right, that is that Torah can be disregarded and disobeyed with impunity. The Genesis writer wants this to be fully appreciated. Nonetheless he also wants to show that such impunity is in fact superficial and illusory. This he achieves by inviting the reader to see that death may be real in a qualitative sense in both the personal and public life of humanity. The story is thus first and foremost a profound study of the nature of morality and integrity in the Hebrew context of living by Torah.[47]

---

[44] Order and disorder in the moral and natural realms are frequently connected in the Old Testament; see, for example, Deut. 28; Hos. 4:1-3, Ps. 72.

[45] E.g. Gen. 6:5-7, Exod. 32:35, Lev. 10:1-2, Num. 16, 21:5f, Jer. 28:15-17.

[46] E.g. Isa. 5:19, Jer. 17:15, Zeph. 1:12.

[47] This understanding of personal deterioration as the most serious consequence of wrongdoing is extensively developed in the New Testament, especially the Johannine writings. It is an insight that is also shared by moralists who do not stand in the Judaeo-

V

An interpretation along these lines, whatever may be its weaknesses in detail, does offer a coherent reading of the story as a whole, and is, as far as I can see, the only way of making sense of God's words and actions that is consistent with the rest of the Old Testament and with the story's own normative setting at the beginning of Genesis. Does it, however, raise any particular difficulties of its own? One will be briefly considered.[48]

This is the difficulty posed by the words of curse and judgement in 3:14-19. For these do not sound like a description of what is true only when humanity is disobedient to God, but as a description of the constant and unchanging experience of life of the ancient Hebrew. The divine words apparently describe regular conditions, rather than conditions which only apply when people are disobedient, and as such it is unclear how well they illustrate the moral point at issue.

It should be noted here that it has sometimes been proposed that the story originally existed in a shorter, simpler form in which the act of disobedience was followed directly by expulsion from the garden, symbolizing alienation from God.[49] Since such a form of the story would closely fit the interpretation we have proposed, our analysis would tend to support the hypothesis of the story's growth in this way. One may conjecture at least two reasons why the words of curse and judgement were added to the tradition. First, a desire to make explicit the link between human disobedience and the painful realities of daily life, in the sort of way that is common elsewhere in the Old Testament.[50] Secondly, a concern to link the story of Gen. 2-3 to the wider context of the primeval history, the motif of the curse upon the ground being one of several

---

Christian tradition. For a discussion of the whole issue, see Sir W. Moberly, *The Ethics of Punishment* (London: Faber, 1968), chaps. 6-9, esp. pp.178-85, 204-11.

[48] One issue, which is not as such a difficulty but which touches on an interesting and obscure area, is the relationship of Gen. 2-3 to Deuteronomy. There are two notable affinities. First, there is a similar Torah theology (see esp. Deut. 30:11-20). Secondly, there is a significant wisdom element in Gen. 2-3 in its concern with the limits of knowledge and a right relationship to creation (cf. W. Brueggemann, (*Genesis* [Atlanta: John Knox Press, 1982], p.51); and it is also in Deuteronomy that there is a marked convergence between Torah and Wisdom (e.g. Deut. 4:6, 29:29). Both these affinities are with material in Deuteronomy (Chaps. 4, 29-30) that are generally considered to represent a distinctive editorial contribution to the book. At the same time, however, there is a complete absence in Gen. 2-3 of the terminology and expressions characteristic of Deuteronomy. The possible implications of all this for the date and life-setting of Gen. 2-3 will best be left for another occasion.

[49] See Westermann, *Genesis*, pp.195,256f.

[50] Cf. n.44 above.

factors that skilfully link the originally independent stories of the primeval history (compare 3:17 with 4:11, 5:29, 8:21).

When one considers the text with 3:14-19 as an integral part, it is clear that the regular painful conditions of ancient life are being seen as consequent upon human sin. If one asks whose sin in particular is envisaged, the answer must be either the one sin of the man and the woman, or the sin of everybody in every generation. The difficulty with the first of these is that the story as a whole gives the impression of being a portrayal of what is generally true, rather than what was true on one particular occasion: moreover, the punishment would hardly fit the crime, which would seem inappropriate given the exemplary concern of the text as a whole. The condition of the world, therefore, is presumably to be seen as the result of the constant disobedience of humanity. Such an understanding of human nature as constantly disobedient to God need not be alien to the concerns of the story, for precisely this point is made by the flood narrative (esp. Gen. 6:5, 8:21). There the writer (generally considered to be the same as in Gen. 2-3) stresses that the regular condition of humanity is that of being disobedient to God and deserving of judgement (as in the flood), even though he equally makes the point that it is undeserved mercy that people normally receive.[51] It is significant that in 8:21 the cursed state of the ground is specifically connected with general human sinfulness,[52] which would support the contention that the same point is also present in Gen. 3.

We find that the story in fact contains two distinct points, depending upon how one reads it. If one takes the story as a whole, then the words of judgement in 3:14-19 are part of what happens *when* humanity is disobedient. If one takes the words in 3:14-19 in their own right, they show *that* humanity is disobedient. The former reading implies that disobedience is not inevitable - obedience to Torah is a real possibility for people (cf. Deut. 30:11-14). The latter implies that disobedience is in fact universal. Although there is a certain tension between these points, their conflation in the text can be understood in the same sort of way as one of the theological paradoxes of the flood narrative. There, although humanity is universally sinful (Gen. 6:5), Noah finds favour in the eyes of God (6:8) and is explicitly said to be righteous (6:9).[53] Even more strikingly, God's final pronouncement of the enduring sinfulness of the human

---

[51] For the interpretation of these verses, see my *At the Mountain of God*, JSOTS 22 (Sheffield: JSOT, 1983), pp.91-3, 113-15.

[52] The position of `od in 8:21a means that it qualifies *leqallel* and not *lo'-'osip* (as it does in 8:21b), and must mean that the curse remains valid but will not be added to.

[53] A recognition of the possible compilation of distinct sources should not mean that the paradox of the completed text is thereby explained away. In any case, the P material in Gen. 6:9-22 itself specifies that "all flesh" was corrupt (6:12), as well as affirming that Noah was righteous (6:9), and so contains the paradox within itself in exactly the same way that the J material does (6:5,8).

heart (8:21) must, in terms of the story, refer primarily to Noah himself and his family, even though Noah at the time is offering an acceptable sacrifice. Such a paradoxical assessment of people as profoundly sinful and yet also capable of true obedience to God is clear in the flood story. I propose that Gen. 2-3 should be read in a similar way. The main thrust of the story is the demonstration of the kind of death that disobedience to God entails, and the paradoxical point about human nature lies in the background. Nonetheless, the paradox is present in the text. This well illustrates the methodological point that, although the text can and should be read as a whole, the text does nonetheless contain emphases which are best appreciated when the likely historical development of the text is taken into account.

VI

Finally, it will be appropriate to consider certain points of detail that were previously passed over but which touch on some of the larger issues that the story raises.

First, there is the question of the importance that should be attached to the fact that the forbidden fruit was on the tree of the knowledge of good and evil.[54] Despite the inherently suggestive nature of the phrase "the knowledge of good and evil", it is unclear whether it is as significant as is sometimes supposed. Enormous energy has been expended upon elucidating the meaning of the phrase, but the results are somewhat disappointing, mainly because Gen. 2-3 leaves the meaning of the phrase open - apart from the awareness of nakedness in 3:7 the text gives no clear indication of the way in which the man and woman become more knowing than they were before. Gen. 3 certainly implies that knowledge of good and evil is a regular feature of the human condition (so esp. 3:22), but attempts to pinpoint its meaning suffer from exactly the same problems as attempts to pinpoint the meaning of the "image of God" in humanity (Gen. 1:26) - the suggestive and elusive nature of the phrase gives interpreters great scope to read their own understanding of humanity into it.

Although one might hope that the question could be resolved on the basis of usage elsewhere in the Old Testament, it is unclear both how far usage of "good and evil" elsewhere is consistent, and whether or not apparent parallels to Gen. 3 are true parallels. The content of "knowing good and evil", for example, can be moral awareness,[55] but it can also be the non-moral ability to distinguish

---

[54] For discussion and bibliography with regard to the tree of the knowledge of good and evil, see Westermann, *Genesis,* pp.240ff.

[55] So Deut. 1:39, where the point seems to be that the children of the Israelites are not yet morally responsible and so do not share in the guilt of their parents.

between what is pleasant and unpleasant.[56] At least one point, however, does seem clear. This is that knowledge or discernment of good and evil is characteristic of maturity and adult life, and is lacking in small children (Deut. 1:39; 1 Kgs. 3:7,9), or someone whose advanced age has brought on "second childishness and mere oblivion" (2 Sam. 19:35 [Heb. 36]).[57] On the assumption that this usage is a genuine parallel to that in Gen. 3, it is these references to adult awareness that have provided much of the exegetical basis for the widespread modern reinterpretation of Gen. 3 whereby the story portrays the painful but necessary transition from childish innocence and transparence to adult awareness and experience which is marked by profound ambiguity - a "fall upwards".[58]

Further justification for such a reading of the text is an apparent parallel in the most famous story outside the Old Testament to have survived from the ancient Near East - the Epic of Gilgamesh.[59] The story of Enkidu in the early part of the Epic contains some interesting echoes of motifs in Gen. 3. Enkidu, the primitive wild man who lives with the animals is seduced by a prostitute with the result that he loses his familiarity with the animals and enters the world of civilized humanity. The narrator comments that Enkidu "now had wisdom, broader understanding", and the prostitute says to him "Thou art wise, Enkidu, art become like a god."[60] However, later Enkidu has to die and he curses the prostitute, apparently (though this is unclear) because she had set him on this

---

[56] So 2 Sam. 19:35 (Heb.36), where Barzillai is no longer able to enjoy the pleasures of adult life. In Isa. 7:15-16 it is uncertain whether "refusing the evil and choosing the good" means incipient moral awareness, i.e. when the child could begin to know what it ought or ought not to do, or simply the ability to express likes and dislikes of what it eats.

[57] An apparent exception may be Isa. 7:15-16 where the Immanuel child's capacity to "refuse the evil and choose the good" is probably envisaged as taking place within a relatively short time, perhaps two years, after its birth; that is while the child is still a child and not yet an adult. Yet even here the point is that this capacity must be grown into.

[58] So, for example, S. R. Driver, "They had passed in a moment - as we all pass, though only in the course of years - from the innocence of childhood into the knowledge which belongs to adult age" (*Genesis* (London: Methuen, 1904), p.46); cf. J. R. Lucas, "There is an account of our moral and spiritual maturation from a state of innocence to a state of adult autonomy.... We are impelled to seek the knowledge of good and evil, however much it may hurt us. It is part of our development to adulthood, part of our becoming rational agents" ("The Origin of Sin" in his *Freedom and Grace* [London: SPCK, 1976], p.43).

[59] See J. B. Pritchard, *Ancient Near Eastern Texts Relating to the Old Testament* (Princeton: Princeton University Press, 1969), pp.72f; also N. K. Sandars (ed.), *The Epic of Gilgamesh,* Penguin Classics (Harmondsworth: Penguin, 1964, 1972).

[60] Tablet I.iv, lines 29,34 (*ANET*, p.75).

path leading to death.[61] The whole Epic of Gilgamesh displays a deep awareness of the limitations and ambiguities of human existence, and Enkidu's ambiguous entry into wisdom and civilization is an important part of this. Given certain similar motifs,[62] one might suppose that the Hebrew story is making the same sort of point as the Mesopotamian story.[63]

It must certainly be admitted that the Genesis story does in some ways lend itself to this sort of interpretation. Such an interpretation is also particularly congenial to a twentieth-century culture that is familiar with both Freudian psychology and existentialism. Nonetheless, as a serious interpretation of Gen. 3 it cannot be sustained.[64] Primarily, this is because of the centrality to the Genesis story of prohibition, disobedience, and death, as outlined above. The knowledge of good and evil is something deadly for humanity, not a painful but necessary part of its development. On this proposed reading, one would have to allow that the serpent was right, especially in his insinuation that the prohibition was not for the man's good, but that God was holding back something desirable. Such an implication about Torah would be intolerable for any Hebrew who accepted Torah as God's good and life-giving will for Israel.

Moreover, the oft-revived suggestion that the condition of the man and the woman before they took the fruit was essentially that of a child is unlikely. Our analysis of 2:15-17 as depicting the basic condition of Hebrew people (that is, adults living responsibly under Torah) tells against it, as does the significance attached to nakedness in 2:25, 3:7.[65] Also, in the parallel account of the king of Tyre (Ezek. 28:12-19) the key figure is an adult, as is Enkidu in the Epic of Gilgamesh or Adapa in the Myth of Adapa.[66]

The meaning of "the knowledge of good and evil" is not therefore resolved by usage elsewhere in the Old Testament or by apparent similarities in other ancient texts. If one allows the context of the Genesis story itself to be the

---

[61] Tablet VII.iii, lines 5-10 (*ANET*, p.86).

[62] The parallels with the Enkidu story become even more striking if one suggests, as has often been done, that either the transgression in Gen. 3 (in some earlier form of the story) or the resultant awareness is to do with sexuality. For a survey of such suggestions, see Westermann, *Genesis,* p.243; J. A. Bailey, "Initiation and the Primal Woman in Gilgamesh and Genesis 2-3", *JBL* lxxxix (1970), pp.144-7.

[63] One might note also that the theme of humanity's development through a painful transition from simplicity to complexity is well known in Greek mythology, for example, the stories of Prometheus and Pandora.

[64] Insofar as a transition from simplicity to complexity is a genuinely significant element in Gen. 3, it could be indicative of the tradition-history of the story. The writer could have deliberately transformed a story that was initially more similar in outlook to that of Enkidu or Pandora, in order to highlight the distinctive *theological* understanding of life entailed by Hebrew faith in YHWH.

[65] Cf. Westermann, *Genesis*, p.235.

[66] See *ANET*, pp.101-3.

decisive factor in determining the details of the story, it would appear most likely that "knowledge of good and evil" signifies *moral autonomy,* that is the adoption of a stance whereby one decides right and wrong for oneself rather than in obedience to divine Torah.[67] Or if, as is often argued, "knowledge of good and evil" means knowledge of everything, moral and non-moral alike,[68] the meaning would be that of autonomy generally. Either way, the point is similar - that acquisition of such knowledge means stepping out of the position of creaturely dependence and trust in the creator. Such an autonomous stance could well be what the Genesis writer saw as the general stance of humanity and also as the fundamental root of humanity's problems.

Next, there is the question of the serpent and the problem of evil. Although the serpent is the agent of disobedience and is hostile to humanity, the serpent itself is not described as evil. This is no doubt because of the strong Hebrew sense that all that God had created was good, and the serpent is specifically one of the creatures that YHWH God had made (3:1, cf.2:19,20). To characterize the serpent as evil in this context would imply that God had created evil, and despite the theoretical puzzle that the existence of evil poses for monotheism, mainline monotheistic theology, both Jewish and Christian, has always resisted ascribing to God the creation of evil. The writer of Gen. 3 shares this resistance and simply bypasses the theoretical problems that evil poses. The serpent is described not as evil but as the most cunning (`arum`) of the creatures God had made, and two possible reasons for the writer's choice of this term can be discerned.

First, the most obvious point to a reader of the Hebrew text is the play on words between the serpent as `arum` (cunning) and the man and woman as `arum` (naked)![69] Presumably the point of such word play is to introduce a sense of pleasure at the narrator's skilful use of language, and serves to remind the modern reader that Hebrew literature is rarely purely functional or didactic, but is to be *enjoyed* as well as profited from.[70]

---

[67] So, for example, W. M. Clark, "A Legal Background to the Yahwist's Use of 'Good and Evil' in Genesis 2-3", *JBL* lxxxviii (1969), pp.266-78.

[68] So, for example, von Rad, *Genesis,* p.89.

[69] This point depends upon the juxtaposition of 2:25 with 3:1. Elsewhere (3:7,10,11) the alternative form of the adjective, `erom` is used. Had `erom` been used in 3:1, the word play would have been diminished.

[70] The word play is also a standing temptation to commentators to exercise their ingenuity and imagination. So, for example, G. W. Coats speculates about a possible earlier form of the tradition "that casts the tempter not as a naked (wise) snake, but as a naked (and wise) woman (cf the Gilgamesh Epic)" *(Genesis, with an Introduction to Narrative Literature,* FOTL I [Grand Rapids: Eerdmans, 1983], p. 58).

Secondly, a study of the use of `arum elsewhere in the Old Testament is revealing. The word appears to be used in two ways.[71] The most frequent usage is in Proverbs, where it is invariably a good and commendable quality - "prudent" or "shrewd".[72] Outside Proverbs, however, the word is never clearly good or commendable and should probably always be rendered "cunning" or "crafty", that is a quality that is inherently ambiguous from a moral perspective; for cunning naturally arouses both admiration and suspicion.[73] It is surely not the usage of `arum in Proverbs but that elsewhere in the Old Testament that explains the writer's choice of the term for the serpent. The serpent is not evil as such but is possessed of a morally ambiguous quality that easily lends itself to evil. Thus the depiction of the serpent ignores the theoretical issue of how God's good creation can become evil, but rather illustrates the disastrous consequences of a classic misuse (for reasons unstated) of a rather unusual and ambiguous God-given quality.

With regard to the theological problems posed by the existence of evil, it is worth remembering that most of those earlier commentators who were happy to read Gen. 3 as literal history still recognized that the story at best showed the first appearance of evil in the world but left unresolved the more fundamental issue of how such evil could exist in the first place. The traditional answer was to trace evil and the Fall back to some premundane catastrophe.[74] On any reckoning, therefore, Gen. 3 leaves the fundamental enigma of evil unresolved. It is rather a classic picture of what disobedience to God involves and entails, which is certainly compatible with a traditional doctrine of the Fall but is not itself the basis for it.[75]

---

[71] For these purposes it is unnecessary to distinguish between the adjective and the related noun and verb.

[72] Prov. 1:4, 8:5,12, 12:16,23, 13:16, 14:8,15,18, 15:5, 19:25, 22:3, 27:12.

[73] Saul says of David that he needs to be watched carefully as he is "very cunning" (I Sam. 23:22), and the Gibeonites deceive the Israelites by employing crafty tactics in the way that the Israelites themselves had done previously at Jericho and Ai (Josh. 9:3f). Cunning could easily be harnessed in murdering someone (Exod. 21:14), and it is clear from Job that `arum can designate a kind of human intelligence that is opposed to God and so brought low by him (Job 5:12,13, 15:5).

[74] See, for example, N. P. Williams, *The Ideas of the Fall and of Original Sin* (London: Longmans, 1927).

[75] The doctrine of the Fall is an issue of pure theology, which is necessitated by two basic convictions; first, that God is good and whatever he creates is likewise good, and secondly, that the condition of the world as we know it is of good that is corrupted and distorted by evil and so in need of God's salvation. The Fall is the traditional explanation of this paradoxical situation. If one resists the notion that evil is somehow inherent in creation, as is often suggested, and maintains the traditional Christian understanding of evil as a corruption of original good, then one is apparently forced to maintain that evil is not eternal but originated within the sphere of time, i.e. that in some sense there was an

VII

Finally, there is the question of the relationship between the meaning of the story in its Hebrew context and its meaning in the context of traditional or contemporary Christian theology. This is best approached through reflection upon the fact that Adam is clearly "everyman", a point made both by his name,[76] and by the context of the garden of God in which he is set, a context which is impervious to the usual divisions and distinctions of human life. Although the shape of the story is moulded by the presuppositions of Hebrew theology, these presuppositions are not allowed to obtrude upon the universality of the story. Thus, for example, although 2:15-17 is shaped by Torah theology, the actual term "Torah" is not used, for it specifies what is God's special gift to Israel alone. The narrator has so presented his material that it can be read in the light of any authentic moral code. Christian theology, which does not see the pattern for life as constituted by Torah, and which has a more complex understanding of the place of moral codes than does the Old Testament, nonetheless still recognizes the importance of the commandments of both Old Testament and New Testament and the centrality of obedience and trust. Moreover, the metaphorical sense of death as alienation and estrangement and the understanding of eternal life as inherent in a right and obedient relationship with God are both likewise congenial to Christian theology. The story thus naturally lends itself to transposition into a Christian context.

It is also no surprise to a modern Western reader that this archetypal story of human sin should include reference to the effects of sin upon humanity's natural environment, a fact which give the story an immediate relevance to one of the pressing problems facing modern society. However, the precise way in which the text envisages the earth being affected, through a divine curse, is somewhat problematic, and a thorough study of the meaning of this within its Hebrew context is necessary before the hermeneutical issue can be properly tackled.[77]

In conclusion, it is not difficult to see not only why the story of Gen. 3 has had such an impact in the past, but also why it is important that the story should

---

historic Fall - though in saying this the inadequacy of traditional categories for comprehending the nature of this profound mystery must be stressed. Whatever one's resolution of the mystery, however, the point is that it is entirely a matter of the examination and explication of fundamental theological principles .

[76] Hebrew 'adam, like Latin "homo" or English "man" (in traditional usage) is a generic term for humanity.

[77] For a recent discussion of the bearing of the early chapters of Genesis upon ecological issues, see B. W. Anderson, "Creation and Ecology" in his (ed.) *Creation in the Old Testament* (Philadelphia/London: Fortress Press/SPCK, 1984), pp.152-69.

still be heard today. Sadly, in much popular thought the waters have been muddied by misleading debates about the relationship between science and the Bible and also by the popular pejorative sense of the term "myth". This means that the intelligent appropriation of the story in contemporary theology will not always be straightforward. Nonetheless one can feel confident that the profound and suggestive qualities of the story should enable the story in itself to prove both more enduring and more interesting than all the various debates and commentaries that become attached to it.

ABRAHAM'S RIGHTEOUSNESS (GENESIS 15:6)

Few individual texts from the Old Testament have a more weighty history of interpretation than the famous words of Gen. 15:6: "And he [Abraham][1] put his faith in YHWH, and he [sc. YHWH] reckoned it to him as righteousness". Paul used Gen. 15:6 as a key text in his argument for the nature of the Gospel (Gal. 3; Rom. 4) in a way that was foundational for Christian theology. Other interpreters in the Graeco-Roman world were also agreed about the importance of the verse, although the Jewish tradition of reading it in close conjunction with Gen. 22 meant that its significance could be developed in a way somewhat different from that of Paul (e.g. James 2:14-26).[2] Later, the centrality for Luther of the concepts of "righteousness" and of "faith" ensured that Gen. 15:6, as interpreted by Paul and Luther, would have an important role within Protestant theology.

It should be appreciated that these interpreters were in no way arbitrary when they attributed great significance to Gen. 15:6, for the verse is clearly remarkable on its own terms within its Old Testament context. First, the text uses two important theological terms, "have faith" (*he'emin*) and "righteousness" (*ṣedaqah*), which only here in the Old Testament occur in conjunction with each other. Moreover, *ṣedaqah* is one of the central concepts of the Old Testament, which means that Gen. 15:6 necessarily resonates within the wider context of the theology of the Old Testament and its interpretation must in one way or another take that wider context into account. Secondly, the verse represents an interpretative comment about Abraham of a kind otherwise unparalleled in the patriarchal narratives. Usually, editorial comments within the Abraham stories relate to circumstances observable within the normal context of life, noted from a temporal perspective ("at that time", "to this day", Gen. 12:6, 13:7, 22:14), and do not purport to give access to the mind and purposes of God. So far as the stories contain explicit theological interpretation they present it within the world of the story, most obviously within certain divine speeches (e.g. Gen. 12:1-3, 18:17-19). Only in Gen. 15:6 does the writer express a theological judgement

---

[1] For convenience I will use the familiar form "Abraham" throughout the essay, even though within Gen. 15 the form "Abram" is used.

[2] Another striking example is I Macc. 2:52, *Abraam ouchi en peirasmō heurethe pistos* [i.e. Gen. 22:1,12], *kai elogisthe autō eis dikaiosunen* [i.e. Gen. 15:6]. On the understanding of Gen. 15:6 in Tannaitic literature and the New Testament, see e.g. F. Hahn, "Genesis 15.6 im Neuen Testament", in H. W. Wolff (ed.). *Probleme biblischer Theologie* (Munich, 1971). pp. 90-107; J.D.G. Dunn, *Romans 1-8* (Waco, Texas, 1988), pp. 200- 1, 226-7.

that to some extent stands outside the story,[3] so far as he describes a divine attitude in the third person ("he [sc. YHWH] reckoned it to him as righteousness") rather than presenting a statement by YHWH in the first person as elsewhere. In terms of the customary "I - thou" dialogue between YHWH and Abraham one might perhaps have expected the text to be something like "And YHWH said to him, 'You are righteous before me'" (*wayyo'mer yhwh 'elayw ṣaddiq 'atta l^{e}panay*). It is the presentation of the theological judgement in the third-person form that has enabled the verse to be used as a theological principle independent (to some extent) of the story in which it is set.[4] Thus both the content and the form of Gen. 15:6 mark it out as exceptional within the Abraham traditions.

I

At first sight, the interpretation of Gen. 15:6 does not appear to present any obvious problems. Its context presents no difficulty: it is a dialogue between YHWH and Abraham.[5] YHWH opens with words of assurance and promise (15:1) to which Abraham responds with a question seeking further assurance (vv.2-3).[6] YHWH gives this in the form of a twofold promise, first that a child of Abraham's own body will be his heir and secondly that the descendants of Abraham will be as numerous as the stars (vv.4-5). It is Abraham's response to this promise that is recounted in v. 6.

The Hebrew of Gen. 15:6 likewise presents relatively little difficulty, although two points of meaning, with regard to *w^{e}he'emin* ("he believed"), and

---

[3] The same is also true to a lesser degree with regard to Gen. 15:18a, "On that day YHWH made a covenant with Abram", which functions as an interpretation of the accompanying narrative. However, it stands out less from its context, both because it continues a third-person narrative, and because of the way it serves to introduce the following speech. On 15:18a see further below, p.52.

[4] So, for example, von Rad comments that Gen. 15:6 is a "solemn statement" which "almost has the quality of a general theological tenet": *Genesis* (3rd ed, London, 1972) p. 185.

[5] It is commonly argued that the dialogue should be understood against the traditio-historical background of human address and divine oracle in a cultic context (so e.g. O. Kaiser, "Traditionsgeschichtliche Untersuchung von Gen. 15", *ZAW* 70 [1958], pp. 107-26; N. Lohfink, *Die Landverheissung als Eid* [Stuttgart, 1967], pp. 48-9; H. H. Schmid, "Gerechtigkeit und Glaube. Genesis 15, 1-6 und sein biblisch-theologischer Kontext", *Ev Th* 40 [1980], pp. 398-9). But even if this is correct (the main difficulty being that the precise sequence in Gen. 15:1-6, with the divine assurance at the outset, is otherwise unparalleled), it lies sufficiently in the background to be of only limited assistance in interpreting the passage as it stands in its present narrative context.

[6] For the theological importance of a faith in God which allows questioning of God, see R. Davidson, *The Courage to Doubt* (London, 1983), pp.42ff.

one ambiguity, as to the subject of *wayyaḥš̌ebeha* ("and he reckoned it"), need some comment.

The Hebrew phrase *he'emin bᵉ* means "to have faith in" in the sense of making a personal response of confident trust in someone,[7] and is usually distinct from *he'emin lᵉ* which tends to have the sense simply of "credit a report", "accept what someone is saying as true".[8] Of course, the sense of accepting something as true may also be present in *he'emin bᵉ* as is the case in Gen. 15:6, but *he'emin lᵉ* does not necessarily carry the further implications of trusting self-commitment as does *he'emin bᵉ*.[9] The second point of meaning is that *wᵉhe'emin* is, apparently, a perfect with *waw* consecutive, which makes the verb frequentative with the sense of repeated action.[10] The most natural meaning of this is that Abraham's faith in YHWH was his constant response, and therefore the reference in Gen. 15:6 constitutes one particular example which represents and summarizes a regular occurrence.[11]

With regard to the subject of the second verb *wayyaḥš̌ebeha*, it is usually assumed without discussion that the subject is YHWH. It should be noted, however, that there has been a recurrent proposal among Jewish commentators (although even among Jewish commentators it has always been a minority option) to understand Abraham as the subject, i.e. "And he (Abraham) reckoned it to him (YHWH) as righteousness". The most notable advocate of this position

---

[7] See e.g. Exod. 14:31, 19:9; Num. 14:11, 20:12; 1 Sam. 27:12; Jer. 12:6; Ps. 119:66; 2 Chron. 20:20. Also *he'emin bᵉ* can be used in parallelism to *baṭaḥ* as in Mic. 7:5, Ps. 78:22.

[8] Gen. 45:26; 1 Kgs. 10:7//2 Chron. 9:6; Isa. 53:1; Jer. 40:14; Prov. 14:15.

[9] Although there is a general idiomatic distinction between *he'emin* with *bᵉ* and with *lᵉ*, the distinction is not absolute. Sometimes *he'emin lᵉ* may imply a trusting personal response as a corollary of accepting someone's word as true; so Exod. 4:1,8; Deut. 9:23; 2 Chron. 32:15. Note also the apparent parallelism between *bᵉ* and *lᵉ* in Ps. 106:12,24. For general discussion of the usage of *he'emin*, see A. Jepsen, *"'aman"*, in G. J. Botterweck and H. Ringgren (ed.), *Theological Dictionary of the Old Testament* I (Grand Rapids, 1974), pp.299-309.

[10] *GK* 112ss classifies Gen. 15:6 as a unusual use of the perfect with *waw* consecutive, and suggests it represents "constant continuance in a past state". The precise significance of the grammatical form is a matter of continuing debate, see e.g. K. Seybold, *"ḥašab"*, in Botterweck and Ringgren (ed.), *TDOT* V (1986), p.242.

[11] B. Vawter comments on Gen. 15:6 that *wᵉhe'min* should be rendered "he continued to believe" since the Hebrew form "suggests that a continuous rather than an incipient act is meant", and moreover in context "Abraham has already been presented as one totally abandoned to the designs of God" (*On Genesis* [London 1977]. p. 207). This point is lost in the LXX which renders *wᵉhe'emin* not with the imperfect but with the aorist, *kai episteusen*, which is the form in which the verse is cited in Gal. 3:6; Rom. 4:3; James 2:23.

was Ramban.[12] Since this has also been proposed recently in two studies by L. Gaston and M. Oeming,[13] it is a possibility that must be taken seriously.[14]

The classic advocacy of this interpretation by Ramban involves a twofold argument, based on the wider context.[15] First, since there is no good reason for Abraham not to have believed YHWH's word (Abraham being a prophet, and God being a faithful God who does not lie; Ramban also notes that a similar promise had been made previously, Gen. 13:1-17, which Abraham had believed), it would be otiose for YHWH specially to commend him on this occasion for doing so. Secondly, and more specifically, if Abraham could believe YHWH in the hard matter of sacrificing his son (Gen. 22), his faith in YHWH's beneficial promise of descendants would seem a light matter by contrast and so hardly worthy of being singled out. Ramban therefore argued that the sense of the verse was that Abraham recognized YHWH's promise as utterly sure, guaranteed in despite of either his merit or his sin, a word of irreversible $s^{e}daqah$ as in Isa. 45:23.

Ramban's argument has received little attention, not least because of the weight of interpretative tradition against him, and, in modern times (at least prior to certain recent literary trends), a reaction against a timeless and ahistorical use of the biblical text. The modern advocacy of the position is therefore based on grammatico-historical exegesis. Nonetheless, Ramban's basic

---

[12] Apart from standard editions of the *Mikraot Gedolot,* see esp. M. Zlotowitz (ed.) *Bereishis: Genesis/A New Translation with a Commentary Anthologized from Talmudic, Midrashic and Rabbinic Sources* 1(a) (New York, 1977,1986), pp.512-13; also B.Jacob *Das Erste Buch der Tora: Genesis* (New York, n.d., reprint from edn of Berlin, 1934) p. 394; J.D. Levenson, "Why Jews Are Not Interested in Biblical Theology", in J. Neusner, B. A. Levine and E. S. Frerichs (ed.), *Judaic Perspectives on Ancient Israel* (Philadelphia, 1987) p. 303.

[13] L. Gaston, "Abraham and the Righteousness of God", *Horizons in Biblical Theology* 2 (1980), pp. 39-68; M. Oeming, "Ist Genesis 15:6 ein Beleg für die Anrechnung des Glaubens zur Gerechtigkeit?", *ZAW* 95 (1983), pp. 182-97.

[14] As far as I am aware, Gaston's article has not been noted by Old Testament scholars who have recently discussed Gen. 15:6. Oeming's proposal has been noted, but the tendency has been to pass over it without argument as selfevidently mistaken. Thus E. Blum comments that it "gibt in Kontext kaum einen Sinn" *(Die Komposition der Vätergeschichte* [Neukirchen-Vluyn, 1984], p. 369, n. 53), while M. Köckert dismisses it with a "(!)" *(Vätergott und Väterverheissungen* [Göttingen, 1988], p.217, n.260). G. J. Wenham, *Genesis 1-15* (Waco, Texas, 1988), p. 330, makes the valid point against Oeming that elsewhere in the Pentateuch $s^{e}daqah$ always applies to human rather than divine activity. But since $s^{e}daqah$ can be an attribute of God elsewhere in the Old Testament and is used in that way frequently, Wenham's point is of limited value.

[15] A full translation of Ramban's commentary on Gen. 15:6 is conveniently available in Gaston (n.13), pp. 42-3. Curiously, Ramban's proposal is never mentioned by Oeming.

sense of a difficulty in the text when read in the light of the wider story of Abraham is, I suggest, a sound insight, to which we will return in due course.

Gaston and Oeming put forward two major exegetical arguments. First, they argue that in the light of the Hebrew predilection for parallelism it is natural to take Abraham as the subject of "reckoned", so that the verse then portrays Abraham's two related responses to YHWH. Secondly, they appeal to Old Testament usage elsewhere, in which people, and not only God, can be the subject of *ḥašab* (e.g. 2 Sam. 19:20), and *ṣᵉdaqah/ṣedeq* can be an attribute or action of YHWH, especially a gracious act of deliverance, a usage widespread in the Old Testament (e.g. I Sam. 12:6,8; Mic. 6:4,5; Neh. 9:8) though especially common in the Psalms and Second Isaiah, whose language has many affinities to the Psalter (e.g. Ps. 7:17, 22:30-1 [Heb. 31-2], 31:1 [Heb. 2]; Isa. 41:10, 46:13, 51:6). They therefore understand "reckoning as righteousness" as Abraham's response of recognition and gratitude to YHWH's gracious and salvific act of granting descendants to Abraham. Such a sense is certainly not inappropriate in context, and indeed it would fit the wider Old Testament pattern of divine promise being met by human praise.[16] It was only at a later stage when the LXX made Abraham the recipient of righteousness, by rendering *wayyaḥšᵉbeha* with the passive *kai elogisthe autō*, that the verse acquired the sense which it has had in most subsequent interpretation.

Gaston and Oeming have certainly shown that it is possible to construe the Hebrew in the way they propose. Nonetheless, there are good reasons why the consensus understanding, with YHWH as subject of *wayyaḥšᵉbeha*, should be retained. First, there is the idiomatic usage of *ḥašab*, which, when used with the technical sense of "reckoning", consistently denotes the situation of people before God, both when the verb is Niphal (Lev. 7:18b,17:4; Num. 18:27,30; Ps. 106:31)[17] and when it is Qal (Ps. 32:2). Even 2 Sam. 19:20, where Shimei begs David "not to reckon his sin to him", is less of an exception than may initially appear, partly because of the obvious religious overtones of "reckoning sin" and partly because of the king's position as God's vicegerent on earth. This regular idiomatic usage creates a strong presumption that Gen. 15:6 also portrays God reckoning something to a person, i.e. Abraham, rather than vice versa.

Secondly, one must give weight to the only other passage in the Old Testament in which *ḥašab* and *ṣᵉdaqah* are combined, that is Ps. 106:31. Here it is unambiguous that it is Phinehas to whom righteousness is reckoned by YHWH, which again creates a strong presumption that Gen. 15:6 should be

---

[16] See Gaston (n. 13), pp. 45-9. Interestingly, the widespread formcritical analysis of Gen. 15:1-6 (see n.5) has not usually been brought to bear upon the exegesis and interpretation of 15:6, despite the fact that v. 6b does not, on its common interpretation, fit the form-critical pattern.

[17] Prov. 27:14 is an unusual usage, yet even here the language of blessing and curse presumably envisages the invoking of particular divine dispositions towards people.

construed similarly with Abraham as recipient. It may be concluded, therefore, that a traditional translation should be maintained and that Gen. 15:6 should be rendered, "And he (Abraham) put his faith in YHWH, and he (YHWH) reckoned it to him (Abraham) as righteousness".

II

If it is not difficult to determine what Gen. 15:6 says, it is quite another matter when it comes to deciding what it means. This is partly because the terms "faith", "reckon" and "righteousness" have a range of meanings in the Old Testament, and there has not always been agreement as to their precise meaning in Gen. 15:6. The problem is compounded by the fact that these terms resonate not only within the Old Testament but also within the two religions, Judaism and Christianity, which relate themselves to the Old Testament as scripture, with the result that commentators have a certain tendency to attribute to the words of Gen. 15:6 that meaning which is congenial to their own theological understanding.

Thus, on the one hand, Protestant Christians (whose views have formed the modern scholarly consensus) tend to find a meaning that is consonant with Paul's interpretation in Gal. 3 and Rom. 4. "Reckon" and "righteousness" are given a less technical sense than they have in Paul, but the general thrust is similar: the text is concerned with *faith* and its *approval* by God: "it is stated programmatically that belief alone has brought Abraham into a proper relationship with God";[18] "A particular attitude to God is declared correct";[19] "Abraham...is a man who responds in trust to what God promises, and on this basis he is in a right relationship with, acceptable to, God",[20] "YHWH 'reckoned it to him as righteousness', that is, certified him to be in a right relationship before God".[21]

On the other hand, many Jewish interpreters have tended to read the verse in a way that is consonant with their traditional belief in the "merit of the fathers" (z^ekut 'abot), a belief which, among other things, includes the notion that many blessings have come to Israel because of their ancestors' obedience to

---

[18] Von Rad, *Genesis,* p.185.

[19] C. Westermann, *Genesis 12-36* (London, 1986), p.223.

[20] Davidson, *Courage to Doubt,* pp.42-3.

[21] B. W. Anderson, "Abraham, the Friend of God", *Interpretation* 42 (1988), p.361 . For an older, thorough study of Gen. 15:6 from a Protestant perspective see H.W. Heidland, *Die Anrechnung des Glaubens zur Gerechtigkeit* (Stuttgart, 1936), or his shorter statement in the article "*logizomai*" in G. Kittel (ed.), *Theological Dictionary of the New Testament* 4 (Grand Rapids, 1967), pp. 284-92.

God.[22] Biblical $ṣ^edaqah$ is interpreted in terms of the rabbinic notion of z^ekut, and Gen. 15:6 is seen as a classic example of a life of obedience being rewarded by God (with blessing for Israel in view). Thus Gen. 15:6 is understood as referring to *faithfulness* and its *reward* by God. A. B. Ehrlich commented, "Das verbum hat seine gewöhnliche Bedeutung, und *ṣdqh* ist = Verdienst (cf. Neh. 2,20 und sieh zu Deut. 24,13). JHVH rechnete Abraham den Glauben an seine Verheissung, deren Erfüllung unter den obwaltenden Umstanden kaum wahrscheinlich erscheinen musste, als Verdienst an";[23] E. A. Speiser translated the verse, "He put his trust in Jahweh, who accounted it to his merit";[24] B. Jacob commented, "$ṣ^edaqa$ ist dasselbe wie das neuhebraische z^ekut, der durch ein löbliches Verhalten erworbene Anspruch auf Anerkennung und Lohn (*lpny yy'*, vor Gott)" ([n. 12], p.394). The interpretation of Gen. 15:6 is thus a classic illustration of the fact that it is extremely difficult to determine the theological meaning of the Old Testament apart from the appropriation of the material within historic and contemporary communities of faith.

III

The obvious way to attempt to understand Gen. 15:6 more clearly is to consider it in the light of its historical context of meaning as represented by the other writings of the Old Testament. By general consensus,[25] the most significant modern study of Gen. 15:6 in this regard is G. von Rad's short article "Faith Reckoned as Righteousness".[26] His thesis is that Gen. 15:6 should be interpreted traditio-historically; that is, he argues that the theological sense of the verse is best understood when its terminology is viewed against the matrix of meaning from which it was derived, a matrix different from that within which

[22] For recent discussion and bibliography, see E. P. Sanders, *Paul and Palestinian Judaism* (London, 1977), pp.183ff.
[23] *Randglossen zur hebräischen Bibel* (Leipzig, 1908; reprinted in Hildesheim, 1968), p.59.
[24] *Genesis* (Garden City, New York, 1964), p. 110. Curiously, Speiser offers no comment whatever on his rendering of the text.
[25] All subsequent discussions refer back to von Rad, for the most part accepting his case as established (so, e.g. W. Eichrodt, *Theology of the Old Testament* 2 [London, 1967], p.279; J. Van Seters, *Abraham in History and Tradition* [New Haven, Connecticut, and London, 1975], pp. 257, 268-9; Schmid [n. 5], pp. 400, 408; Westermann [n. 19], p.223; D.G. Buttrick, "Genesis 15:1-18", *Interpretation* 42 [1988], p.395), though sometimes there is disagreement (so e.g. Lohfink [n. 5], Seybold [n. 10], Gaston and Oeming [n. 13]).
[26] The essay is available in his *The Problem of the Hexateuch and other Essays* (Edinburgh and London, 1966), pp.125-30 = "Die Anrechnung des Glaubens zur Gerechtigkeit", *Gesammelte Studien zum Alten Testament* (Munich. 1958), pp.130-5 = *ThLZ* 27 (1951), cols 129-32.

it is now used. First, von Rad argues that the verb *ḥašab* designates a formal "reckoning" pronounced by a priest on YHWH's behalf within the cult as a response to a worshipper's offering (Lev. 7:18, 17:4; Num. 18:27). Secondly, he argues that the priest's judgement was communicated to the worshipper through a declaratory formula such as can be discerned in Lev. 19:7b or Ezek. 18:9b (where a person is pronounced to be *ṣaddiq*). Thus both *ḥašab* and *ṣᵉdaqah* have a clear cultic meaning. Although *ḥašab* and *ṣᵉdaqah* are never actually combined in any of these texts, such a silence is not significant but is an accident of the differing functions of the texts in question.

Von Rad concludes that when Gen. 15:6 is read in the light of these cultic antecedents, "it is revealed as a polemical and indeed revolutionary declaration. The process of 'reckoning' is now transferred to the sphere of a free and wholly personal relationship between God and Abraham." Further, "The most astonishing difference... is that the cultic 'reckoning' depended on something done by the human worshipper, by way of sacrifice or specific obedience... Here, however, in a solemn statement concerning the divine purpose, it is laid down that it is *faith*[27] which sets men on a right footing with God... only faith (*nur der Glaube*), which is the wholehearted acceptance of Yahweh's promise, brings man into a right relationship."[28] After making this grand assertion von Rad seems to have had second thoughts and backtracks somewhat. He allows that there may in fact be no deliberate polemic against cultic "reckoning", in which case "what is contrasted in *Gen*. xv. 6 with the cultic process of 'reckoning' (brought about through a multiplicity of particular acts) is actually the whole process of the relationship between Yahweh and mankind. Above all, this process is subjective and inwardlooking, so that the accent is now upon the inward and personal attitude of the worshipper."[29]

These are indeed remarkable conclusions to be founded upon such unremarkable evidence, and it is astonishing that the article should have been so frequently referred to by later scholars without demur or criticism.[30] As a piece of theological argument it seems unduly indebted to von Rad's own Lutheran convictions (even though von Rad makes no reference to the history of interpretation). When he universalizes the significance of what is said of Abraham, portrays faith as something inward, and says that it is the sole requirement for a right relationship with God, it is clearly the Protestant understanding of faith in the light of Paul and Luther that is the determining

---

[27] The italics are provided by the translator, and are not in the German.

[28] E. tr., p.129 = p.133-4 = col. 132.

[29] E. tr., p.130 = p.134 = col. 132.

[30] Such criticism as there has been has generally been directed to the question of the precise nature of the relationship of the language of Gen. 15:6 to the cult (see the discussions in n. 5). The sharpest criticism from a theological point of view has been that of Levenson ([n. 12], pp.301-4), though see also Blum (n. 14), p.369.

factor in the argument. It is probably because von Rad himself realized that his conclusion outran his evidence that he expressed himself a little more moderately in his *Old Testament Theology* I:[31] "If it is there [i.e. Gen. 15:6] emphasised that faith was 'counted' as righteousness, this was certainly a striking and perhaps even revolutionary formulation for those contemporary with it... it represents the thesis that taking Jahweh's promise seriously, and responding to it as something perfectly concrete, was the true attitude in relationship to Jahweh." However, "we must not make the words absolute and exclusive, as if they ruled out any other possible way for men to exhibit righteousness, for they are of course bound up with Abraham's peculiar situation as the recipient of a promise with wide historical implications. Different situations might have demanded different expressions of faithfulness in relationship to Jahweh" (p.379 = German, pp.376-7).

Although von Rad himself appears to have recognized that his original conclusions may have been overstated, he nonetheless maintains a substantially similar position in the later work. The first step, therefore, will be to argue that, even if the premises about the cultic nature of the language of reckoning and righteousness are correct (a matter to which we shall return), von Rad's conclusions, even in modified form, are unwarranted.

First, even if "reckoning as righteousness" normally had cultic associations, on what grounds could one know that its use within the non-cultic context of Gen. 15:1-6 should be understood as polemical? Within the context of Gen. 15 there is no hint of an anti-cultic polemic. Indeed, Gen. 15:6 is followed by the description of a ritual which, although unique in the Old Testament, has obvious affinities with the practices of the cult.[32] To read Gen. 15:6 in sharp contrast to the cultic uses of reckoning is to import concerns which are nowhere expressed in the text and may in fact be irrelevant to it.

Secondly, the problem of knowing whether to read Gen. 15:6 in the light of cultic concerns is exacerbated by the question of the dates of the respective texts. When von Rad wrote his original article (1951) the dating of pentateuchal sources had not yet become as problematic as it was soon to become. Yet even on the dating scheme that he accepted with reasonable confidence, it is odd that a text which von Rad ascribes to the Elohist (9th/8th century) should be seen as in some way dependent upon material ascribed to Ezekiel and the Priestly school (6th/5th century). Of course, because of the inherently conservative nature of cult, much of the content of P may be older than the literary context in which it now appears; but in any given case this needs to be argued and not just assumed, especially when the thesis depends upon it. In terms of the literary

---

[31] (Edinburgh, 1962) = *Theologie des Alten Testaments* I (Munich, 1957).

[32] Von Rad discounted the significance of Gen. 15:7ff. on the grounds that it came from a source other than the Elohist to whom he ascribed 15:1-6 ([n.26], E. tr., p.130 = p.134 = col. 132).

dates that von Rad accepted it would be just as reasonable to argue that an originally non-cultic understanding of righteousness (Gen. 15:6) was subsequently incorporated within the cult, rather than vice versa. (This problem is avoided by most recent scholars who tend both to be doubtful about the ascription of Gen. 15:1-6 to E and to bring the date of composition of Gen. 15 down to the exile.)[33]

Thirdly, it is likely that von Rad did not give much thought to the two issues just raised because of his wider views about the history of Israel's religion. His whole discussion of Gen. 15:6 appears to be a sort of microcosm of his understanding of the origins of Israel's theological traditions within a world of wholly sacral/cultic practice and thought;[34] it was only subsequent to a fundamental shift from sacral to nonsacral in the early monarchical period ("The Solomonic Enlightenment") that traditions developed in the wider contexts of Israel's everyday life.[35] Although all the texts under discussion here were dated by von Rad later than the "Solomonic Enlightenment", he seems to have regarded the move of traditions from within to outside the cult as a basic and recurring feature of Israel's experience. But while there is much of value in this conception, it is highly debatable exactly how widespread such a process was (and, in particular, the central notion of a "Solomonic Enlightenment" has been heavily criticized as being unfounded);[36] its heuristic value for interpreting Gen. 15:6 is therefore doubtful.

Fourthly, there is one particular deficiency in von Rad's view of the sacral nature of Israel's premonarchical traditions that is of importance for Gen. 15:6. Within the early sacral traditions von Rad allows for no major distinction between the patriarchal and Mosaic traditions, but rather groups all the material together as belonging to a "patriarchal cultic world".[37] Here, "patriarchal" is not used specifically with reference to Abraham, Isaac, and Jacob, but rather as a general term to convey the early, premonarchical ethos as a whole; and the fact that he can thus classify all Israel's early traditions without distinction supports

---

[33] See e.g. Westermann (n. 19), pp.209-10, 214-16 for bibliography and an overview of recent discussion; also R. Rendtorff, "Genesis 15 im Rahmen der theologischen Bearbeitung der Vätergeschichten", in R. Albertz et al. (ed.). *Werden und Wirken des Alten Testaments (Festschrift für C. Westermann)* (Göttingen and Neukirchen-Vluyn, 1980), pp.74-81.

[34] Von Rad asks rhetorically "Is it conceivable that the statement that faith is reckoned as righteousness arose wholly and solely from the reflections of a theologian?", and goes on to say that the pronouncement of 15:6 is "inconceivable...except on the basis of quite specific sacral traditions" ([n. 26], p.125 = p.130 = col. 129).

[35] See (n. 31), E. tr., pp. 33-4, 37-8, 263 = pp.42-3, 45-6, 262, also his essay "The Beginnings of Historical Writing in Ancient Israel" in his *Problem of the Hexateuch* (n. 26), pp. 166-204.

[36] See e.g. J.L. Crenshaw, *Old Testament Wisdom* (London, 1982), pp. 52-3, and n.25.

[37] (n. 31), E. tr., pp. 37, 39, 396 = pp. 45-6, 47, 394.

the contention that in von Rad's understanding no major distinction between patriarchal and Mosaic traditions is envisaged. Yet the Old Testament itself clearly makes a distinction between the religion of the patriarchs and Yahwistic religion as mediated to Israel through Moses.[38] Despite the fact that all the patriarchal traditions as they now stand have been told from the perspective of Mosaic Yahwism, a perspective which has in varying degrees moulded the content of the traditions, there is clear evidence that the Yahwistic tradents of the patriarchal traditions were aware of the distinctiveness of the religion of the patriarchs (imbued as it is with attitudes and practices that are at variance with Israel's Torah), and on the whole imaginatively retained this distinctiveness even when retelling the traditions within the context of Israel. This distinctiveness is essentially that the context within which the patriarchs are set precedes Israel, Sinai and the Torah, a context in which the commandments given to Israel had not yet been given and therefore did not necessarily apply. It is vital that any interpretation of the patriarchal traditions takes this context seriously.[39] Yet to compare Gen. 15:6 with Lev. 7:18, etc., and to argue that the non-cultic context of the former may represent a significant shift from the cultic context of the latter precisely fails to allow for the possibility that the crucial consideration may be that Gen. 15:6 is not anti-cultic or even simply non-cultic but rather pre-cultic. It is not the case, of course, that the patriarchs are depicted as without a cult of their own, but their cult is different from, and antecedent to, Israel's cult, and it is the relationship between Abraham's righteousness and that mediated through Israel's cult that is the point at issue. A comparison on von Rad's terms is not to the point.

IV

I propose that a fresh approach to the interpretation of Gen. 15:6 is needed. In terms of method, I suggest that the discussion should begin with the nearest parallel to Gen. 15:6 in the Old Testament, the one other passage in which "reckon" and "righteousness" occur in conjunction, that is Ps. 106:31. It is

---

[38] For the argument in the rest of this paragraph, see the fuller discussion in my book *The Old Testament of The Old Testament* (Minneapolis, 1992).

[39] Of course, von Rad recognized both the distinctiveness ofthe patriarchal period ([n.31], E.tr., p.175 = pp. 176-7) and the appropriation and reinterpretation of this material within a Yahwistic context (pp. 166-7). My point of disagreement is with his apparent supposition that once the patriarchal material had been appropriated within a Yahwistic context then the significance of the distinctive salvation-historical context of the patriarchs (before Moses, Sinai and the Torah) was forgotten. Von Rad says, "J and E seem to be completelv unaware of it [the patriarchal stage in cultic history], and even if memories of it did live on into their time, the storytellers attached no importance to them" ([n. 31], E.tr., p.166 = p. 170). It is against this that I argue in my *The Old Testament of the Old Testament* (n.38).

indeed customary for commentators to note the parallel, but simply to note it without comment,[40] an omission which is surprising given that the action of Phinehas which occasions the "reckoning as righteousness" (Ps. 106:30; cf. Num. 25:6-13) is strikingly different from the faith of Abraham as generally understood (Franz Delitzsch once observed that Ps. 106:31 "bears the same relation to Gen. 15:6 that St. James does to St. Paul").[41] In most studies it appears that two assumptions are made. First, not unreasonably, it is assumed that because the same formula is used in both Ps. 106:31 and Gen. 15:6 it has the same meaning in each passage. Secondly, more questionably, it is assumed that since the meaning of Gen. 15:6 is already known, Ps. 106:31 is not needed to illuminate Gen. 15:6 but simply illustrates another use of the same already-known formula. So, for example, after he has noted that Abraham's faith is an attitude to God that is declared correct and noted the related use of $s^e daqah$ in Deut. 24:13, Westermann comments, "similarly Ps. 106:31: 'that has been reckoned to him (Phinehas) as righteousness' (correct comportment in a critical situation); 'the attitude of a good, pious, loyal servant of God' (H. Gunkel)".[42]

In terms of method, I propose that this procedure should be reversed. Instead of starting with Gen. 15:6, whose meaning is controversial because of its history of interpretation, it would be better to start with Ps. 106:31, which has little significant history of interpretation and whose meaning is therefore not controversial. If the meaning of the latter can be ascertained, then it may be able to serve as a control for deciding the meaning of the former. It is of course hardly possible to rule out the possibility that the phrase "reckon as righteousness" may be used in Ps. 106:31 with a sense different from that which it has in Gen. 15:6. Nonetheless, the natural assumption is that where the same (and otherwise unparalleled) phrase is used the same meaning is intended, unless there are good reasons to suppose the contrary, and so similarity of meaning will be the heuristic assumption in this discussion.[43]

---

[40] So   e.g. S.R. Driver, *The Book of Genesis* (12 edn, London, 1926), p.176; J. Skinner, *Genesis* (2nd edn, Edinburgh, 1930), p.280; Wenham (n. 14), pp.329-30. Likewise, commentators on Ps. 106 usually do no more than simply note the parallel with Gen. 15:6 without probing its possible significance; e.g. H. Gunkel, *Die Psalmen* (Göttingen, 1926), p.467; H.-J. Kraus, *Psalmen 2* (Neukirchen Kreis Moers, 1960), p. 731; A. A. Anderson, *Psalms* 2 (London, 1972), p. 745; L. C. Allen, *Psalms 101-150* (Waco, Texas, 1983), p.49.

[41] *A New Commentary on Genesis* II (Edinburgh, 1889), p.166.

[42] (n 19), p.223. Similarly Hahn ([n. 2], p. 92) notes the parallel between Gen. 15:6 and Ps. 106:31, and assimilates the latter to the former; he comments that although Ps. 106:31 does not use the term *he'emin* a reference back to Gen. 15:6 may nonetheless be intended, in which case Phinehas' action would be understood as an act of faith.

[43] Identity of meaning is a heuristic assumption which must be tested by its practical fruitfulness. If it could be shown that one usage significantly antedated the other, it would

If we turn to study Ps. 106:31, it should first be noted that the formulation of the crucial words "reckon as righteousness" is not in fact identical with that in Gen. 15:6:

Ps. 106:30-1: *wayya`amod pinhas way$^e$pallel    watte`aṣar hammaggepah wattehaśeb lo liṣ^{e}daqah   l^{e}dor wador `ad-`olam*
Gen. 15:6: *w^{e}he'emin bayhwh wayyaḥ$\check{s}^e$beha lo ṣ^{e}daqah*

The two differences are that *haśab* is Niphal in Ps. 106:31, but Qal in Gen. 15:6, and that *ṣ^{e}daqah* in Ps. 106:31 is preceded by *l^e*. It is unlikely, however, that either of these differences is significant. It has already been seen that *haśab* can bear the same technical meaning of "reckon" in both Niphal and Qal; while the *l^e* probably functions in Ps. 106:31 simply to show that *ṣ^{e}daqah* is not the subject of the passive verb *wattehaśeb,* which is an impersonal form with God as the implied agent, but the outcome or result of the act of reckoning, as in Gen. 15:6.[44] Thus despite these small differences, the central formula "reckon as righteousness" is essentially the same in both texts.

There remains, however, one other difference between the two texts. This is the fact that Phinehas' righteousness is said to be "to all generations for ever". It is this that surely creates severe difficulties for the consensus view that *ṣ^{e}daqah* means "correct behaviour" in Gen. 15:6 and is no different in Ps. 106:31. For what sense would it make to say that "correct comportment in a critical situation" or "the attitude of a good servant" lasts for ever? It may be that Ps. 106:31 has a significance that has been generally overlooked, and the point of departure for a fresh study must be the fact that the psalmist envisages Phinehas' *ṣ^{e}daqah* as something enduring.

It should be noted that the rendering of Ps. 106:31 is not in fact without ambiguity. The crucial syntactical question is whether the temporal phrase "to all generations for ever" qualifies the verb "reckoned" or the noun "righteousness". If the former, then the sense would be: "in every generation for ever this action of Phinehas is reckoned to be a righteous deed"; the one specific action is constantly recalled and extolled as a righteous action, presumably

---

be possible to argue that the later passage might be reusing an old formula in a new way. Even if the two usages were contemporary with each other, that would not guarantee similarity of meaning. Nonetheless, despite the difficulty of dating Gen. 15:6, it will be argued that it probably dates from the same period as Ps. 106:31 and that it also has a similar meaning. Since any argument as to the relationship between date and interpretation can easily become circular, it seems best to give attention primarily to linguistic and contextual evidence and to leave the question of dating until the end.

[44] The LXX rendering of *ṣ^{e}daqah* in Gen. 15:6 by *eis dikaiosunen,* which interprets *ṣ^{e}daqah* as though it were *liṣ^{e}daqah,* is a natural interpretative explication of no great significance.

primarily by God but also, by natural implication, by Israel. If the latter, then the sense would be "this was reckoned to Phinehas as righteousness of a sort that endures to all generations for ever"; the one specific action had lasting effects, effects expressed by the term "righteousness". This latter sense would presumably include the former, since the enduring effects of the action would obviously cause it to be constantly recalled. Nonetheless it is markedly different, for it is the enduring quality of $ṣ^e daqah$, rather than its constant recall, that would be the concern of the text.

It is the former interpretation that seems to have been preferred by scholars so far as they have addressed the issue.[45] It gives $ṣ^e daqah$ its common meaning of a morally commendable action, and it makes obvious sense, for the story of the zeal of Phinehas (Num. 25) was no doubt frequently retold in biblical as well as postbiblical times.[46] There are, however, two surely decisive considerations which favour the correctness of the second interpretation.[47] First, there is the form of the verb $wattehašeb$, imperfect with waw consecutive, which naturally refers to a completed action (as e.g. $watte{\grave{\;}}aṣar$ in Ps. 106:30b), not a continuous one, for which one would expect waw consecutive and perfect, i.e. $w^e nehš^e bah$. The verb form indicates a single reckoning, not a repeated one. Secondly, the psalmist is clearly alluding to the tradition recounted in Num. 25 where the central concern is that Phinehas' zealous action on YHWH's behalf results in YHWH giving to Phinehas a covenant of peace, which is specified as a "covenant of perpetual priesthood" ($b^e rit\ k^e hunnat\ {\grave{\;}}olam$) for both "himself and his descendants after him" ($lo\ ul^e zar{\grave{\;}}o\ 'aharayw$, Num. 25:13). It is the empirical reality of the priesthood that the psalmist must have in mind when he says "to all generations for ever", a priesthood which, no doubt, was part of

---

[45] Some commentators and translators offer a rendering that simply preserves the ambiguity of the Hebrew (e.g. Gunkel [n. 40], Kraus [n. 40], A. Weiser, *The Psalms* [London, 1962], p.678. Also the *Revised Standard Version* and the *New English Bible*) . Sometimes, however, an explication is offered. So, for example, Allen renders the verse, "It has been regarded by God as a virtuous act / throughout all generations forever" ([n. 40], p.46). The *Jerusalem Bible* has "Hence his reputation for virtue / through successive generations for ever". This would appear also to be the implication of M. Dahood's rendering "This was credited to his virtue / from generation to generation, forever" *(Psalms 101-150* [Garden City, New York, 1970], p.65). Cf. P. J. Budd's comment that "in view of the tradition preserved by the psalmist in Ps. 106:28-31 it seems possible that Phinehas was one of those who acted decisively as 'judge,' and who thereby won for himself a lasting reputation as a righteous man" *(Numbers* [Waco, Texas, 1984], p.281).

[46] For early Jewish use of the story and example of Phinehas, see M. Hengel, *Die Zeloten* (Leiden/Köln, 1961), pp. 154-81.

[47] This rendering seems to have been preferred by Gunkel, who commented that $ṣ^e daqah$ in Ps. 106:31 has the sense of "Verdienst", "Lohn", that is a reward constituted by the perpetual priesthood ([n. 40], p.467).

Israel contemporary with himself, and which validated its position by reference to Phinehas. This priesthood for Israel was understood as the lasting legacy of Phinehas' action. Thus the meaning of Ps. 106:31 is not that Phinehas' action was often recalled and cited as righteous, though no doubt that was the case, but that Phinehas' action had enduring effects for Israel because God reckoned it to Phinehas as $s^e daqah$.

If this construal of Ps. 106:31 is correct, it raises the question precisely what $s^e daqah$ means in this context. But before we consider this, it will be worthwhile to return to Gen. 15:6 and see whether the proposed general sense of "reckon as righteousness" in Ps. 106:31, that a specific action can be given enduring effects by God, would be applicable to Gen. 15:6. Admittedly, Gen. 15:6 does not use the language of "to all generations for ever", but it may be that "to all generations for ever" does not alter the meaning of "reckon as righteousness" but simply makes explicit, in the light of Num. 25:13, the sort of implications that may also be present in Gen. 15:6. The likelihood of this is increased when one considers certain fundamental similarities between the stories of Phinehas and Abraham.

In order to set Gen. 15:6 in context and compare it with the story of Phinehas, two points must be made. The first is the fact that all the patriarchal stories, as they now stand, are told from the perspective of Israel. Although the stories contain much evidence of originating in a context which was not that of Israel with its Mosaic Yahwism, that original context is of real but restricted significance for the storytellers and editors who recount the stories from within the context of Israel and its faith. The stories have been appropriated by Yahwism and so have become Israel's stories. They are told from the point of view of Israel looking back to its origins and seeking to understand its contemporary position in the light of those origins. Although, therefore, the storytelling is imaginatively consistent in maintaining the world and perspective of the patriarchs as the primary focus, it is always legitimate to seek to discern whether the perspective of Israel may not also be present in the text.

Secondly, it is important to ask why the writer of Gen. 15:6 should have mentioned Abraham's faith and God's response to it at all, and why in this particular context - the basic issue that was seen by Ramban. For it is clear that a trusting and obedient attitude to YHWH was Abraham's consistent response. It is highly doubtful that Abraham's believing response to the promise of Gen. 15:4-5 should be seen as a deeper or truer response than his response to the initial command to leave home, family and country (Gen. 12:1-4). Likewise, it is doubtful that his response to the promise of Gen. 15:4-5 should be seen as in any way different to his response to the promise of 13:14-17. The promise of 13:14-17 is in fact more amazing than that of 15:4-5, for it not only promises countless descendants in a similar way (the dust of the earth is hardly less than the stars of heaven) but also promises land at the same time. Although Abraham's response is not specified as such, it is hardly to be supposed that he was seen as disbelieving; rather, a trusting attitude is clearly presupposed by the writer. The promise of 13:14-17 has received much less attention than that of 15:4-5, not least because it lacks the imaginative appeal of the scene envisaged in the latter. Nonetheless, it sharply poses the question why Abraham's faith and YHWH's response should be specified at 15:6 rather than elsewhere.

The answer to this question must be sought by looking at the context of Gen. 15 as a whole, and specifically the remarkable narrative of 15:7-21. Although the content of the double promise of both descendants and land (v.18b) is not new within the Abraham story (cf. Gen. 12:1-3,7, 13:14-17), what is unprecedented is the strange and elaborate ritual that now accompanies it, and which the writer interprets as constituting a covenant (v.18a). Whatever the precise significance of the ritual, it suggests a formal and symbolic commitment on YHWH's part which furthers and enhances the promises already made.[48] Thus Gen. 15 gives the impression of being the fullest and most formal portrayal of YHWH's commitment to Israel (both people and land) in the whole Abraham cycle, a portrayal of unusual and imaginatively suggestive character.

It is this, I suggest, that accounts for the writer's inclusion of the statement in Gen. 15:6. The effect of 15:6 is to link Israel's existence as a people in the land (i.e. the concern of Gen. 15 as a whole) to Abraham's trust in YHWH. It was not only the promise of YHWH that gave existence to Israel, primary and fundamental though that was, but also the faithful response of Abraham. It was because Abraham put his faith in YHWH, and YHWH reckoned this to him as ṣᵉdaqah, that YHWH entered into the ritual that constituted his covenant with Israel.

The perspective of the writer of Gen. 15:6 is therefore analogous to that of the psalmist in Ps. 106:30-1. As the psalmist writes in the time of the priesthood of the house of Phinehas, and relates it back to the story of Phinehas' faithful zeal, so the Genesis writer works from the perspective of Israel as YHWH's people and relates this back to the stories of Abraham's faithfulness to YHWH, and in particular the moving and mysterious story of Gen. 15. As Phinehas' faithfulness led to a perpetual covenant of priesthood, so Abraham's faithfulness led to a covenant (presumably perpetual)[49] of YHWH's commitment to Israel as

---

[48] From a traditio-historical perspective it has been suggested that Gen. 15 may represent the earliest form of the tradition of divine promise (so e.g. Lohfink [n. 5]) which would mean that the other promises in Gen. 12-14 which now precede it in the literary tradition were once dependent on it. But whether or not this is so does not affect the central point of the argument that only in Gen. 15 are the divine promises linked to a symbolic ritual.

[49] Admittedly, the term bᵉrit in Gen. 15:18a is not qualified by `olam, but such a sense may nonetheless have been considered by an ancient writer to be implicit in the text. On the one hand, there is the promissory form of the bᵉrit, analogous to the promissory covenants with Noah, Phinehas and David, all of which are specified as "perpetual" (`olam, Gen. 9:16; Num. 25:13; 2 Sam. 23:5), and there is nothing in the text of Gen. 15

people and land. As Phinehas stands to the priesthood, so Abraham stands to Israel. As Ps. 106:31 (with Num. 25) shows how the priesthood owes its covenant status to YHWH's response to Phinehas, so Gen. 15:6 shows how Israel owes its covenant status to YHWH's response to Abraham.

If this general understanding of Ps. 106:31 and Gen. 15:6 is along the right lines, it can be seen that our proposed interpretation of Gen. 15:6 is, broadly speaking, closer to the traditional Jewish interpretation, i.e. that the concern of the text is the faithfulness of Abraham and its value for Israel, than to the traditional Christian interpretation, i.e. that the concern of the text is the faith of Abraham in relation to Abraham's own standing before God. The latter interpretation is not, of course, thereby excluded, and may to some extent be included within the former, but the point is that the Jewish emphasis appears closer to the original concerns of the text. Nonetheless, however much the rabbinic conception of the "merit of the fathers" may represent a theological development that is sensitive to, and a legitimate extension of, the nuances of the biblical text, it remains an important task not to import too quickly into our interpretation the overtones of postbiblical interpretation, but rather still to seek to understand the meaning of the text in its biblical context.

V

What, then, is the precise meaning of the expression "to reckon as righteousness"? I suggest that the question may best be approached via von Rad's thesis about the cultic origins of such language. Although I have rejected the inferences von Rad drew from his thesis, it does not follow that his thesis in itself may not still be substantially correct and able to shed light upon Gen. 15:6 in a different way. There are two important insights in his thesis that I wish to affirm and extend; first, when *ḥašab* is used with accusative and *le* of recipient (reckon something to somone), a usage akin to a double accusative (cf. GK 117*ii*,119*t*), it has a meaning distinct from that of other uses of *ḥašab*;

---

to suggest that the covenant was contingent or temporary in nature. On the other hand, there is the covenant with Abraham in Gen. 17, which is specified as "perpetual" (v. 7). As the text stands, this must be understood as a fuller unfolding of the the covenant of Gen. 15. Moreover, whatever the relationship between Gen. 15 and 17 may have been traditio-historically, it is unlikely that P ever envisaged its Abrahamic covenant as depicting a covenant different from that in Gen. 15 (also Old Testament tradition elsewhere never implies that there was more than one covenant between YHWH and Abraham; it understands the one covenant as "perpetual"; Ps. 105:8-11 // 1 Chron. 16:15-18). If, therefore, the consistent understanding elsewhere in the Old Testament is that the covenant between YHWH and Abraham is "perpetual", it may well be that such a sense is implicit in Gen. 15:18a in its own right. In any case, it is likely that the text would have been understood in such a way from the exilic or early post-exilic period (which, as I shall argue below, may in fact have been the time when it was written).

secondly, *ḥašab* in this sense is consistently used as a religious term with reference to human standing before God.

The significance of the distinctive usage of *ḥašab* has not always been sufficiently taken into account. For example, Gunkel argued that the meaning of Gen. 15:6 is that Abraham's trusting response to God's promise is appropriate behaviour that indicates that he is truly a pious, righteous man: "diese Tat des Glaubens wider. alle Wahrscheinlichkeit war in Gottes Augen ein deutlicher Beweis, dass Abraham gerecht sei: darum hat ihn Gott fur seinen treuen und frommen Knecht gehalten".[50] However, if the writer had wished to say that God regarded Abraham as a righteous man *(ṣaddiq)*, he would have used a different idiom. When *ḥašab* is used to express an assessment of a person or thing as having a particular quality or character, the person under consideration is in the accusative, and the quality attributed to him is usually expressed by *l^e* (Gen. 38:15; I Sam. 1:13; Job 13:24, 19:15, 33:10, 41:27,32 [Heb.19,24]; cf. Isa. 29:17, 32:15; Lam. 4:2); although sometimes the quality attributed may be expressed without a preposition (Isa. 53:4; cf. Gen. 31:15). Thus, had the writer wished to say "and he considered him to be a righteous man" he would surely have written *wayyaḥš^{e}behu l^{e}ṣaddiq* (or perhaps *wayyaḥš^{e}behu ṣaddiq)*. However, in Gen. 15:6 and Ps. 106:31, and other related uses of *ḥašab,* the person under consideration is referred to with *l^e*, and the thing reckoned to him is in the accusative (or nominative, if the verb is passive). The idiom used in Gen. 15:6 indicates that the sense cannot be "consider someone to be something", but must rather be "reckon something to somone". It is important that this latter sense be recognized as distinct and not confused with the former.

It is also possible to extend von Rad's thesis about the idiom "to reckon something to someone". Although von Rad was correct in pointing to the cultic uses of the phrase, it is unnecessary to suppose that it was always a cultic phrase. Apart from Gen. 15:6 there are at least three uses in clearly non-cultic contexts (2 Sam. 19:20; Ps. 106:31; Prov. 27:14).[51] However, in every instance the context is religious, that is there is always reference in some way to human standing before God. The evidence suggests that although von Rad was right to argue that the idiom of "reckoning something to someone" was at home in the cult, and may well have originated there, it nonetheless became an idiom that could be used in religious language in a variety of contexts.

It may further be noted that the historical likelihood of "reckoning righteousness to someone" as a recognized religious idiom is increased by the fact that "reckoning iniquity *(`awon)* to someone" also appears to have been a recognized idiom (2 Sam. 19:20; Ps. 32:2). The fact that *ṣ$^e$daqah* and *`awon* are sometimes explicitly contrasted to each other (Ps. 69:28,29; 2 Sam. 22:24,

---

[50] *Genesis* (3rd edn, Göttingen, 1910), p.180.

[51] The cultic nature of Ps. 32:2 is a matter of debate because of the psalm's many affinities with Wisdom literature.

25//Ps. 18:23,24 [Heb. 24,25]; Isa. 53:11),[52] and that they are both used in a similar way with *ḥašab*, suggests that the phrases *ḥašab ṣᵉdaqah lᵉ* and *ḥašab ʿawon lᵉ* should be seen as correlative expressions, representing two opposite pronouncements upon a person's position before YHWH. It is against this general idiomatic background that the specific meaning of "reckon righteousness" in Gen. 15:6 and Ps. 106:31 may now be explored.

VI

In the use of the idiom "to reckon righteousness/iniquity to someone" there appear to be four assumptions. First, there is a recognition of the inherent quality or value of what the addressee has done; an unacceptable sacrifice (Lev. 7:18), wrong conduct (2 Sam. 19:20), or right conduct (Ps. 106:31; Gen. 15:6). Actions are subjected to a moral and religious assessment within the context of Yahwism.

Secondly, there is an assumption that actions have moral and religious consequences. As von Rad put it, "Israel was convinced that there was a definite and even clearly recognisable connexion between what a man does and what happens to him, such that the evil deed recoils banefully upon the agent, the good one beneficially." "...the presupposition... is the closest possible correspondence between action and fate: what is in question is a process which, in virtue of a power proper alike to all that is good and all that is evil, comes to a good or an evil end. Israel regarded this as a basic order of her whole existence, to which Jahweh had given effect and over whose functioning he himself kept watch."[53] In this context we may note the wellknown point that *ʿawon* can signify both an evil act in itself and the result of that act, in such a way that it can sometimes be hard to distinguish between the different meanings;[54] the same difficulty in distinguishing between act and consequence is true also for *ṣᵉdaqah* (e.g. Deut. 6:25, 24:13; Isa. 56:1).

Thirdly, despite the close connection between action and consequence, there is little sense in the Old Testament that the relationship is inflexible or inevitable. Rather, Old Testament writers often emphasize that the outcome of actions is open to change, particularly with reference to the possibility of nullifying *ʿawon*, through either forgiveness *(salaḥ,* e.g. Exod. 34:9; Ps. 130:3-4) or expiation *(kipper,* e.g. Isa. 27:9; Prov. 16:6).[55] Indeed, the two explicit uses of the phrase "reckon iniquity" (2 Sam. 19:20; Ps. 32:2) both

---

[52] When the root *ṣdq* is used in adjectival or verbal form, then it is usually contrasted with the root *rš*ʿ (e.g. Ps. 1, Ezek. 18).

[53] (n.31), E. tr., pp.384,265 = pp.382,264.

[54] Cf. von Rad (n.32), E. tr., pp.262ff, 385-6 = pp.261ff, 382-4.

[55] Also important in this context is the common occurrence of divine "repentance" which I have discussed briefiy in "Did the Serpent Get It Right"? (above, pp.10-12).

depend on the possibility that actions designated as `awon should not be
followed by their expected consequences.

Fourthly, when the phrase "reckon righteousness/iniquity" was used in the
cult, it would have been spoken by the priest as an authoritative pronouncement
on YHWH's behalf, a "performative utterance" designed to enact what it says
and looking to the future. However, in Gen. 15:6 and Ps. 106:31, the reckoning
is made directly by YHWH himself and is set as something completed in the
past. By giving this insight into the mind of YHWH the writer lays emphasis
both upon the validity of the judgement thus given and upon the certainty that
what was reckoned was indeed enacted.

What, then, would be understood as the outcome of "reckoning
righteousness"? In general terms, there is a consistent Old Testament
understanding that $ṣ^edaqah$ leads to an enhanced quality of life for both
individual and community. For example, the idealized descriptions of a
righteous king consistently portray a life of blessing and peace for his subjects
that will be the result of the king's righteousness (e.g. Ps. 72; Isa. 11:1-9,
32:1-8,15-20, esp.v.17; Jer. 23:5-6, 33:15-16). Or, in certain exemplary
narratives, the ṣaddiq not only can expect life for himself, even at a time when
divine judgement threatens, but can also cause life to be granted to others
(Noah, Gen. 6:9, 7:1; Cf. Abraham's dialogue with YHWH over Sodom, Gen.
18:16-33).[56] One would therefore expect that the reckoning of righteousness to a
person would lead to enhanced quality of life in some form or other.

More specifically, we may note with regard to $ṣ^edaqah$ that, just as it may
be difficult to distinguish between the righteous act and its consequence, so it
can be difficult to distinguish between $ṣ^edaqah$ as a human quality (correct
behaviour) and as a divine quality (deliverance, vindication, blessing).
Particularly significant is the statement in Deut. 6:25 that if Israel is careful to
observe all that YHWH has commanded them "it shall be righteousness for us"
($uṣ^edaqah$ $tihyeh$-$llanu$). In the wider context of Deuteronomy, the result of
obedience is characteristically expressed in terms of blessing (28:1-14), and so
in general terms there is clearly a close connection between $ṣ^edaqah$ and
b^erakah.[57] Moreover, the wording of 6:25 is noteworthy. The basic sense of the
construction of noun with l^e and suffix is possessive, i.e. "we will have
righteousness". The construction also appears to be analogous to that of
"reckoning righteousness", for the related passage in Deut. 24:13, where it is

---

[56] The question of the manner and extent to which the ṣaddiq could benefit others by
his $ṣ^edaqah$, or the raša` involve others in his `awon, could become a difficult issue
to determine (Ezek. 14:12-20; 18; Jer. 31:29-30).

[57] Cf. Ps. 24:5 where b^erakah is used in parallelism with $ṣ^edaqah$, in the context of
YHWH's response to the worshipper who lives righteously (v.4: the term ṣaddiq is not
used, but the concept is present).

said of the person who behaves generously in the matter of a loan and a pledge that "it shall be righteousness to you *(ul^{e}ka tihyeh ṣ^{e}daqah)* before YHWH your God", shows that the phrase signifies some kind of divine approval of the action. The righteous action will be seen by YHWH who will respond to it by ensuring that the person receives what is appropriate to, because it arises out of, that action - the person can be sure of divine blessing. The point, therefore, of Deut. 6:25 is not that Israel will be doing the right thing, i.e. will be righteous *(w^{e}hayinu ṣaddiqim),* if they are obedient, which would be redundant in context; nor is it that they will be regarded as righteous by YHWH *(w^{e}nehṣabnu ṣaddiqim);* rather, their obedient behaviour will be approved by YHWH in such a way that they will "have righteousness": their relationship with YHWH will be enhanced and they can fully expect to receive the appropriate outcome of such an enhancement in the form of the bestowal of divine blessing. In this usage ṣ^{e}daqah as right human behaviour merges with ṣ^{e}daqah as divine blessing. I suggest that it is the same in Gen. 15:6 and Ps. 106:31 also.

Finally, we should return to the striking statement about ṣ^{e}daqah in Ps. 106:31 (and, as I have suggested, by implication in Gen. 15:6 also) that it represents something enduring. Although initially this may appear odd in the light of the discussion of ṣ^{e}daqah thus far, two points should be noted. First, there is the fact that ʿawon, which we have argued can function as an opposite to ṣ^{e}daqah, is well known as representing a condition that can endure for a prolonged period of time. Three examples will suffice to illustrate the point. (i) There is the pronouncement in two of the central ethical and theological texts of the Old Testament, the ten commandments and the divine self-revelation to Moses (Exod. 20:5, 34:7), that ʿawon may be visited by God upon several generations. (ii) There is the archetypal sin of Israel at Baalpeor (Num. 25; cf. Num. 31:16; Deut. 4:3; Ps. 106:28-31; Hos. 9:10), from whose ʿawon, according to one tradition, Israel was still not cleansed when in the promised land (Josh. 22:17). (iii) There is the divine pronouncement about the permanent exclusion of the house of Eli from the priesthood (I Sam 3:11-14), where it is explicitly said that the iniquity of the house of Eli will never be expiated by sacrifice *('im-yitkapper ʿawon bet-ʿeli b^{e}zebaḥ ub^{e}minḥah ʿad-ʿolam).* This last example may be particularly significant because of possible links between the house of Eli being excluded from priesthood "for ever" and the descendants of Phinehas being granted a priesthood "for ever" (Num. 25:13; Ps. 106:31). But whatever the historical processes and interrelationship underlying these texts,[58] the important point for our purpose is the theological conception of ʿawon as depicting a lasting condition of human guilt and exclusion before God. Against this background it becomes easier to understand ṣ^{e}daqah as also depicting something lasting.

---

[58] See e.g. F.M.Cross, *Canaanite Myth and Hebrew Epic* (Cambridge, Massachusetts, 1973), pp. 201-3.

Secondly, it is likely that the conception of both Ps. 106:31 and Gen. 15:6 of $ṣ^edaqah$ as enduring is related to the bestowal of the covenants on Phinehas and Abraham respectively. So far as each covenant was understood as enduring, so the usage of $ṣ^edaqah$ has been influenced by the theological conceptions associated with each covenant.

It is in the light of all these considerations that the meaning of "reckon as righteousness" in Ps. 106:31 and Gen. 15:6 can be understood. The writers are using a recognized religious idiom with regard to human obedience to God and what can be expected to flow from it, in the context of a wider understanding of the integral, though not inevitable, relationship between good or evil behaviour and its consequences for human life. The statement that YHWH "reckoned righteousness" indicates both the divine recognition of the true quality of the behaviour of Abraham and Phinehas and the affirmative response which brought lasting blessing. It was a bold but appropriate idiom for the psalmist and the Genesis editor to use as they interpreted the traditions of Phinehas and Abraham respectively. In each case there was an outstanding example of human faithfulness to YHWH, to which YHWH had responded in a way that was of enduring benefit to Israel. The writers use this idiom of "reckoning righteousness" to show how YHWH's bestowal of blessing on Israel, in the form of the two covenants, was integrally connected with, and grew out of, the human behaviour that occasioned it.

In theological terms this represents a profound understanding of the value of human behaviour in relation to God. The semantic point that it can be difficult to distinguish between $ṣ^edaqah$ as human behaviour and as action of God reflects the theological point that when a person lives in full obedience to God there is a convergence between human and divine action. Not only is there the general point that righteous behaviour can enhance a relationship with God in a way that leads to blessing for the person(s) in question. There is the further and deeper point that in two archetypal and paradigmatic traditions, those of Abraham and Phinehas, the enhanced relationship with God led to a kind of overflow such that enduring blessing was bestowed on Israel also.

VII

In the light of this interpretation, is it possible to determine the context and date of the writer of Gen. 15:6? Although any proposal must necessarily be tentative, there are three converging indications which give just sufficient justification for advancing a thesis.

First, there are the similarities between Gen. 15:6 and Gen. 22:15-18. The striking theological conception of the value of Abraham's faithful response in Gen. 15:6 is in fact closely paralleled in Gen. 22:15-18. In a study of the latter passage I concluded that: "A promise which previously was grounded solely in the will and purpose of YHWH is transformed so that it is now grounded *both* in the will of YHWH *and* in the obedience of Abraham. It is not that the divine promise has become contingent upon Abraham's obedience, but that Abraham's obedience has been incorporated into the divine promise. Henceforth Israel owes its existence not just to YHWH but also to Abraham."[59] Both passages display a similar concern to show how Israel's existence as a people is dependent upon both YHWH and Abraham.

If the similarity of outlook justifies postulating a common hand at work, two further points may follow. (i) In my study of Gen. 22:15-18 (below, pp.66-7,72) I noted certain linguistic peculiarities with affinities to texts of the 7th and 6th centuries. Although these are hardly compelling, they nonetheless suggest some such date for Gen. 22:15-18, and so for Gen. 15:6 also. (ii) In my study of Gen. 22:15-18 I argued that the verses repesent a theological commentary on the otherwise already complete story of 22:1-14,19. I suggest that the same is true of Gen. 15:6. The text of Gen. 15 could easily be read without v.6, and indeed we have already noted how v.6 does not conform either to the customary practice of theological interpretation in a divine speech or to the form-critical pattern of divine address and human response of lament or praise. The addition of v.6 as a distinctive theological interpretation subsequent to the composition of the rest of the story is a not-unlikely explanation of this departure from normal practice.

Secondly, there is the likely date of Ps. 106 in the 6th century, either during or after the exile. Admittedly, the psalm is difficult to date. The most specific evidence it affords is the reference to exile in vv.46-7. Although this may well be a reference to the Babylonian exile as something contemporary, it must be recognized that it need not be so. The exile might not be the Babylonian exile,[60] and the prayer to be gathered from the nations could belong to many different centuries. Nonetheless, the reference to exile together with the general theological tone of the psalm make a date in the mid 6th century as likely as any, and there is no good reason to reject the scholarly consensus which locates the psalm at about this period. If this is the correct date for the psalmist's use of "reckon as righteousness", the same may be the case for the Genesis editor also.

Thirdly, there is the fact that it was in the period of the exile that the figure of Abraham came into prominence in Israel's theological reflection (Ezek. 33:24; Isa. 41:8, 51:1-2).[61] It seems clear that part of Israel's response to the exile as it sought a hope for the future was to look to the traditions of Abraham and to seek in them a pattern for their own self-understanding. The appeal of the prophet to "look to the rock from which you were hewn...look to Abraham your father" may have been precisely the concern that motivated the writer of Gen.

---

[59] "The earliest commentary on the Akedah", below, p.71.
[60] See the cautionary comments of Weiser (n.45), p. 680.
[61] This point is central to the thesis of Van Seters (n.25), although he develops it differently from the way proposed here.

15:6, 22:15-18 as he sought to understand the implications of the stories of Gen. 15 and 22 (the only two stories in the Abraham cycle in which active participation is restricted essentially to YHWH and Abraham, and in which the nature of the relationship between YHWH and Abraham is explored most deeply),[62] and to draw out from them a theological basis for Israel's future.[63]

In the light of these factors I suggest that the likely context and date for the writer of Gen. 15:6, 22:15-18 is the period of the exile, probably in the latter part, c.550-540 B.C., roughly contemporary with Second Isaiah.

The question whether this same writer made further contributions to the interpretation of the Abraham stories lies beyond the scope of the present essay. However, it should be noted that within Gen. 15 there is one other part that could well be the work of the same writer, that is 15:18a, *bayyom hahu' karat yhwh 'et-'abram b^{e}rit le'mor*. V.18a shares five characteristics in common wth v.6. First, it is a third-person theological statement about YHWH, rather than a first-person statement by him. Secondly, it uses the term *b^{e}rit*, which, like the language of 15:6 but unlike most of the other vocabulary of Gen. 15, resonates within a context of mature Hebrew theology. Thirdly, it functions as does 15:6 to provide a specific interpretation of the surrounding narrative and discourse. Fourthly, it specifies Abraham as the object of YHWH's dealings, but just as in 15:6 a concern for Israel is in view. Fifthly, it can easily be removed from the text without disturbing the flow of the story, as long as there was some speech introduction, such as *wayyo'mer yhwh*, in its place. It would be consistent with my thesis if 15:18a came from the same hand as 15:6.

This study, therefore, to some extent supports the current growing scholarly consensus that also dates Gen. 15:6 to the time of the exile. This was indeed a period when theological interpretation of the Abraham traditions came to the fore, and this has become incorporated into the traditions as we know them. However, I disagree with the consensus so far as it dates Gen. 15 as a whole to the exile, for I see Gen. 15:6 (and perhaps 15:18a), like 22:15-18, as a distinct theological commentary on an already-existing and authoritative tradition. For

---

[62] The restriction of focus to YHWH and Abraham is also the case in Gen. 17. However, in Gen. 17 dialogue predominates to such an extent that there is little narrative context or development, with the consequence that the relationship between YHWH and Abraham is not explored in the same sort of way as in the stories of Gen. 15, 22.

[63] It may be the case that the kind of interpretation of Gen. 15, 22 for which I have argued with regard to 15:6, 22:15-18 should be seen as part of a wider tendency, beginning perhaps in the exile, to revere Israel's past as normative for the present and future and to consider its texts as sources of appropriate guidance. For an account of such a process with regard to prophecy, see J. Barton *Oracles of God* (London, 1986), esp. ch.3. The phenomenon of inner-biblical exegesis is discussed extensively by M. Fishbane. *Biblical Interpretation in Ancient Israel* (Oxford, 1985), who does not, however, refer to either Gen. 15:6 or 22:15-18.

the composition of the story of Gen. 15 as a whole, it is to a time prior to the exile to which we must look.

VIII

Finally, although I cannot at present offer any thorough re-examination of the New Testament use of Gen. 15:6 in the light of my discussion, one or two pointers for possible lines of argument may be noted.

First, the tradition of interpretation represented in James 2:14-26, whereby Gen. 15:6 is understood in conjunction with Gen. 22, stands in continuity with the editorial interpretation of Abraham in the Old Testament itself. Moreover, the point that Abraham's faith cannot be understood apart from his whole life of obedient response to God is entirely in keeping with the concerns of the Old Testament text. It is notable, however, that despite his continuity with mainstream Jewish interpretation James makes no use of the rabbinic conception of $z^e kut$ 'abot, perhaps simply because it was not appropriate to his ethical exhortations.

Secondly, although Paul's use of Gen. 15:6 is strikingly different from that of James, it too is genuinely sensitive to the Old Testament text. (i) Paul takes with utmost seriousness the overall context of the Abraham stories within a period of salvation-history prior to, and distinct from, that of Moses and Israel. He argues that if faith and righteousness were possible in this pre-Sinai, pre-Torah context, then that, among other things, relativizes the claim that obedience to Torah is a *sine qua non* of faith and righteousness. (ii) In Gal. 3 Paul uses Gen. 15:6 as part of an argument that God's promises made to Abraham apply to Gentiles as much as to Jews. That is, Paul is concerned with the implications of God's dealings with Abraham for those who come after in a way analogous to what we have argued for Gen. 15:6 in its own right - though with the crucial difference that Gen. 15 is concerned solely for Israel, while Paul argues that when it is read in the light of Gen. 12:3 then its scope may legitimately be extended to include Gentiles also.

The use of Gen. 15:6 thus remains a classic case-study for the wider question of the use of the Hebrew Bible as scripture by both Jew and Christian.[64] I have argued that the rabbinic tradition of $z^e kut$ 'abot probably stands closer to the concerns of the Genesis writer than does the usage of either James or Paul, and yet both James and Paul were themselves developing genuine implications of the Genesis text in its wider context. Different

---

[64] For a recent study which seeks to overcome the impasse between Jewish and Christian approaches to Gen. 15:6, though touching only briefly on the hermeneutical issues at stake, see R.W.Klein, "Call, Covenant, and Community" *Currents in Theology and Mission* 15 (1988), pp.120-7. Fuller attention to these hermeneutical issues is given by Gaston (n. 13).

interpreters developed different implications because of their own differing theological contexts, and this will necessarily continue to be the case with contemporary interpreters, both Jewish and Christian. Nonetheless, while it would be idle to seek unanimity as to *the* meaning of the text, it remains the case both that some interpretations are better than others and that misunderstanding of alternative interpretations should be avoided.[65]

---

[65] I am grateful to Dr A. Gelston for his comments on a draft of this essay.

THE EARLIEST COMMENTARY ON THE AKEDAH

Few stories within the Old Testament have received more commentary than the story of the testing of Abraham - widely known as the Akedah, the Binding of Isaac - in Gen. 22:1-19. Particularly within Jewish faith and thought the story has been reflected on and commented on so extensively that any survey of all the commentary material becomes a major undertaking.[1] Within recent years the regular appearance of articles and monographs devoted to the story attests its continuing fascination for the biblical commentator.[2] The thesis of this further addition to the literature of commentary is that there is in fact one part of the story that has been generally neglected, and that, rightly understood, it constitutes the earliest of all the story's recorded commentaries.

I

The part of the story in question is Gen. 22:15-18, the words of the angel of YHWH when he calls a second time from heaven. The reason for its comparative neglect is obvious - the main action and drama of the story is contained in 22:1-14. So, for example when Rembrandt interprets the story as an artist, it is the first call of the angel (v.12) and never the second call (v.15) which captures his imagination.[3] Likewise Kierkegaard's famous reflections on the story in his *Fear and Trembling*[4] concentrate exclusively on 22:1-14 without even the slightest passing reference to 22:15-18. At least one modern writer of a major commentary on Genesis manages to pass over 22:15-18 with no comment on their content whatsoever,[5] while most commentators content themselves with a brief paraphrase and the observation that the divine promises,

---

[1] A stimulating introduction to the history of interpretation is provided by S. Spiegel, *The Last Trial* (New York: 1979).

[2] For a general bibliography, see C. Westermann, *Genesis 36* (NeukirchenVluyn, 1981), pp. 429-30, E. tr. (Minneapolis, 1985; London, 1986), pp. 351-2, to which may be added the further works noted in J. L. Crenshaw, *A Whirlpool of Torment* (Philadelphia, 1984), p. 13, n. 10. A useful survey of the major trends of modern interpretation is provided by J.-L. Duhaime, "Le Sacrifice d'lsaac (Gn 22, 1-19): L'Héritage de Gunkel", *Science et Esprit* 33 (1981), pp. 139-56.

[3] Four of Rembrandt's pictures are included in G. von Rad's monograph *Das Opfer des Abraham* (Munich, 1971), pp. 86-95.

[4] Available in numerous editions, most recently Penguin Classics (Harmondsworth, 1985).

[5] E. A. Speiser, *Genesis* (Garden City, New York, 1964), pp. 165-6.

here renewed, are an important element elsewhere in the patriarchal narratives. Even those who notice that there is something distinctive about the verses do not linger to explore.[6] To the best of my knowledge no article has ever been devoted to the study of these verses,[7] which may enable the present writer to lay claim to a modest "first".

It might be claimed that such neglect is a relatively modern phenomenon, since there is at least one element in 22:15-18 that was of great significance for traditional Jewish interpretation of Gen. 22. As R.J.Daly puts it, "Of the several texts which mention the blessings promised to Abraham and his descendants, this is the *only* one in which these blessings are explicitly presented as a reward of a *particular* virtuous act on the part of Abraham. No great imagination is needed to see how important such a text would be for a theology whose basic soteriological theory centered around the idea of justification by works of obedience to the Law".[8] But while it is certainly true that the apparent doctrine of merit in 22:15-18 contributed to the importance the Akedah acquired in Jewish thought,[9] I still have the impression that relatively little attention was given to 22:15-18 as a significant unit in itself within the Akedah, once this theological principle had been extracted from it.[10] So a sense of the secondary

_____

[6] So, for example, R. Davidson notes the distinctiveness of 22:15-18, but simply comments, "Why they should be expressed in this particular form is unclear" *(Genesis 12-50* [Cambridge, 1979], p. 97). Likewise, G. von Rad notes that "This finale ends powerfully and celebrates the victor from Moriah in highest superlatives... The development is almost excessive", but offers no further reflection upon this *(Genesis* [2nd edn, London, 1972], p. 242, = *Das erste Buch Mose-Genesis* [5th edn, Göttingen, 1958], p. 207).

[7] Westermann's sectional bibliography ([n. 2], p. 430; E. tr., p. 352) lists three items specifically on these verses: R. Smend, *Jahwekrieg und Stammebund* (Göttingen, 1963); J. C. H. Lebram, "Nachbiblische Weisheitstraditionen", *VT* 15 (1965), pp. 167-237; D. E. Gowan, "The use of ya`an in Biblical Hebrew", *VT* 21 (1971), pp. 168-85. The relevance of the first two escapes me entirely (Lebram has only a passing reference to the Targum of 22:17 [p. 188]), while the third is simply a study of a linguistic issue of limited significance for the interpretation of this passage. The nearest to a study of 22:15-18 is the article by T. D. Alexander, "Genesis 22 and the Covenant of Circumcision" *JSOT* 25 (1983), pp. 17-22, but this is not an exegetical study and is concerned primarily with a proposed reading of 22:15-18 in relation to Gen. 17, as will be discussed below.

[8] "The Soteriological Significance of the Sacrifice of Isaac", *CBQ* 39 (1977), p.47.

[9] The question of what kind of doctrine of merit is contained in these verses is discussed below, pp.69-72.

[10] In, for example, the Targum of Ps. Jonathan on Gen. 22 (for a convenient presentation of which see J. Bowker, *The Targums and Rabbinic Literature* [Cambridge, 1969], pp. 224-34), vv. 15-18 are the one part of the story which is recounted almost unchanged, apart from a reference to merit (z^ekut) added in v.18.

importance of 22:15-18 within the story as a whole appears to have been a constant feature, in one way or another, in the history of interpretation.

It lies beyond the scope of this present study to examine the ways in which 22:15-18 was understood in ancient and medieval biblical commentary.[11] Rather, the approach will be initially to consider such interpretation as the verses have received in modern study, and then subsequently, building on this, to offer proposals for a fresh interpretation of their likely original significance.

II

The primary concern of modern study of 22:15-18 has been a source-critical analysis, which has led to the strong consensus that the verses are not original to the story in 22:1-14,19 but are a later editorial addition. The reasons for regarding vv.15-18 as an addition are threefold, but easily the most important is the structure and content of vv.1-14 which are such that the story is in a real sense complete by v.14. This will best be appreciated through a brief outline of the story's three major concerns.

First, the overarching concern of the story is God's test of Abraham (v.1) which is completely resolved by Abraham's obedience (v.12). The meaning of this is illuminated when it is appreciated that the two key words, test *(nissah)* and fear *(yare')* occur in conjunction in one other context of fundamental theological importance, that is Exod. 20:20. Here it is explained that God has given Israel his torah, supremely the ten commandments, to test *(nissah)* them and so that the fear *(yir'ah)* of God should be before them so that they do not sin. The general sense of the connection between testing and fearing (which in Exod. 20:20 as much as in Gen. 22:12 means moral obedience rather than religious awe)[12] is that God seeks by his commandments to draw out his people into fuller obedience and righteousness;[13] a sense which seems well captured by

---

[11] With regard to the current debate about the interpretation of Gen. 22 in the New Testament and Tannaitic period, see esp. C. T. R. Hayward, "The Present State of Research into the Targumic Account of the Sacrifice of Isaac", *JJS* 32 (1981), pp. 127-50. This also includes references to other relevant bibliography.

[12] B. S. Childs, *Exodus* (London, 1974), p. 373.

[13] M. Greenberg notes a widespread uncertainty as to the precise sense of *nissah* among commentators both medieval and modern ("*nsh* in Exodus 20:20 and the Purpose of the Sinaitic Theophany", *JBL* 79 [1960], pp. 273-6). Unfortunately his own proposals miss the mark because he discounts the present position of Exod. 20:20 after the ten commandments, on the grounds that because 20:18-21 appears to be an appropriate continuation to 19:19, and may once have been the actual continuation, the verses should therefore be interpreted in the context of 19:19, i.e. solely with reference to the theophany.

the analogy between divine testing and the refining of metals in Prov. 17:3.[14] This remarkable verbal and conceptual similarity between Gen. 22 and Exod. 20 suggests that we should discern a common editorial hand (the consensus of scholars has ascribed both passages to E), and also that the passages should be interpreted in the light of each other. The likely significance, I propose, is that Abraham supremely exemplifies the meaning of living by torah. He as an individual demonstrates the quality of response to God that should characterize Israel as a whole.[15]

Secondly, it is clear that the ancient practice of child sacrifice constitutes an important part of the background against which the story should be read. Although there is no general agreement as to how precisely Gen. 22:1-14 relates to this practice, I suggest that it relates in a way that may be said to be characteristic of classic Hebrew theology. It appears to have been a widespread belief in ancient Near Eastern religion that the first of all new life belonged to God, the fundamental assumption apparently being that God, as God, has absolute rights over human life. This assumption is shared by Gen. 22 which does not question but rather presupposes God's absolute right over human life, in a way reflected also in various strata of Old Testament laws (cf. Exod. 22:29-30 [Heb. 28-9], 13:2; Num. 3:13a). However, it is characteristic of Hebrew theology to maintain that, while YHWH does indeed have absolute right to demand the first and best of human life, he does not in practice exact his right but is prepared to forgo it, allowing some token to be offered instead (e.g. the ram, 22:13; cf. Exod. 34:19-20, and Exod. 12-13, esp. 13:11-16 and Num. 3:11-13 which ground Israel's normative practice in the traditions of the Passover). As Gen. 22 stands, however, the issue of God's inherent right to the firstborn, although important to the story's resonance, remains in the background. It is not so much that Isaac is the firstborn who belongs by right to God, for that issue should, in principle, be resolved at birth,[16] but rather he is the long-awaited child of God's promise who bears all Abraham's hopes for the future. As such the writer appears to be generalizing the basic principle of God's rights, so that God can require of Abraham whatever is most valuable to him, even though he only has Isaac through the gift of God in the first place; and it is

---

[14] The verb in Prov. 17:3 is *bahan* rather than *nissah* but the usage of the two verbs is similar.

[15] This means that the rabbinic tradition that Abraham observed *torah* before it was revealed to Moses (on which, see Bowker [n. 10], pp. 235-6) is developing a point that is more deeply rooted in the biblical text than the traditional appeal simply to Gen. 26:5b would indicate. On this whole question see now my *The Old Testament of the Old Testament* (Minneapolis, 1992), pp.142-6.

[16] Gen. 17:12 may well be interpreting the ancient law of Exod. 22:29-30 in its making circumcision the mark of a child being given to God (and also extending the principle to every male child and not just the firstborn).

only as the initial gift is freely surrendered that YHWH restores it again with renewed blessing. Thus both the sovereign rights and the mercy of God are strikingly presented in the story.

Thirdly, the story's concern of God "seeing" *(ra'ah),* i.e. providing (v.8), is likewise resolved (v.13).[17] Moreover, this is then related as a general principle to one place where God supremely sees (v.14a) and is seen (v.14b), that is, apparently, none other than the holy hill where the Temple stands in Jerusalem. Here God is specially present as Israel offers the *tamid,* the twice daily sacrifice of burnt offering *(`olah,* Exod. 29:38-46), just as Abraham offered the ram as a burnt offering *(`olah,* v.13). The link of Gen. 22 with the Temple is not explicit, probably because of the context of the story within the overall history of Israel long before the Temple was built, which makes foreshadowing and subtle allusion the appropriate mode of reference. Nonethe less the link is twofold.

First, there is the name Moriah (v.2), which, when taken in conjunction with v.14, the story probably understands as "the place of seeing"[18] through play on the Hebrew root *ra'ah.*[19] Although in itself this does not specify any particular place, within the Old Testament generally there are two places, *par excellence,* where the vision of God is granted: first, Sinai (esp. Exod. 24:9-11; cf. 33:11-34:35; 1 Kgs 19:9-18), and secondly Jerusalem (e.g. 2 Sam. 24:15-17; Isa. 6:1; Ps. 48, esp. vv. 5,8 [Heb. 6,9]). Since the story envisages a location within the central territory of Israel (three days' journey from Beersheba), it is of Jerusalem that an ancient Hebrew in, say, the period of the monarchy would naturally have thought. It is no surprise, therefore, when 2 Chron. 3:1 later identifies Mt. Moriah as the site of the temple.[20]

Secondly, there is the use of the phrase "mount of YHWH" (v.14b),[21] which is used elsewhere of Jerusalem (e.g. Ps. 24:3; Isa. 2:3). This subtle

---

[17] For reflection on the theological implications of this "seeing", see esp. W. Brueggemann, *Genesis* (Atlanta, 1982), pp. 191-2.

[18] This is not of course to prejudge the question whether this was always the form and mean ing of the name.

[19] There may additionally be a play on the root *yare',* i.e. "place of fearing".

[20] It is true that Gen. 22:2 mentions only the land *('ereṣ)* of Moriah and not mount *(har)* Moriah. But it is unlikely that this difference would have been significant to the Chronicler who presumably is simply combining the name Moriah with the specified mount *(har)* of Gen. 22:14.

[21] It is of course possible to argue that the Massoretic pointing of *har* in the construct with *yhwh* reflects the post-exilic interpretative tradition represented by 2 Chron. 3:1, and to repoint with *bāhar yhwh yir'eh/yera'eh;* for it is notable that these two options are represented by the LXX, *en tō orei kurios ophthe,* and the Vulgate, *In monte Dominus videbit.* Even so, a phrase like "the hill/mount" within the general context of the Old Testament would still more naturally refer to Jerusalem than to anywhere else. Moreover,

allusion to the Temple as the place where YHWH always "sees" and so provides for his people makes v.14 the natural conclusion to the story.[22] It is thus clear that all the major concerns of the story are resolved and completed by v. 14.

The other two reasons for considering vv.15-18 to be an addition to the story may be stated more briefly. One is that the style of vv.15-18 differs from that of vv.1-14. The story is noted for its taut and economic style of telling, heavy with suggestion of background context and meaning which is passed over in silence.[23] By contrast, the style of vv.15-18 is repetitive and cumulative, with use of synonyms and similes. It is a long address with no reference to any response by Abraham, unlike the short addresses to which Abraham responds in the preceding narrative.

The other reason for considering vv.15-18 an addition is that its vocabulary is in some ways distinctive (though of course one can only be highly tentative in formulating judgments in such a short passage). While for the most part it is composed of phrases which are common elsewhere in the patriarchal narratives,[24] it also contains two phrases which are otherwise unparalleled in Genesis but are common in prophetic literature (v.16a, *bi nišba'ti* and *n^e'um yhwh*). It will suffice here simply to note this unusual terminology.[25] Its significance for the meaning of the text will be discussed further below.

---

the significance of the LXX and Vulgate interpretations is problematic, since the tradition of identifying Moriah with Jerusalem, as indicated by the Massoretic pointing, was clearly well established before even the LXX, as 2 Chron. 3:1 makes clear.

In any case, the important point is that although the explicit identification of the story with Jerusalem is attested only at a relatively late period (4th century?), the concerns and language of the story so naturally lend themselves to a connection with Jerusalem that the Chronicler was probably drawing on an already well-established tradition.

[22] For the significance of Moriah/Zion as a place of visionary experience which validates subsequent Temple worship, see J. D. Levenson, *Sinai and Zion* (Minneapolis, 1985), pp. 94-5. For Gen. 22 as a validation of the Temple cult in later tradition, see Hayward (n. 11), pp. 132-4.

[23] See esp. the famous literary analysis by E. Auerbach, *Mimesis* (Princeton, 1953,1968), ch.1, and the fine treatment by von Rad (n.6), pp.203-10, E tr., pp.237-45.

[24] So Gunkel, for example, comments that the passage contains "nothing new" (*Genesis* [3rd ed., Göttingen, 1910], p.240.

[25] The criterion of usage of divine names, which has often been appealed to in this context, is problematic. Gen. 22:1-14 does in general use *'elohim*, while vv.15,16 both contain *yhwh*. But 22:1-14 is not in fact consistent, as *yhwh* is used twice in v.14, and the angel in v.11 is the angel of *yhwh*. This last usage is particularly significant since there is no good reason to consider it redactional, unlike part or all of v.14. Admittedly "angel of YHWH" is a regular Old Testament idiom and so could be used here in a purely formulaic way. But the fact that "angel of God" (*mal'ak 'elohim*) is an attested usage and occurs in Gen. 21:17 which, like Gen. 22:1-14, is generally ascribed to E, tells against such a supposition. The usage of divine names in Gen. 22:1-19 is not therefore of such a

It is the cumulative weight of all these considerations that has led to the consensus that vv. 15-18 are a separate addition to the preceding story. The strength of this conclusion can be usefully tested by a consideration of the arguments that have occasionally been raised in disagreement with the consensus.

G. W. Coats, for example, sees vv.15-18 as "an integral part of the narration developing from the test".[26] His main argument is that in the story as it now stands the entire focus is upon Abraham's obedience, which makes a reward for his obedience an entirely appropriate part of the story. Vv.1a,18b with their references to testing Abraham's obedience form a framework for the story, and the recurring motif of the "only son" (vv. 2,12,16) forms the content of the test. Coats does not deny, however, that in an earlier form of the story, prior to its incorporation in the Pentateuchal sources, the divine promise would not have been present.[27] His argument, therefore, is a helpful pointer to the skilful way in which vv.15-18 have been integrated into their present context, but does not really meet the above points about the inherent completeness of 22:1-14 nor deny the point at issue about the divine promise as an addition to the tradition, even though Coats sees this happening at the traditio-historical rather than the literary level of the text.

The most substantial criticism is offered by J. Van Seters, who notes the obvious plausibility of seeing vv.15-18 as an addition, but quite rightly comments that "the fact that such a notion of an addition is very plausible is not enough to conclude that this is actually the case".[28] He argues that the promise would overburden the initial divine address in v.12 and delay the action v.13, and so as a matter of dramatic necessity is placed in a second speech from heaven (p. 238). That is, if the promise were original to the story it is difficult to see how else it could be appropriately expressed other than in the way the text in fact presents it. It is unreasonable, therefore, to argue that the position of vv.15-18 shows them to be secondary if their content requires that position.

Such an objection has weight. It seems to me an unsatisfactory response simply to dismiss it, as J. A. Emerton does, by the questionable stylistic assessment of vv.15-18 as a "clumsy addition...after the climax of what is otherwise a beautifully written story".[29]

---

nature as to allow source-critical inferences to be drawn - although it may still be of significance for the meaning of the text (on which, see Spiegel [n.1], pp.121,124).

[26] "Abraham's Sacrifice of Faith: A Form-Critical Study of Genesis 22", *Interpretation* 27 (1973), p.395.

[27] A point which he develops more fully in his *Genesis, with an Introduction to Narrative Literature* (Grand Rapids, 1983), pp. 157-62.

[28] *Abraham in History and Tradition* (New Haven, Conn., and London, 1975)), p.230.

[29] "The origin of the promises to the patriarchs in the older sources of the book of Genesis", *VT* 32 (1982), p.18.

Nonetheless, Van Seters's argument still does not show that the promise was in fact original to the story, but only that in terms of its position it could be. Moreover, even apart from the cumulative appeal to style and vocabulary as well as position, it is not in fact the case that dramatic necessity requires the promise in its present position. While the promise would indeed be out of place in v.12, it would not be out of place if inserted between v.13 and v.14. By the end of v.13 the dramatic action is complete, and a second divine address at that juncture would be entirely appropriate. V.14 would follow v.18 just as smoothly as it follows v.13. Indeed, from the point of view of reading vv.1-19 as an integral unity it would even improve the flow and coherence of the text to read it in the order vv.1-13,15-18,14,19, for the obviously concluding v.14 would then conclude the drama on Moriah as a whole and lead naturally into the final narrative note in v.19. It remains more likely then that the present position of vv.15-18 after v.14 indicates that they are not original to the story but are the work of an editor who respected the already complete unit vv.1-14 but added to it.[30]

We may also briefly note the recent study of T. D. Alexander which questions the "apparent secondary nature of 22:15-18" on the strength of ingenious arguments to the effect that Gen. 22 in its present form should be read as the ratification of the covenant in Gen. 17 ([n.7], p.21, and n.8). Alexander interprets Gen. 17:1 as a promise of a covenant which is dependent upon Abraham's obedient response, a condition which is not fulfilled within Gen. 17 but is fulfilled in Gen. 22. He further argues that a similar pattern of divine promise and human response is to be found in the account of the covenant with Noah in Gen. 6-9. He thus maintains that both Abraham's act of obedience (22:12; cf. Gen. 6:22, 7:5) and offer of sacrifice (22:13; cf. Gen. 8:20) were necessary before God could confirm his promised covenant (22:15; cf. Gen. 9:8-17). Therefore the angel had to call a second time, after Abraham's sacrifice.

Although this shows one possible way in which the text of Genesis may be read, it is open to exactly the same objection as made to Van Seters, and overall the proposal seems somewhat forced, especially since the argument lacks exegetical depth and nowhere takes into account the possible significance of the traditio-historical, source-critical and redactional dimensions of Gen. 6-9, 17, 22 respectively. At best, it is one possible reading of the final form of the text.

Finally, we may note that J. L. Crenshaw has expressed some uncertainty about the consensus view of 22:15-18: "In my judgment, the prominence of

---

[30] Van Seters also argues that if the story ended in v. 14 "the whole purpose of testing would have no real consequence. Nothing would be changed. It is only with the inclusion, in the second speech, of the divine confirmation of the patriarchal promises, vv. 15-18, that the ultimate aim of the testing becomes clear. Because of Abraham's obedience his children will be blessed" (p. 239). This however simply misses the meaning of vv.1-14 as outlined above.

formulaic language in the so-called Yahwistic supplement and the likelihood of citation render the reigning theory problematical" ([n.2], p.13, n.11). His passing comment, however, scarcely amounts to an argument, and so hardly merits discussion here, especially since the characteristics of 22:15-18 that he notices will be discussed in our own interpretation below.

It may be concluded, therefore, that the consensus view of 22:15-18 as an addition to the story of 22:1-14,19 has not been seriously challenged, and should continue to be maintained as the most likely explanation of the textual peculiarities of structure, style and vocabulary as outlined above.

III

The second dominant concern in modern discussion of 22:15-18 has been to relate this passage to the study of the divine promises to the patriarchs in Genesis as a whole. This is an area of complex debate, but since helpful surveys are readily accessible there is no need to attempt any survey here.[31] Rather, three brief observations will suffice.

First, there is a general consensus that 22:15-18 has been added to the story in Gen. 22 as part of an overall editorial process within Genesis which has had two aims: on the one hand to link individual patriarchal traditions to the wider context of other patriarchal traditions within Gen. 12-50, and on the other hand to link the patriarchal traditions as a whole to the wider context of the Pentateuch (or Hexateuch). There is no agreement, however, whether this represents the consistent work of just one or two editors, or whether this was a process extended over several centuries of editorial moulding of the patriarchal traditions.

Secondly, it follows from the presence of so many divine promises in Genesis that it is necessary to relate the interpretation of the promises in any given passage, such as 22:15-18, to the interpretation of other promises. As Westermann puts it, "It is generally agreed that the texts containing the promises cannot be interpreted solely on the basis of their present contexts; they have an extended context also in the group of identical or similar promises in Genesis 12-50 and also beyond Genesis" ([n.31], p.119). It is interesting, however, that while the promises in 12:1-3 and 15:1-6 have received much attention both in relation to their immediate context and in relation to the wider context, the same cannot be said of 22:15-18. Discussion of 22:15-18 within the context of 22:1-14,19 has been perfunctory and superficial, and interest in them has focussed on the extended context of Genesis at the expense of their immediate context.

---

[31] See C. Westermann, *The Promises to the Fathers* (Philadelphia, 1980; E tr. of *Die Verheissungen an die Väter* [Göttingen, 1976]), pp.95-118, and Emerton (n.29), pp.14-32.

Thirdly, despite the lack of consensus as to the identities and dates of the editors responsible for the addition of those patriarchal promises which are recognized to be secondary, a notable concern of recent study has been less an understanding of the promises in themselves in their immediate or wider context within Genesis than an attempt to relate them to the concerns of the supposed historical context within which the editors were working. So, for example, Van Seters argues that the promises may represent assurances to a nation in exile in the 6th century ([n.28], pp.310-11), Emerton tentatively suggests the mood of confidence associated with Josiah's reform ([n.29], p.31), E. Blum argues for a Deuteronomic reworking (*Bearbeitung*) of the patriarchal traditions,[32] while the earlier work of von Rad related the promises to the intellectual endeavours of the supposed Solomonic enlightenment.[33] But while there is of course value in attempting to contextualize the biblical text within Israel's historical experience, there are important limitations to what this can achieve.

The main limitation is that since there is simply insufficient evidence available to allow any definitive resolution of date and context, surmises about which must necessarily remain hypothetical,[34] any interpretation which substantively depends on relating the text to an historical context must itself be for ever tentative and hypothetical. This then fails to do justice to the fact that the text has an integrity and meaning in its own right, a point rightly urged (though sometimes to excess) by many literary critics.[35] Moreover, it seems clear that in many Old Testament texts a hermeneutical process has been at work precisely to loosen the text from its original context, so that it can have meaning for readers within a wide range of different situations (this has been extensively argued by Brevard Childs). Neither of these points denies the value of relating a text to its supposed original context, but they relativize its significance within the total work of interpretation.

The following interpretation, therefore, will seek to build upon the debate about the patriarchal promises in an attempt to relate Gen. 22:15-18 both to its immediate and its wider context within Genesis. But while historical concerns will not be ignored, the interpretation will be primarily literary and theological in outlook.

---

[32] *Die komposition der Vätergeschichte* (Neukirchen-Vluyn, 1984), esp. pp.363-5.

[33] "Der Anfang der Geschichtsschreibung im alten Israel", in his *Gesammelte Studien zum Alten Testament* (Munich, 1958), pp. 148-88, E. tr. *The Problem of the Hexateuch and Other Essays* (Edinburgh and London, 1966), pp. 166-204.

[34] The important recent study of R. N. Whybray, *The Making of the Pentateuch* (Sheffield, 1987) is a sobering reminder of how little we really know about the origins and composition of the Pentateuch.

[35] For helpful surveys of literary approaches to the Old Testament, see R. J. Coggins, "The Literary Approach to the Bible", *Exp.T.* 96 (1984), pp. 9-14, and J. Barton, *Reading the Old Testament:Method in Biblical Study* (London, 1984), chs. 8-12.

IV

Before turning to the detailed study of 22:15-18, it will be helpful to make two preliminary points to set the exegesis in context. First, there is the question of the genre of the verses and the terminology generally used to refer to them. I suggest that one of the major obstacles in the way of a positive assessment of the passage has been an unreflective, and yet implicitly pejorative, use by the vast majority of scholars of terms such as "secondary", "addition", "supplement", "appendix". The use of these terms has generally carried the implicit corollary that the passage is somehow of inferior quality and is of no great importance for understanding the meaning of the story within which it stands - hence its general neglect.[36] But while the assessment of 22:15-18 as an addition to an already complete story would certainly appear to be correct, such a recognition does not of itself give any understanding of the genre and purpose of the verses in themselves. So far as this question has been addressed, the verses have simply been considered as part of the editing of Genesis as a whole, as noted above. I propose, therefore, the use of different terminology. If one takes seriously the position of vv. 15-18 within the context of 22:1-19, the natural assessment of them is surely as an interpretation, or commentary, on the preceding story.[37] In context, vv. 15-18 are clearly drawing out the implications of what has preceded - "because you have done this...". Since this interpretation relates to what is clearly the central concern of the story as it now stands, that is the obedience of Abraham to God's testing command, and since it has become part of the received text of the story, I propose that vv.15-18 should be described as the earliest and canonically recognized commentary on the story.

To say this is in no way to deny the various interpretative elements that have already been incorporated within 22:1-14,19. Nor is it to suggest that one could not properly interpret the story without reference to vv.15-18 - for numerous profound and valuable interpretations have done so. Nor is it to deny that one can legitimately develop the implications of the story in ways different from vv.15-18; as, for example, much Jewish interpretation has imaginatively developed the role of Isaac as the model martyr, often in the context of finding a

---

[36] The use of "secondary" has been particularly equivocal. What should be a purely temporal assessment has also been allowed to function - without justification - as a value judgement.

[37] As far as I am aware, the only scholar who has explicitly recognized 22:15-18 as a commentary ("eine Art kommentar") is H. G. Reventlow, but his own reflections on its significance are only briefly developed *(Opfere deinen Sohn* [Neukirchen-Vluyn, 1968], pp. 73-4). More generally, the phenomenon of inner-biblical commentary within the Old Testament is well treated in M. Fishbane, *Biblical Interpretation in Ancient Israel* (Oxford, 1985).

pattern and meaning in the suffering of pogroms (see Spiegel [n.1], passim). Nonetheless, while it is indeed true that a story as profound and suggestive as Gen. 22 cannot be said to have only one meaning, and that its implications may indeed legitimately be developed in more than one direction, the fact remains that vv.15-18 are the commentary that the Old Testament itself contains. As such they are surely deserving of more careful attention than they have in general hitherto received.

The second preliminary point relates to the possible significance of the fact that the commentary is put in the mouth of the angel of YHWH. It may be that this is simply a matter of dramatic necessity. Given the general convention of Hebrew storytelling that the narrator does not stand outside the story to offer comment upon it but rather lets the story contain its own interpretation, especially in the speeches that the characters make, the writer had little choice: God, or his angel representing him, is the only significant figure in the story apart from Abraham (and Isaac), and so any interpretative comment would have to be on his lips. Moreover there is the compelling precedent that all the similar promises previously have been spoken by God himself. Nonetheless, the fact that the speech is on the lips of God's angel is still probably intended to be taken seriously by the writer; indeed, the way the speech is presented virtually as a soliloquy, without reference to any response from Abraham, makes it reminiscent of the divine soliloquies in Gen. 1-11, some of which are major theological statements about the purposes of God.[38] It is likely that here too the reader is meant to recognize a serious interpretation of the mind and purposes of God.

V

As we turn to a detailed study of vv.15-18, it will quickly be seen that while the angel's words certainly contain elements familiar from previous divine promises in Genesis, there are also strikingly unusual aspects in them.

First, there is the phrase "By myself I have sworn" (*bi nišba`ti*). On three other occasions in Genesis reference is made to God swearing an oath (24:7, 26:3, 50:24), each time in connection with the promise of the land which he will give to Abraham's descendants. In fact the "swearing to give the land" is a regular formulaic expression, occurring often elsewhere in the Pentateuch.[39] The notable feature about Gen. 22:16 is that the divine oath is uniquely not

---

[38] On, for example, the significance of Gen. 6:5-8, 8:21, see my *At the Mountain of God* (Sheffield, 1983), pp. 91-3.

[39] Exod. 13:5,11, 33:1, Num. 11:12, 14:16,23. 32:11, and regularly in Deuteronomy (1:8,35 etc). Many scholars consider Gen. 15:18 to be the fundamental text underlying this tradition, though the text mentions only a promise and does not specify an oath; on this, see Westermann's discussion of N. Lohfink in (n. 31), pp. 112, 145.

connected with the giving of the land, as the entire concern of vv.16-18 is with Abraham's descendants. The usage is in no way formulaic, and therefore carries particular weight.

Further emphasis is added by the idiom "*By myself* I have sworn". This is unique in the Pentateuch, with the exception of Exod. 32:13 which is a generalized reference back to Gen. 22 and other promises in Genesis. It is, however, to be found sometimes in the prophets and the psalms, either in identical or related form.[40] In itself the formula is naturally one of unusual emphasis, as indeed noted and reflected upon by the writer to the Hebrews (Heb. 6:13-18). Although admittedly its usage can occasionally appear slightly formulaic, it certainly can be used to lay as great emphasis as possible upon the divine saying in question (so esp. Isa. 45:23; Ps. 89:36). Given its combination here with the unusual usage of the oath, such special emphasis would appear to be its intended meaning.

The second element "says YHWH" (n^e'um $yhwh$) is again unusual. Although a frequent idiom in the prophets, especially Jeremiah and Ezekiel, it is rare in narrative texts, and occurs elsewhere in the Pentateuch only in Num. 14:28, a divine pronouncement of exceptional seriousness, the judgement that the generation of rebellious Israelites will die in the desert. The use of this formula in Gen. 22:16 should again be seen as a means of drawing attention to the exceptional nature of the pronouncement which follows.

As we turn now to the content of the divine pronouncement, it will be appropriate for the time being to pass over the opening words (v.16b), which recall what Abraham has done (cf. v.12) and so give the reason for what follows, and focus directly on the content of the promises in vv. 17-18.

The promises are introduced by the particle *ki*, which could simply be a grammatical introduction, "that". However, the divine words have already been introduced in this way (v.16b). So although the usage in v.17a could be simply resumptive with no further significance, it is perhaps more likely that the *ki* has asseverative force, "surely", "indeed", to add extra emphasis to what follows.

First comes a promise of blessing, in the emphatic form with infinitive absolute, *barek 'abarek^{e}ka*. This is notable, because while the theme of divine blessing is indeed common in the patriarchal narratives,[41] nowhere else is this emphatic verbal form used.[42] Such a usage is indeed found elsewhere in the Old

---

[40] In identical form, Isa. 45:23, Jer. 22:5, 49:13. In related form, Jer. 51:14, Amos 6:8 (*b^{e}napšo*), Amos 4:2, Ps. 89:36 (EVV. 35) (*b^{e}qodšo*), Ps. 89:50 (EVV. 49) (*be'emunateka*).

[41] It occurs in divine promises, Gen. 12:2, 17:16,20, 26:3,24, in narrative comment, 24:1,35, 25:11, 26:12, 32:30, 35:9, and once each on the lips of Isaac and Jacob, 28:3, 48:3.

[42] If the promise of blessing is strengthened, it is usually by the addition of *m^{e}od*, e.g. 24:35.

Testament, especially with reference to Balaam's pronouncement of blessing upon Israel,[43] but within Genesis the present passage is unique.

Next comes a promise to multiply Abraham's descendants, which again uses the emphatic verbal form, *harbah 'arbeh* (this is missed by the *RSV*). This, though unusual,[44] is not unique within Genesis, as the divine promise to Hagar about her descendants (16:10) uses the same emphatic form. Nonetheless 22:17 is the only instance where the formula is used for the "official" line of Abraham's descendants through Isaac.

The divine promise next contains two similes to express the unimaginable number of Abraham's descendants who will be "like the stars of heaven and like the sand on the seashore". Both these similes are used elsewhere in divine promises in Genesis,[45] but always singly and never in combination. Their unique juxtaposition in Gen. 22:17 further highlights the unusually emphatic nature of the promise.

The final element in v.17, "and your descendants shall possess the gate of their enemies", is the sole element within this promise that is not in some way paralleled in other divine promises in Genesis. Its sole other occurrence is in Gen. 24:60, the blessing pronounced on Rebekah and her offspring by her family. The point is not, as sometimes suggested, an oblique reference to the promise of the land,[46] but is rather to make explicit the enviable condition which the numerous descendants of Abraham will enjoy; their lot will not be the misery of the downtrodden, but rather the joy and prosperity of the victorious.

In v.18a the familiar promise of the blessing of the nations (cf. 12:3, 18:18) is included, though with the difference from previous occurrences that it is by Abraham's descendants, rather than Abraham himself, that people will bless themselves, a usage found elsewhere only in 26:4b.[47] Probably, the difference of wording results from the promise being moulded to suit the present context.[48] It appropriately continues the picture of the unique blessing to be enjoyed by Abraham's descendants, which will be such that they will be the admiration of all other peoples.

---

[43] Num. 23:11,25, 24:10, Josh. 24:10; elsewhere Deut. 15:4, Ps.132:15, 1 Chron. 4:10.

[44] If the promise of multiplication is strengthened, it is by the addition of m^eod (26:4, 28:3, 49:4) or m^eod m^eod (17:2,20).

[45] Stars, Gen. 15:5, 26:4; cf. Exod. 32:13; sand, Gen. 32:12 (Heb. 13).

[46] So e.g. B. Jacob, *Das erste Buch der Tora: Genesis* (Berlin, 1934; repr. New York, n.d.), p.503; D. J. A. Clines, *The Theme of the Pentateuch* (Sheffield, 1978), p.36.

[47] On Gen. 26:2-5 see further below, p.72.

[48] From the point of view of method, therefore, it is highly questionable to attempt to interpret this and related phrases in isolation from their present contexts as, for example, R. Rendtorff does *(Das überlieferungsgeschichtliche Problem des Pentateuch. BZAW* 147 (Berlin and New York, 1977), pp. 40ff, esp. pp.42-8).

The promise then ends with a reiteration of Abraham's obedience as the reason for what is promised, the significance of which will be considered below.

It has now become clear that although the divine promise in Gen. 22:16-18 uses the language of promise familiar from elsewhere in Genesis, it does more than simply reaffirm the promise. The phrases that are familiar elsewhere are used here in a uniquely emphatic way, and formulae of emphasis which are otherwise unparalleled in Genesis are also used. Moreover the promise focusses exclusively on the blessing of Abraham's descendants, with no reference to the oft-repeated promise of land. The reason for this clearly lies in the close and specific relationship of vv.15-18 to the story in which it is set. It is easy to see, in general terms, that the remarkable obedience of Abraham in 22:1-14 has been met with a divine promise of remarkable emphasis. And since the test of Abraham focussed entirely on his son (and so, by implication, on all his descendants who were thereby at risk), it is likewise appropriate that the divine blessing should concentrate entirely on those descendants. The match between the content of the promise and the quality of Abraham's obedience is readily apparent.

VI

Is it, however, the sole point of this commentary on the story that extraordinary obedience brings extraordinary blessing? If so, it would certainly represent an important reflection on the story's implications. But I suggest that there is a further dimension. This emerges through consideration of the one element in the angel's words that has thus far been passed over, that is the repeated reference to Abraham's obedience as the reason for the promise (vv. 16b,18b). It is precisely here that the extended context of related divine promises elsewhere in Genesis becomes of crucial interpretative significance.

One of the most notable features about the divine promises elsewhere in Genesis is that they always constitute a unilateral and unconditional offer on God's part. The promise precedes an initial obedient response on Abraham's part (Gen. 12:1-3,4) and is reaffirmed (e.g. 15:5, 18:18) independently of any notable action on Abraham's part to occasion it.[49] No passage gives any explicit reason for the promises, but the clear tacit assumption is that the promises are rooted in the goodwill and purposes of YHWH for Israel. What then is one to make of 22:15-18 where the promise is given because Abraham was obedient? How does this relate to the other promises? Westermann, for example, comments, "The promises to the fathers are, in essence, free assurances by God. To ground them, as here, on Abraham's achievement is to alter the understanding of them. The Deuteronomic theology with its conditioned promise is presupposed... By way

---

[49] The one partial exception is Gen. 18:19, but the significance of this passing reference is unclear.

of conclusion, the obedience of Abraham is again underscored in v.18b; it is understood as meritorious" ([n.2] E.tr., pp.363-4=445-6). More commonly commentators have just briefly noted that this passage introduces a doctrine of merit, but then have pursued the matter no further.[50]

By contrast, Emerton doubts whether the linkage between divine promise and human obedience here is of any particular significance at all, significance having been attributed anachronistically in the light of subsequent theological developments: "Later ideas should not be read back into the Old Testament, and it may be doubted whether an ancient writer would have been conscious of any conflict of ideas here".[51]

How should this be assessed? First and foremost, I suggest that the choice of the term "merit" by commentators is unfortunate. "Merit" is a loose and imprecise category with a long, and sometimes controversial,[52] history within both Jewish and Christian theology. It is too overladen with the overtones of subsequent theological debate to be a helpful category for appreciating Genesis on its own terms. As such, Emerton's caution is entirely appropriate. But this does not mean that 22:15-18 is in fact without special significance in this regard, only that it is vital to be careful in the way one describes it.

It is clear that the crucial issue is how precisely to understand the relationship between 22:15-18 and previous divine promises. In order to do this, two preliminary points of clarification are in order. First, the promise in 22:15-18 is evidently not a novel promise, but derives much of its significance from the fact that a promise in similar terms is presupposed as having previously been given. This remains equally true whether one interprets the text in its received, canonical form, in which case it presupposes everything presently contained in Gen. 12-22, or whether one interprets it on the editorial level at some stage or other within the composition of Genesis, when it is arguable precisely how much of Gen. 12-22 may have lain before the editor.[53] This means that the writer of 22:15-18 was familiar with the normal form of the divine promise as an unconditioned offer as part of the patriarchal traditions, and indeed presupposed it.

---

[50] So e.g. S E. McEvenue, "The Elohist at Work", *ZAW* 96 (1984), p.331.

[51] (n.29) p.24; cf. p.30. The context of the statement is an attempt to refute those who find here evidence of the work of more than one hand. Professor Emerton tells me that he did not intend to suggest that the linkage between divine favour and human obedience had no significance, but only that there was no conflict such as to suggest different authorship.

[52] So, for example, Calvin's comments on Gen. 22:15 explicitly engage with the Reformation debate about the theological significance of merit and good works: J King (ed), *Commentaries on the first book of Moses called Genesis,* Calvin Translation Society (Edinburgh, 1847-50; repr London, 1965), p. 572.

[53] It is probably mainly Gen. 14 and 17 whose presence within the editor's *Vorlage* might be disputed.

Secondly, it is not in fact the case that the promise of 22:15-18 has been modified in accordance with Deuteronomic theology. The classic Deuteronomic expression of conditional promise in Deut. 28 envisages both Israel's obedience and blessing as future. The blessing is dependent upon what Israel may do in the future, and is nowhere pronounced as a reward for what Israel has already done. On the contrary, when Deuteronomy refers to what Israel has done, Israel is depicted as consistently unfaithful and disobedient (e.g. 1:26-33, 9:6-10:11, esp. 9:24).

Two vital features thus distinguish Gen. 22:15-18 from the typical Deuteronomic conditioned promise. On the one hand, 22:15-18 asserts that the act of obedience which brings blessing is already an established fact, not a future possibility. On the other hand, the promise of blessing which ensues upon Abraham's obedience is not a new factor which did not previously obtain but a reaffirmation of an already existing promise of blessing. It is in the light of these two factors that one can now assess the true significance of 22:15-18.

Abraham by his obedience has not qualified to be the recipient of blessing, because the promise of blessing had been given to him already. Rather, the existing promise is reaffirmed but its terms of reference are altered. A promise which previously was grounded solely in the will and purpose of YHWH is transformed so that it is now grounded *both* in the will of YHWH *and* in the obedience of Abraham. It is not that the divine promise has become contingent upon Abraham's obedience, but that Abraham's obedience has been incorporated into the divine promise. Henceforth Israel owes its existence not just to YHWH but also to Abraham.

Theologically this constitutes a profound understanding of the value of human obedience - it can be taken up by God and become a motivating factor in his purposes towards humanity. Within the wider context of Hebrew theology I suggest that this is analogous to the assumptions underlying intercessory prayer. Here too faithful human response to God is taken up and incorporated within the purposes and activity of God.

One particularly clear example is the portrayal of Moses as mediator and intercessor in Exod. 32-34, which I have discussed elsewhere ([n.38] ch.2). Here the renewal of the covenant between YHWH and Israel is dependent not only upon the absolute and undeserved mercy of YHWH towards disobedient Israel (Exod. 33:19, 34:6-7,9), but also upon the faithful intercession of Moses which constitutes the essential channel through which the divine mercy flows (Exod. 32:10,11-14, 33:11,12-18, 34:27,29-35). In my study of Exod. 32-34 it is concluded that "it is through the faithful man of God that this mercy is given. God's mercy does not override man, but man is given an indispensable role within God's purposes... So the position of Israel in the restored covenant is not identical to what it would have been had the people never sinned. Henceforth their life as a people depends not only upon the mercy of God but also upon the intercession of God's chosen mediator" ([n.38], pp.93,106).

Admittedly the analogy between Abraham and Moses is only an analogy, since Abraham's obedience when tested is different from Moses' intercession when Israel is under divine judgment, and each story has its own distinctive tradition-history. But there are two crucial similarities which, I believe, make the analogy fruitful; in each story the very existence of Israel is under threat, and in each story God's assurance that Israel has a future is called forth by the total faithfulness of a man of God.

One consequence of this, therefore, is that part of the function of the theological commentary in Gen. 22:15-18 is to draw out the significance of Abraham's obedience in such a way that Abraham can be seen to have a role within the salvation-history of Israel akin to that of Moses. It is a commentary that shows the Hebrew understanding of human significance and potential in relation to God at its most profound and positive, and characteristically relates this to Israel's very existence as the people of God.

VII

In conclusion, three further points may briefly be made. First, it is hardly possible in the light of the available evidence to resolve the question of the date and context of the commentator responsible for Gen. 22:15-18. Certain of the linguistic peculiarities noted above would appear to have most affinities with texts of the 7th or 6th century, and some such period is not unlikely, but one is basically reduced to intelligent guesswork.[54] In any case, this issue does not substantially affect an appreciation of the commentator's work.

Secondly, although it is notable that the rest of Genesis as a whole shows no knowledge of our commentator's interpretation of Abraham's obedience - in particular, the promises to Jacob never mention it -the one exception to this is the Isaac tradition in Gen. 26. The only divine promises given to Isaac are those in Gen. 26:2-5,24, and both link the promised blessing with Abraham's obedience in a way reminiscent of 22:15-18. The precise relationship between these texts cannot be discussed here.[55] If it is correct to discern a deliberate editorial strategy, the restriction of reference to Isaac may be because Isaac was the only other person involved in the drama of Gen.22.[56] Such a reminder to Isaac may possibly contain the seeds of the later tradition which did not

---

[54] See now my further reflections, above, pp.50-1.

[55] Three brief points may be noted. First, the primary concern of 26:2-4 is the land rather than descendants. Secondly, the most significant parallel is that of 26:5a with 22:18b; 26:5a might well be an addition by the same commentator as in 22:15-18. Thirdly, one should probably see 26:5b as a fuller expansion of the understanding of Abraham as a model of living by torah, either by the same commentator again or by a later glossator.

[56] The young men of 22:3,5,19 take no part in the main action.

envisage the drama on Moriah as abhorrent to Isaac but rather emphasized his own willing participation.

Finally, it should be noted that 22:15-18 is the last of the divine promises to Abraham within Gen. 12-25, and as such makes a fitting conclusion. Indeed 22:15-18 are the final words of any sort exchanged between God and Abraham in the Abraham cycle, for nowhere in 22:20-25:11 does either YHWH speak to Abraham or Abraham speak to YHWH. Whether or not Gen. 22:15-18 was deliberately intended to be the final communication between God and Abraham is difficult to judge. But the recognition that it is so cannot but enhance the reader's appreciation of its significance. If our interpretation of 22:15-18 as a profound theological commentary on the story of 22:1-14,19 is correct, it becomes peculiarly appropriate that this earliest, and canonically recognized, commentary should be given a position of climactic significance within the Abraham cycle as a whole.

"YHWH IS ONE":THE TRANSLATION OF THE SHEMA

One of the fundamental theological statements of the Old Testament is Deut. 6:4, the Shema. It is notable, however, that while the importance of the verse is not in doubt, its interpretation is a matter of continuing and unresolved debate. Much of the debate revolves around disagreement as to the translation of the Hebrew, whose possible different renderings give rise to significantly different meanings. It is the thesis of this essay that the disagreement about translation can in fact be satisfactorily resolved. If the thesis is correct it will not of itself resolve all the problems of interpretation, since the proposed translation raises particular interpretative difficulties of its own; but it will provide the necessary foundation on which any true interpretation must be built.

The Hebrew text of Deut. 6:4 reads: *šᵉmaʿ yisrael yhwh 'elohenu yhwh 'eḥad*. It is generally agreed that *šᵉmaʿ yisrael* is unproblematic and should be rendered "Hear, O Israel" (cf. Deut. 9:1, 20:3), serving as an introduction to what follows. The problem of translation centres on the fact that in the next four words *yhwh 'elohenu yhwh 'eḥad* there is no verb, and therefore a verb must be supplied by the translator. The natural assumption is that this verb should be the verb "to be", for it is a common idiom of Biblical Hebrew to use verbless clauses whose construction is that of noun and predicate juxtaposed and related by an implied verb "to be".[1] Further, it is also a natural assumption that the tense of the verb is present, since no other tense is suggested by the context[2] and Hebrew tends to indicate past or future by the specific inclusion of *hayah* or *yihyeh*.[3] If, then, one is to understand the verb "is", the crucial question is precisely where in the sentence it should be understood.

To put the same point differently, the question is how much of the sentence is subject and how much is predicate. What precedes the verb that the translator must supply will be the subject and what follows the verb will be the predicate. But the division between subject and predicate can be put at any point in the sentence. The four words of the clause offer three possible positions in which the verb can be understood; and if the verb is understood in the first position

---

[1] On noun-clauses see GK 140, 141.

[2] A future sense was given to the second part of the verse by Rashi who interpreted it "canonically" in the light of the wider context of Zeph. 3:9 and Zech. 14:9 to give the sense that the Lord who is now God of Israel alone will in future be the one God of all the earth (M. Rosenbaum & A.M. Silbermann [ed.], *The Pentateuch with the Commentary of Rashi:Deuteronomy* [Jerusalem: Silbermann, 1972], p. 37).

[3] Cf. GK 141 *f g, i*.

then it can also be understood in the third, thereby making a sentence with two subjects and two predicates. There are thus four basic alternatives:[4]

(i)   *yhwh - 'elohenu yhwh 'eḥad*: "YHWH is our God, YHWH alone".[5]
(ii) *yhwh 'elohenu - yhwh 'eḥad*: "YHWH our God is one YHWH".[6]
(iii) *yhwh 'elohenu yhwh - 'eḥad*: "YHWH our God, YHWH is one".
(iv) *yhwh - 'elohenu yhwh -'eḥad*: "YHWH is our God, YHWH is one".[7]

If one examines these four renderings (with their variations), two basic differences among them become apparent. First, if *yhwh* is subject and *'elohenu* is predicate, as in (i) and (iv), then we have a statement about the relationship between YHWH and Israel, while if *'elohenu* is part of the subject and not the predicate, as in (ii) and (iii), then we have a statement about the nature or character of YHWH. Secondly, (i) is different from all other renderings in translating *'eḥad* as "alone" rather than "one". It is not absolutely necessary that if *yhwh* is subject and the rest of the sentence predicate that *'eḥad* should be rendered "alone" (see n. 5), but "alone" makes better sense than "one" and is therefore widely adopted. Given these two basic differences, there is a general tendency to regard the four alternatives as essentially reducible to two: either "YHWH is our God, YHWH alone", which states the exclusive relationship between YHWH and Israel, or "YHWH our God, YHWH is one" which states the oneness of YHWH. The first rendering is generally preferred by modern

---

[4] Cf. e.g. S.R. Driver, *Deuteronomy* (3rd edn, Edinburgh: T. & T. Clark, 1902), pp. 89-90. It should be noted that yet other renderings have been proposed. For example, F.I. Andersen suggests "Our one God is Yahweh, Yahweh" (*The Hebrew Verbless Clause in the Pentateuch* [Nashville, 1970], p. 47), while M. Dahood suggested "Obey, Israel, Yahweh. Yahweh our God is the Unique" (L.R. Fisher [ed.], *Ras Shamra Parallels* I [Rome, 1972], p. 361). These may perhaps best be described as syntactically adventurous. The present argument with regard to the more common renderings will apply equally to these.

[5] A variant, which avoids giving the unusual sense "alone" to *'eḥad* is "The LORD is our God, one LORD" (*New English Bible*). This variant seems to make better sense with the title "LORD" than with the proper name YHWH. A paraphrastic alternative for "alone" can be found in the *Revised English Bible* which translates "The LORD is our God, the LORD our one God".

[6] This was the rendering of the LXX: *kyrios ho theos hemon kyrios heis estin.* In this form the text is cited in Mk. 12:29. One modern liturgical rendering of this is "The Lord our God is the only Lord" (*The Alternative Service Book 1980* [Cambridge: CUP, 1980], p. 120). Although this is an attractive rendering, it depends on the implications of the title "Lord" and would be less meaningful if the proper name YHWH were substituted.

[7] Or "YHWH is our God, YHWH is 'One'", if *'eḥad* is taken as a name or title (C.H. Cordon, "His Name is 'One'", *JNES* 29 [1970], pp. 198-9).

scholars,[8] while the second was generally preferred in traditional Jewish usage,[9] and still has some modern advocates.[10]

With regard to these two alternatives, two observations would, I think, command a wide consensus. The first is that it is not possible to make a definitive choice between the two renderings, because each is an acceptable translation of the Hebrew. It is common practice in modern translations of the Old Testament that, whichever rendering is chosen in the text, at least one alternative, and sometimes all three alternative options, are noted in the margin as possibilities.[11] Secondly, the rendering "YHWH is our God, YHWH alone" is more obviously in keeping with the central concerns of Deuteronomic covenant theology than is a statement about the oneness of YHWH whose precise sense is not immediately apparent and which is all too easily interpreted in the light of the monotheistic concerns of later periods. The obviously appropriate sense of "YHWH alone" is recognized even by those who do not think it is the correct rendering (see Janzen [n. 10], p. 281).

Despite the obvious appropriateness of "YHWH is our God, YHWH alone", and despite the fact that it is preferred by a majority of modern scholars, I shall argue that it cannot be the correct translation because of a simple fact of Hebrew idiom.

The translation "YHWH is our God, YHWH alone" involves two crucial judgements about the Hebrew. The first is that it is possible to render 'eḥad as "alone". It is this that has most often been called in question, because it involves giving 'eḥad a sense that is otherwise apparently unparalleled in the Old Testament. Although the usage of 'eḥad is not our primary concern, it is still necessary briefly to consider the point.

A.D.H. Mayes, for example (n. 8), cites five passages in support of the meaning of 'eḥad as "alone": Isa. 51:2; Ezek. 33:24, 37:22; Zech. 14:9; I Chr. 29:1. But in fact none of these is a clear example, and in all of them 'eḥad probably retains its basic meaning of numerical singularity. In both Isa. 51:2 and Ezek. 33:24 there is a numerical contrast between Abraham who was but one and the large number of his descendants. In Ezek. 37:22 the point is that

---

[8] See e.g. S.D. McBride, "The Yoke of the Kingdom", *Interpretation* 27 (1973) esp. pp. 274, 293; P.D. Miller, "The Most Important Word: The Yoke of the Kingdom", *Iliff Review* (1984), pp.17-29; J.D. Levenson, *Sinai & Zion* (Minneapolis: Winston Press, 1985), p. 82; and, more tentatively, A.D.H. Mayes, *Deuteronomy* (Grand Rapids and London: Eerdmans/MMS, 1979), p. 176.

[9] See e.g. L. Jacobs, *A Jewish Theology* (London: DLT, 1973), p. 21.

[10] See e.g. J.F.A. Sawyer, "Biblical Alternatives to Monotheism", *Theology* 87 (1984), p.175; J.G. Janzen, "On the most important word in the Shema (Deuteronomy vi 4-5)", *VT* 37 (1987), pp. 280-300.

[11] So the *Revised Version, Revised Standard Version, Jerusalem Bible, New International Version,* though not the *New English Bible or the Revised English Bible*.

Israel shall be one nation with one king as opposed to two nations with two kings, again a numerical contrast. Zech. 14:9 is apparently a citation of Deut. 6:4 and raises problems similar to those of Deut. 6:4; it will be argued below that it probably uses *'eḥad* as a predicate in a numerical sense.

I Chron. 29:1 is the most problematic instance. The Hebrew of v.1aß reads: *šᵉlomoh bᵉni 'eḥad baḥar-bo 'elohim na`ar warak*. It is customary to render this "Solomon my son, whom alone God has chosen, is young...",[12] a rendering advocated or accepted by most commentators.[13] It depends on two assumptions. First, it assumes that *'eḥad* should be construed with *baḥar* on the basis of the idiomatic peculiarity of Chronicles to omit the relative *'ašer*.[14] Secondly, it assumes a contextual linkage with I Chron. 28:5, the point being that Solomon alone of David's many sons was chosen by YHWH. Yet both these assumptions may be questioned, and an alternative construal is probably preferable. First, it is unnecessary to assume the idiomatic omission of *'ašer*. It makes good sense to take *'eḥad* with *šᵉlomoh bᵉni*: "Solomon my son is but one man (*'eḥad* having a sense similar to that in Isa. 51:2, Ezek. 33:24); YHWH has chosen him when he is but an inexperienced youth". Secondly, the contextual contrast is not with David's other sons as in 28:4-5, which in the context of ch. 29 is irrelevant, but with the large number of Israelites whom David is addressing. The point is that because Solomon is but one man (and young and inexperienced), he needs all the help he can get from the many people of Israel, who should therefore contribute generously to the project.

It remains the case, therefore, that the objection to rendering *'eḥad* as "alone" has not been met. But although the objection is strong it has not generally been considered decisive since, despite the lack of other clear examples of such usage, many scholars have thought that the sense yielded is so good that it justifies taking *'eḥad* in an otherwise unparalleled sense.

There is, however, a second crucial judgement involved in the translation "YHWH is our God, YHWH alone". This is that it is possible to take *'elohenu* as the predicate of *yhwh*. It is this that, to the best of my knowledge, has received remarkably little attention.[15] Yet it is, I suggest, the decisive issue.

---

[12] So *RV, RSV, JB*; cf. *NEB, REB*.

[13] See e g. W. Rudolph, *Chronikbücher* (Tübingen: 1955) p. 190; H.G.M. Williamson, *1 and 2 Chronicles* (Grand Rapids and London: Eerdmans/MMS, 1982), p.183; R. Braun *I Chronicles* (Waco, Texas: Word, 1986), p. 277.

[14] See S.R. Driver, *Introduction to the Literature of the Old Testament* (9th edn, Edinburgh: T. & T. Clark, 1913), p. 537; cf. GK 155*d*).

[15] The idiomatic point that is discussed here is mentioned by N. Lohfink in his discussion of Deut. 6:4, but its implications for the debate about translation are not fully spelt out ("*'echadh*" in G.J. Botterweck, H. Ringgren [ed.], *Theological Dictionary of the Old Testament* I [Grand Rapids, 1977], pp. 196-7 = *Theologisches Wörterbuch zum Alten Testament* I [Stuttgart, 1973], cols 213-14).

A survey of Deuteronomic usage[16] (excluding, for the moment, Deut. 6:4) reveals the following statistics.[17] Throughout Deuteronomy the divine name *yhwh* and the epithet *'elohim* in one form or other are frequently juxtaposed. Most frequently, 300 times in all, *yhwh* is juxtaposed with *'elohim* with a first person plural suffix, *'elohenu*, or with second person singular or second person plural suffix, *'eloheka*, *'elohekem*, the three of which are largely interchangeable in Deuteronomic idiom.[18] In 12 further instances *yhwh* is juxtaposed to other forms of *'elohim* (first person singular suffix, third person singular suffix, and the construct with *'abot*, itself with various suffixes). In all these 312 instances where *yhwh* and *'elohim* are juxtaposed, the two words are always in apposition; *'elohim* is always used descriptively, i.e. "YHWH our/your God", and never predicatively, i.e. "YHWH is our/your God". (If *'elohim* is the predicate of *yhwh* it is not directly juxtaposed, but occurs in the form *ha'elohim* and is separated by the insertion of *hu'* [Deut. 4:35,39, 7:9; cf. I Kgs 8:60]). If this is consistent Deuteronomic idiom in 312 instances, it provides strong support for the contention that in the 313th instance, i.e. Deut. 6:4, the same idiom should be discerned. In Deut. 6:4, therefore, *yhwh 'elohenu* must be rendered "YHWH our God", not "YHWH is our God", and the verse must be a statement about the oneness of YHWH and not about the exclusive relationship between YHWH and Israel.

Admittedly, one might attempt to lessen the force of the statistics by arguing, as is often done, that the formula *yhwh 'elohenu yhwh 'ehad* originally existed independently as a cultic formula prior to its present inclusion within Deuteronomy,[19] and may have meant "YHWH is our God..." in that context. But even if this be allowed as a possibility (and by the nature of the case it must remain hypothetical), it must still be asked how the Deuteronomist intended the words to be understood, given the consistency of usage elsewhere. One could reasonably expect some indication of distinctive usage, were that intended, such as the wording *yhwh hu' 'elohenu*. Given the absence of any such marker there is no reason to suppose that the usage of *yhwh 'elohenu* in Deut. 6:4 is in any way different from that elsewhere in the book.

---

[16] For present purposes it is unnecessary to distinguish between different compositional levels within Deuteronomy as there is a consistency of usage in this regard throughout the book.

[17] The survey is based on the MT. There is some variation in other manuscript traditions because in some of the instances where *yhwh* appears in the MT without *'elohim* juxtaposed there is a tendency to conform to the common idiom by adding *'elohim*; see *BHS* at e.g. Deut. 6:12,18, 9:18.

[18] It would be otiose to cite all the references here. Simply within Deut. 6 (apart from v.4) the idiom occurs in vv. 1, 2, 5, 10, 13, 15, 16, 17, 20, 24, 25.

[19] E.g. McBride (n. 8), p.297 and n. 51, Lohfink (n. 15), p.197.

If we return now to the translation of the Shema as a whole, we are left with
the two alternatives "YHWH our God, YHWH is one" and "YHWH our God is
one YHWH". Between these it is more difficult to choose, but it is also less
important as their meaning is similar. Two factors, however, suggest that the
former is preferable. First, the recognition of the consistent idiom of conjoining
yhwh with a form of *'elohim* may explain the otherwise slightly puzzling
resumptive use of *yhwh* as subject before the predicate.[20] If the writer wished to
use *'ehad* as a predicate of *yhwh* and say *yhwh 'ehad* (and if there was a
pre-existing cultic formula it was surely simply these two words), but also
wished to introduce the divine name in his customary idiomatic way, then it was
the idiomatic but intrusive use of *'elohenu* that necessitated a resumptive use of
yhwh.

Secondly, and more importantly, there is Zech. 14:9, which is apparently
the sole citation of Deut. 6:4 elsewhere in the Old Testament. The text of v.9b
reads: *bayyom hahu' yihyeh yhwh 'ehad uš^{e}mo 'ehad*. Although this text raises
problems of its own, only two points need be mentioned here. First, the text
apparently envisages the eschatological fulfilment of Deut. 6:4, which had
perhaps by then already become a recognized confession of faith. As such it
represents the earliest surviving interpretation of Deut. 6:4. Although one cannot
be sure that by the time of Zech. 14:9 the Shema had not undergone some shift
in meaning from its usage in Deut. 6:4, there is no good reason to suppose that
any interpretative shift took place. All the material in Zech. 14 is deeply rooted
in Zion traditions and shows resistance, not accommodation, to the non-Jewish
world, be it Persian or Hellenistic, and so there is no reason to suppose
reinterpretation in the light of wider cultural change. With due caution,
therefore, it is reasonable to use Zech. 14:9 in interpreting Deut. 6:4. Secondly,
the most natural interpretation of the syntax of *yihyeh yhwh 'ehad* is that *'ehad* is
predicate to *yhwh* as subject (and similarly *uš^{e}mo 'ehad*). It is this predicative
use of *'ehad* in Zech. 14:9 that most strongly suggests a similar use in Deut. 6:4.

I conclude, therefore, that the Shema cannot legitimately be rendered
"YHWH is our God, YHWH alone",[21] but should best be translated "Hear, O
Israel: YHWH our God, YHWH is one". It is not, therefore, a statement about

---

[20] S. R. Driver (n.4) commented that "no sufficient reason appears for the resumption of
the subject by the second 'Jehovah'".

[21] In the most recent commentary on Deuteronomy, written since the original appearance
of this essay - D. L. Christensen, *Deuteronomy 1-11* (Dallas: Word, 1991) - the rendering
"YHWH is our God, YHWH alone" is still maintained (pp.137,142f). Although this essay
is included in the bibliography, no attempt is made to justify the chosen rendering, and all
Christensen says is, "The six words of v 4 have been translated in numerous ways, each
of which may have a measure of truth in the poetic form of the present text". Such a
failure to engage with reasoned arguments that present a contrary case raises doubts as to
how far Christensen is making a genuine contribution to understanding the text.

Israel's exclusive relationship with YHWH, although that exclusive relationship is indeed presupposed by the words "YHWH our God". Rather, it is a statement about YHWH; though precisely what it means to say that YHWH is "one" is an issue to which I hope to return on another occasion.

PROCLAIMING CHRIST CRUCIFIED:
SOME REFLECTIONS ON THE USE AND ABUSE
OF THE GOSPELS

One of the major areas of contemporary theological interest is biblical hermeneutics, that is the question of how Christians should responsibly interpret and use the Bible within the modern world. Particularly within evangelical circles there has been a growing appreciation of the fact that a simple insistence upon the authority of scripture - *sola scriptura* - cannot by itself resolve any problems unless it is also accompanied by recognized and agreed principles of interpretation; otherwise, people can "prove anything" from the Bible. Evangelical Christianity has indeed always had certain principles and traditions of interpretation, but their significance has perhaps not always been acknowledged or critically reflected upon as much as they deserve. What I wish to do in this paper is to study two centrally important passages of scripture and explore some of the hermeneutical issues they raise, in the course of which I will give special attention to some of the hermeneutical assumptions embodied in customary evangelical handling of this material.[1]

The material to be considered is the portrayal of the crucifixion in the gospels. This has the advantage of being one of the best known portions of scripture and also one of the most centrally important, for it is the cross that stands at the heart of evangelical Christianity. A further advantage of considering the crucifixion is that the historicity of the episode is not in question. The sort of fundamental problems with regard to miracles and the activity of God within history that tend to bedevil discussions of the resurrection hardly arise here. The crucifixion should therefore be an excellent subject on which to focus basic hermeneutical questions about the interpretation and use of scripture.

Introduction to the Crucifixion Narratives

A quick look at the four gospels shows that they all agree on all the basic facts with regard to the crucifixion; and although there is probably nothing in the gospels that has not been questioned by someone at sometime, there is no good reason to doubt that all these points of unanimous agreement can be accepted as genuine historical facts:

1 *Day:* Jesus was crucified on a Friday, the day before the sabbath (Matt. 27:62, Mk. 15:42, Lk. 23:54, Jn. 19:14, 31).

---

[1] I would like to express my gratitude and indebtedness to my friends in *DEWTHO,* whose discussions have provided the inspiration for this paper.

2 *Place:*   Jesus was crucified at "the Skull" (in Aramaic, Golgotha), just outside Jerusalem (Matt. 27:33, Mk. 15:22, Lk. 23:33, Jn. 19:17).

3 *Cause of Execution:*   Jesus was put to death as a criminal on the official charge of being, or claiming to be, "The King of the Jews", a charge which was affixed to his cross (Matt. 27:37, Mk. 15:26, Lk. 23:38, Jn. 19:19).

4 *Time of Death:*   Jesus died sometime in the late afternoon, between 3pm and sunset (Matt. 27:46, 50, 57, Mk. 15:34, 37, 42, Lk. 23:44, 46, 54, Jn. 19:30-34).

5   *Circumstances of Burial:*   Jesus' body was granted by Pilate to Joseph of Arimathea at the latter's request. The body was then put in wrappings and laid in a tomb that evening (Matt. 27:57-61, Mk. 15:42-7, Lk. 23:50-6, Jn. 19:38-42).

In addition to these basic facts, all four gospels also agree on a number of points of detail, which are in a sense incidental but which were clearly remembered as part of the historical tradition:

6 Two other men were crucified at the same time, one on either side of Jesus (Matt. 27:38, Mk. 15:27, Lk. 23:33, Jn. 19:18).

7 Jesus' garments were divided among the attendant Roman soldiers (Matt. 27:35, Mk. 15:24, Lk. 23:34, Jn. 19:24).

8 Jesus was at some stage given wine vinegar to drink (Matt. 27:48, Mk. 15:36, Lk. 23:36, Jn. 19:29).

9 The crucifixion was witnessed by some women who were followers of Jesus (Matt. 27:55-6, Mk. 15:40-41, Lk. 23:49, Jn. 19:25-7).

Finally, one may note that all four gospels share a similar restraint with regard to the physical sufferings of Jesus and the horror of crucifixion as a spectacle - unlike many subsequent devotional writers, who have used their imagination to develop and emphasize precisely this aspect of the death of Jesus.

Beyond this basic agreement, however, the gospels differ in their portrayal of the crucifixion. This has, of course, always been recognized. It is the *extent* of the differences and the *significance* that should be attached to them that leads to a parting of the ways. The traditional approach of Christians, following the precedent and principles laid down by St. Augustine,[2] has been (i) to minimize the differences between the gospel accounts, and (ii) to assume that such differences as there are are not incompatible with, but rather complementary to, each other. Indeed, in many ways the crucifixion narratives afford a classic example of the plausibility of such an approach, because many of the varying details can, with a little imagination, be combined into an harmonious whole. On the one hand, simple differences of detail can be made complementary to each other; thus, the various sayings of Jesus (1 in Matthew

---

[2] Brevard Childs *(The New Testament as Canon: An Introduction,* [London: SCM, 1984], pp 143-56) gives an important brief survey of traditional and modern approaches to the problem posed by the presence of four gospels within the canon of the New Testament.

and Mark, 3 in Luke, and 3 in John) can be combined and arranged in sequence, the "seven words from the cross". On the other hand, apparent contradictions can be easily harmonized; thus, Jesus initially carried his own cross (Jn. 19:17), but subsequently, because of his already weakened condition, Simon of Cyrene carried it for him (Matt. 27:32, Mk. 15:21, Lk. 23:26); initially both of the crucified thieves mocked Jesus (Matt. 27:44, Mk. 15:32), but subsequently one of them, impressed by Jesus' attitude and words, turned to him in faith (Lk. 23:39-43).

This sort of approach has in fact been abandoned, for a variety of reasons, by the mainstream consensus of modern biblical scholars, and abandoned to such an extent that it is generally viewed with suspicion and hostility. Instead, there is a general tendency to maximize the difference between the gospels and to assume the incompatibility of the respective accounts. Nonetheless, it should be recognized that a harmonizing approach is a natural and instinctive approach to the text for many a reader, and also represents a natural defensive move to any claim that the differences between the gospels show them to be unreliable or contradictory in such a way as to impugn their authority for the Christian believer. This latter is an important reason why a significant degree of harmonization has continued to prevail in much evangelical writing (as will be seen below). The issues that are raised, therefore, should in no way be taken for granted or assumed to be obvious. The present paper is an attempt to clarify some of the issues and to present the paradox that although a consistently harmonizing approach appears to set much store by the literal truthfulness of the gospel text, and is therefore adopted from the best of motives, it is in fact in many ways questionable in principle and also potentially restricting in practice.

The argument will be based upon a study of the crucifixion as it is presented in Mark and Luke, and will be limited (more or less) to those two gospels. Mainly this is to try to keep the essay reasonably short, although the argument would undoubtedly be enhanced by a study of Matthew and John as well. It is, however, only necessary to study two gospels to establish the point at issue, which the reader can then apply elsewhere accordingly.

Mark's Account of the Crucifixion

A careful reading of Mark's account of the crucifixion suggests that the central emphasis of the narrative is the *utter desolation* of Jesus. This is conveyed primarily by the words Jesus cries out, but their force is best appreciated when they are set in context.

First, everyone who speaks to, or about, Jesus speaks with nothing but antipathy, mockery and misunderstanding. Initially, three different groups of people speak: the passers-by "blaspheme" Jesus (Mk. 15:29-30), the chief priests and scribes speak mockingly to each other (15:31-32a), and those crucified with Jesus abuse him (15:32b). Later, those who hear Jesus cry out entirely misunderstand the meaning of his cry, thus heightening his isolation;

and the act of giving him something to drink is not an act of mercy but is simply to keep him alive a little longer (and so prolong his agony) in the hope of being treated to a miraculous display (15:36).

Secondly, those who might be expected to be present and sympathetic, that is Jesus' disciples, are nowhere to be seen. His friends have deserted him. When last mentioned they were fleeing for their lives (14:50), and the mysterious young man in the garden was even prepared to leave his one basic item of clothing behind in his urgent haste to get away (14:52). Peter has denied Jesus with an oath and a curse (14:71) and nothing more is heard of him. Admittedly, some women are present as Jesus is crucified, but they are looking on "from afar off" (15:40), and so provide no support for Jesus. Even the centurion, who recognizes Jesus' true significance as he dies, is not standing beside Jesus but "over against" him (15:39).[3] The isolation of Jesus from human companionship and support is complete.

What, then, of God, the one whom Jesus addressed as "Abba" (Father) (14:36), the one who could surely be depended upon when all others failed? Even he has abandoned Jesus. The only words that Jesus utters are a cry of anguish, not to "Father" but to a God who has abandoned him (15:34). This is further emphasized by the darkness that covers the land (15:33). Darkness is naturally sinister and fearful, and a strange supernatural darkness in the middle of the day could readily suggest divine anger or absence. If, moreover, the well-informed reader is meant to be reminded of Amos 8:9-12, such an interpretation is confirmed, for the darkness at noon in that Old Testament context is explicitly connected with divine judgment and withdrawal.

Finally, it should be noted that Jesus himself does not speak from the cross in any normal tone of voice. The words of Ps. 22:1 which Jesus utters are a cry of pain, and so it is precisely with a loud cry that the words leave Jesus' lips, and it is another loud cry that he utters just before he dies (15:34,37). Both cries are naturally suggestive of the deep anguish and agony of the abandoned Jesus.

Beside this central concern of Mark's narrative, certain other emphases also emerge if one pays attention to the details of Mark's wording. First, it is likely that the careful reader of the gospel should see special significance in the fact that both those groups whose mockery of Jesus is spelt out connect the idea of Jesus saving himself with his coming down from the cross (15:30, 31b-32a). For earlier in the gospel, in the context of his central pronouncement about his mission and the meaning of salvation, Jesus has made clear that salvation only comes through taking up the cross and losing one's life (8:34-35). Thus it is ironic that the mockers miss the central point that it is only by Jesus' remaining on the cross and not coming down that salvation, for himself or anyone else, can

---

3 The precise significance of the Greek *ex enantias* is debatable, but the fact that it is used instead of the usual words for "near" *(eggus, plesion)* makes not unlikely the sort of meaning suggested here.

be gained. They, like Peter earlier, cannot understand things in the way that God understands them (8:33).

Following on from this, it appears that Mark is developing more generally the paradoxical theme of seeing and believing in Jesus, especially in relation to Jesus as king/messiah. Earlier, Pilate twice refers to Jesus as king in the presence of the crowds (15:9, 12), but although the crowds see Jesus they do not recognize him as king, but rather call for him to be killed (15:13-14). The Roman soldiers call Jesus king, but intend it only as mockery (15:16-20). Then the words "The King of the Jews" are fixed to the cross publicly for all to see (15:26). The crucial words are on the lips of the chief priests who mockingly demand that "the Christ, the king of Israel should come down now from the cross, *that we may see and believe.*" They assume that if they see something, then they will believe. The irony is that the truth about Jesus, that he *is* king, is publicly displayed before their very eyes, and yet they do not believe. Later on, they still hope to see something, that is that Jesus should be miraculously taken down from the cross by Elijah if he is not able to come down by himself (15:36). Only one person, the centurion, does recognize Jesus for who he is, and indeed this is because he sees (15:39a) - but what he sees is nothing spectacular or miraculous such as the others had hoped for. He sees simply "that he died thus", ie, in utter desolation. *This* is the only sort of seeing that leads to faith. Jesus has been portrayed consistently as a suffering king, but no one has taken this seriously. Rather, people have ignored, mocked, and looked for something else. The centurion sees the suffering king at the final moment of anguish in death, yet he believes.

Thus Mark may be subtly indicating that simply to view the person of Jesus and the truth about him does not lead to faith. The assumption that to see a miraculous display would lead to faith is likewise mistaken. In both cases people's preconceptions about what the king ought to be like make them blind. Only the centurion who takes with utter seriousness the apparent contradiction before his eyes - a king/messiah who dies in desolation - sees truly and so believes.

One final irony is to do with Jesus and the temple. Accusations with regard to the temple were made at the trial (14:58), and are mockingly repeated at the crucifixion by the passers-by (15:29) - let the one who would perform the great feat of replacing the temple perform the simple feat of saving his own life. But the truth emerges when Jesus dies, for then the curtain of the temple is torn in two. The precise significance of this has been much debated. It has often been suggested (presumably in the light of Hebrews 10:19) to symbolize a new kind of access into the presence of God. This would mean that the fundamental presupposition of temple theology, viz. that the temple is the unique meeting-place between God and humanity, is in principle retained, the difference now being the extent of access available. But in the light of the preceding mocking reference to Jesus destroying the temple, it is perhaps more likely that the tearing of the temple curtain symbolizes precisely what the mockers denied, that is, it symbolizes the destruction of the temple as a whole - the curtain is torn right through ("from top to bottom", 15:38) not so that people can come in but because God is coming out - he is leaving the temple and has finished with it. Henceforth the unique meeting-place between God and humanity is no longer the temple but rather Jesus, the crucified king.

In summary, then, the predominant concern of Mark's narrative is the utter and unrelieved forsakenness of Jesus. Paradoxically, it is only one who dies thus who is the true meeting-place between God and humanity, and who can be recognized as the Christ, the Son of God (15:39, cf. 1:1).[4] Interwoven with this is a strong and painful irony which for the careful reader further draws out the implications of Jesus' death. Such is the crucifixion of Jesus according to Mark.

Before leaving Mark it is important finally to appreciate that this forbidding and uncomfortable portrayal of Jesus at his crucifixion is consistent with the portrayal of Jesus elsewhere in the same gospel. Throughout, Jesus is a lonely and awesome figure. Perhaps this is most notable in the image of Jesus striding out alone, ahead of his awe-struck followers (10:32). More generally, the constant reaction to Jesus is fear *(phobos,* 4:41, 5:15, 9:32, 10:32), astonishment *(thambos,* 1:27, 10:24,32), and amazement *(ekplessomai* 1:22, 6:2, 7:37, 10:26, 11:18). Even his family think he is mad (3:21),[5] and Jesus' response to their anxieties is hardly reassuring (3:31-35). The truth about Jesus is far from clear - his disciples are constantly uncomprehending (6:52, 8:14-21, 9:32), Jesus speaks publicly in a riddling sort of way that may even increase incomprehension (4:11-12), and when his significance does become at all clear it is something that should be kept quiet (1:25, 3:12, 8:30, 9:9). Even the disciples, who are committed to Jesus and have things specially explained to them in a way that is not possible for outsiders (4:11-12, 34), may themselves sometimes be unbelieving in exactly the same way as outsiders with hardened hearts and eyes that do not see (8:17-18). It would be consistent with all this if the original intended ending of the gospel was at 16:8. The point would then be that the resurrection, though real (16:6), does not in itself remove the mystery surrounding Jesus or the possibility of misunderstanding him. For, in the light of all that has preceded, it becomes clear that a true understanding or seeing of Jesus is possible only for those who themselves embrace the way of humility, suffering and death - without that, any seeing of Jesus would be a seeing that fails to see.

---

[4] The reference to "Son of God" in 1:1 is textually uncertain. If, however, the words are a gloss then they are an appropriate and perceptive gloss, which constitutes a valuable addition to the textual tradition.

[5] The precise meaning of the Greek phrase translated here by "family" is uncertain, and a possible alternative rendering is "friends". Either way, the basic point remains that it was people close to Jesus who thought thus.

Luke's Account of the Crucifixion

If we turn now to consider Luke's account of the crucifixion, a very different picture emerges. Here again the basic tone is set by what Jesus says - four distinct sayings in all. First, on the way to crucifixion, Jesus speaks to the women of Jerusalem, showing concern for them and warning them of their own impending doom (23:28-31). Secondly, Jesus shows love for his enemies by praying that his executioners may be forgiven; in his compassion for them he knows that they are acting in ignorance (23:34a).[6] Thirdly, Jesus speaks words of mercy and assurance to the penitent thief (23:43). Lastly, Jesus uses some ancient words of trust in God (Ps. 31:5) to commit himself into his Father's hands at death (23:46). Two aspects of these sayings may particularly be noted. On the one hand, both the times Jesus speaks to God in prayer (the second and fourth sayings) he prefaces his words with his customary address of trust and obedience, "Father". On the other hand, each time Jesus speaks, he *speaks* (and does not shout). What he says is presumably to be understood as being said in a manner appropriate to the content, ie, with quiet assurance and authority. Luke does indeed mention that Jesus gave a loud cry (23:46a), but the content of the cry is not recorded and so it plays no significant role.[7]

A second notable feature of Luke's portrayal is the emphasis that Jesus is innocent of any crime, because he is a truly good and righteous man. This point is made three times by Pilate (23:4, 14-15, 22), once by the penitent thief (23:41b), and finally by the centurion (23:47). It is perhaps also made by Jesus himself (in a characteristically indirect way) in his words to the women of Jerusalem (23:31), where the point of the proverb appears to be, "if this happens to the innocent (ie, Jesus, who is not deserving of such a fate, like green wood which is full of life and not ready for being cut down and burnt), then what will happen to the guilty (ie, the sinful inhabitants of Jerusalem, who are like dry wood which is ready to be cut down and burnt)?". Given such a consistent emphasis in the narrative, what is its likely significance?[8] Luke's aim is

---

[6] The words of 23:34a are textually uncertain. They are, however, totally in keeping with Luke's portrayal of Jesus. If they are a later addition, then, like "Son of God" in Mk. 1:1, they should be appreciated as a valuable enhancement of the tradition.

[7] I am assuming that Jesus' words in 23:46b are to be understood as a separate utterance from the cry in 23:46a (although the point is open to debate). The basis for the assumption is the fact that it is a common idiom of NT Greek in general, and Luke in particular, to say "he did X and he did Y" by "having done [aorist participle] X he did [aorist indicative] Y" - which is the grammatical form of 23:46. Cf. eg, Lk. 4:17, 20, 29, 30 for four examples of this idiom within one story.

[8] The common explanation of this is in terms of Luke's supposed apologetic purpose of commending the political innocence of Christianity to a suspicious Roman Empire, just as Mark's emphasis on suffering is generally explained in terms of the pastoral needs of persecuted Christians in Rome. While such proposals are not unlikely and can help the

probably to show both how Jesus embodies and fulfils the kind of righteousness that is acceptable to God, and how in Jesus goodness overcomes evil. Luke is deeply aware of how faithfulness to God can produce human opposition and hatred (cf Ac. 3:14, 4:27, 7:52), and has already indicated that the real issue in the passion of Jesus is a struggle against Satan and the powers of evil (Lk. 22:3, 31, 53). How are the powers of evil overcome? By a positive goodness which trusts unswervingly in God, repays hatred with love, and is a channel for the mighty power of God to flow through.

This understanding of the death of Jesus is especially indicated by the response of the centurion (23:47), who not only proclaims that Jesus is innocent/righteous but also at the same time *glorifies God*. A human response of glorifying God is often mentioned by Luke (2:20, 5:25,26, 7:16, 13:13, 17:15, 18:43), and it is always a response to a demonstration of the saving and healing power of God. The centurion, therefore, is responding to a demonstration of saving divine power in Jesus on the cross, which consists presumably (since this is what the narrative emphasizes) in Jesus' unswerving compassion towards people and trust towards God in the face of injustice, suffering, hatred and death. Thus are Satan and the powers of evil overcome.

A third notable emphasis in Luke's narrative is the connection which is made between salvation and Jesus as king/messiah. Three times Jesus is mocked, and each mocking is virtually identical in content. The rulers (23:35), and the condemned criminal (23:39) explicitly link Jesus being the Christ/Messiah with his being able to save himself, while the soldiers (23:37) link his being the king of the Jews with his being able to save himself.[9] As in Mark, there is heavy irony here, the words being the words of those who have eyes but cannot see. For although Luke seems to imply that even the charge "This is the King of the Jews" was attached to the cross in mockery (23:38 - the implication lies in the word "also" after the mockery of the previous verse), it is precisely this point, that Jesus *is* king, that is seen by the penitent thief (23:42).[10] And as he recognizes Jesus as king, so he is saved (23:43). In this portrayal, the words "salvation" and "kingship" are seen to have a new meaning.

---

reader imagine a particularly appropriate context for each work, it should be remembered that they are at best *partial* explanations which do not grasp the theological nettle of explaining what the text actually *means*. At worst, such an approach leads to an "explaining away" of the text, similar to that of people who refuse to engage with the content of someone else's argument on the grounds that they know the motives that have caused them to say it.

[9] "Christ" and "King of the Jews" are presumably identical in meaning, the latter phrase, which avoids the specifically Jewish word, being more appropriate on the lips of Roman soldiers.

[10] This essential point is unaffected by the textual uncertainty whether Jesus will come *into* his kingdom (ie, future glory?) or *in* his kingdom (ie, second coming?).

Jesus' kingship means the supremacy of his compassion towards people and trust towards God even in the face of injustice, suffering and death, for through these both sin and death are overcome (23:43). Salvation means recognizing this Jesus as king and looking to him even in the midst of suffering and death.

In short, Luke portrays the crucifixion as a predominantly tranquil scene dominated by the quiet authority and compassion of the suffering Jesus. The unfailing goodness of Jesus is stressed, and this true king of the Jews is thus able to give salvation to the lost and overcome death.

As with Mark, it is important to see how Luke's portrayal of the crucifixion is consistent with his portrayal of Jesus elsewhere. In particular, Jesus' encounter with the penitent thief, which is so central to the crucifixion, is similar to two other stories of encounter that are peculiar to Luke, the prostitute who anointed Jesus (7:36-50),[11] and Zacchaeus (19:1- 10). Each story presents a typical outcast - a prostitute, a tax collector, a criminal - who quite simply responds to the person of Jesus. There is no preaching or explicit challenge in any of the stories, but each person makes a genuine response to Jesus which results each time in an assurance of salvation (7:50, 19:9, 23:43). In particular, the assurance given to the penitent thief that *today* he would be with Jesus in Paradise reminds the reader of the similar assurance given to Zacchaeus (19:5, 9).

A similar note is sounded in some of the parables peculiar to Luke, especially the prodigal son (15:11-32) and the Pharisee and the publican (18:9-14). In each of these parables an attitude of humility and honesty to God is shown (15:18, 18:13-14), similar to that which in the narratives is shown towards Jesus. Humility and openness on the one side, goodness and compassion on the other side - these are the consistent features of God's salvation in Jesus as depicted in Luke.[12]

Comparison of the Two Crucifixion Accounts

If now we set these two crucifixion accounts side by side and compare them, what emerges? Two strikingly different pictures, different both in general tenor and in detail. In Mark, Jesus is an anguished figure, abandoned by both people and God, speaking only in loud cries. There is absolutely nothing to relieve the agony except perhaps the centurion's words, by which time Jesus is already dead. In Luke, Jesus is a compassionate figure, forgiving people, trusting God, and peaceful throughout. The nature of the difference may be well expressed by an artistic analogy. Mark's portrayal is like Grünewald's famous

---

[11] There has naturally been extensive debate about the relationship of this story to that in Mk. 14:3-9, Matt. 26:6-13, Jn. 12:1-8. For present puposes what matters is that the story as it stands is peculiar to Luke.

[12] Luke's general portrayal of Jesus is well expressed in Charles Wesley's famous line, "Jesus, thou art all compassion..."

crucifixion in the Isenheim altarpiece - a stark, agonizing, disturbing picture. Luke's portrayal is like any of the crucifixion scenes of Fra Angelico - always peaceful, dignified, moving.

Given two such different pictures, it is worth comparing points of similarity and difference in some detail.

Similarities

These are mainly the points of basic historical outline, as set out in the introductory section. Otherwise, the major similarity is the strongly ironical portrayal of the mockery of Jesus, which both Mark and Luke use to highlight the significance of Jesus' death, even though each writer nuances this somewhat differently. Beyond this, there are certain details common to both Mark and Luke - the darkness at noon, the cry before death, the tearing of the temple curtain, the witness of a centurion, and women looking on from far off. However, as will be seen below, it is likely that these various details were interpreted differently by the two evangelists.

Differences

In Mark, Jesus' recorded words have only to do with being forsaken. In Luke, Jesus' words are all words of compassion and trust. Whereas Jesus' words in Mark show him to be forsaken by God, Jesus' words in Luke show not the slightest hint of any rupture in the relationship of love and trust between Father and Son.

In Mark, Jesus only speaks in cries. In Luke, Jesus speaks normally. Given the difference in content, in both Mark and Luke there is a consistency between what Jesus says and the way he says it. Luke does indeed allow for a loud cry before Jesus dies (23:46), but this corresponds to the loud cry before death similarly mentioned by Mark (15:37) and so cannot be the cry of dereliction. Because the cry does not enhance the general tenor of Luke's portrayal, it plays a lesser role there than in Mark where it represents a significant furthering of the anguish and pain of Jesus.

In Mark, the significance of Jesus' death is conveyed by the tearing of the temple curtain which accompanies his death. In Luke, the tearing of the temple curtain is recorded *before* Jesus' death (23:45), and in a manner less emphatic and dramatic than in Mark.[13] Luke apparently presents the tearing of the curtain simply as one of two amazing portents that accompanied Jesus' death (the other being the darkness at noon, specified as "the sun failing" [23:44-45a], perhaps a portent of the day of the Lord, cf Joel 2:31, Ac.2:20). No earlier mention of the temple is made in either the mockery at the cross or at the trial as they are presented by Luke. Apparently, therefore, Luke did not see the death of Jesus as

---

[13] In Mark, the curtain is "torn in two from top to bottom" while in Luke it is simply torn "in the middle".

effectively abolishing and replacing the temple, in the way that Mark seems to, for subsequently Luke can still regard the temple positively as an appropriate place for worship (Lk. 24:53, Ac. 3:1 etc.). In any case, however Luke understood the tearing of the curtain, it is presumably the story of the penitent thief, and not the tearing of the curtain, that for him is the primary key to the meaning of Jesus' death.

In Mark, the centurion's reaction to Jesus' death is the recognition of Jesus as son of God - the emphasis is on Jesus in all his suffering as truly related to God. In Luke, the centurion praises God and recognizes Jesus as righteous - the point is a joyful recognition of God overcoming evil through the unfailing goodness of Jesus.

In Mark, Jesus is only spoken to with abuse. In Luke, there is abuse but also the penitent thief speaks with faith.

In Mark, the passers-by (ie those other than the religious leaders or the soldiers) are hostile to Jesus (15:29). In Luke, the crowd (again, those other than the religious leaders or the soldiers) is not actively hostile but simply looks on (23:35), and at the end is deeply moved (23:48, cf 23:27).

In Mark, Jesus' disciples are absent, and only women are present, "afar off" (15:40). In Luke, the onlookers are still "afar off" but now they include "all those known to Jesus" (23:49), which presumably includes his disciples. That this is significant is likely since Jesus' words that the disciples would be scattered (Mk. 14:27) have no place in Luke, who, by contrast, has Jesus' words to the disciples, "You are those who have continued with me in my trials" (22:28), words of reassurance to Peter (22:31-32), and no reference to the disciples fleeing in Gethsemane. In Luke, Jesus is not only not abandoned by God but also he is not abandoned by people.

Just as the portrayal of the crucifixion in each gospel needs to be understood in relation to the portrayal of Jesus in each gospel as a whole, so too the comparison of the two crucifixion accounts needs to be related to a comparison between the gospels as a whole, although at present only a few brief indications can be given.

In Gethsemane, for example, Mark portrays Jesus as going to prayer in great pain and anguish (14:33-34), while Luke's corresponding narrative makes no reference to any disturbance of Jesus' serenity (22:40-41).[14] Where Mark dramatically portrays Jesus as falling to the ground to pray (14:35), Luke simply portrays him as kneeling (22:41). Later, Luke twice shows Jesus' compassionate

---

[14] This may be qualified to some extent by the textually uncertain 22:43-4. Even here, however, the central word, *agonia,* does not simply have the same meaning as the English word "agony". The basic meaning of the word is "contest" or "struggle" and this is the appropriate sense in context, where the point is the intensity of Jesus' wrestling in prayer (presumably to defeat Satan and the powers of evil) rather than any mental anguish as such.

concern for others in incidents unparalleled in Mark; he heals the severed ear of the high priest's slave (22:51b), and he looks at faithless Peter (22:61).

Earlier, one of the key statements in Mark about the meaning of Jesus' death is "For the son of man did not come to be served but to serve, and to give his life a ransom for many" (10:45). In Luke the corresponding passage reads simply, "I am in the midst of you as one who serves" (22:27). The centrality of suffering and death for a true understanding of Jesus is conveyed in Mark by the pivotal significance within the gospel of the episode of Caesarea Philippi (8:27-9:1). In Luke, this episode appears simply as one among many others (9:18-27), and its impact is softened because Peter's misunderstanding and Jesus' rebuke are omitted and the call to discipleship is generalized.[15]

Customary Evangelical Interpretation of the Crucifixion

It will be appropriate now to turn to consider the portrayal and interpretation of the crucifixion in two recent books by evangelical writers. Because the writers, John Stott and Michael Green, are widely recognized as leading figures within contemporary evangelical Anglicanism, their books may reasonably be regarded as representative of a contemporary evangelical outlook.

First, John Stott's *The Cross of Christ*.[16] Much of the book is a fine exposition of scripture, and it is only certain aspects that are questionable. In his discussion of the gospel material Stott gives central place to the cry of dereliction (Mk. 15:34) which he expounds at some length (pp.79-82). He then continues,

> "Almost immediately after the cry of dereliction, Jesus uttered three more words or sentences in quick succession. First, 'I am thirsty', his great spiritual sufferings having taken their toll of him physically. Secondly, he called out, again (according to Matthew and Mark) in a loud voice, 'It is finished.' And thirdly the tranquil, voluntary, confident self-commendation, 'Father, into your hands I commit my spirit,' as he breathed his last breath. The middle cry, the loud shout of victory, is in the Gospel text the single word *tetelestai*... At once the curtain of the Temple, which for centuries had symbolized the alienation of sinners from God, was torn in two from top to bottom, in

---

[15] I appreciate that a possible criticism of my general thesis is that it depends upon an intensive study of two short passages which may find meaning where none was intended, combined with a partial and selective reading of the gospels elsewhere. But while I certainly accept that I may have to some extent "overinterpreted" the two crucifixion accounts, and also that any thorough study of the portrayal of Jesus in Mark or Luke would produce a richer and more differentiated picture than the relatively straightforward one I have drawn, I do not believe that further study in either area will significantly blur the main outlines of my portrayal or show it to be untrue to the text.

[16] Leicester: IVP, 1986.

> order to demonstrate that the sin-barrier had been thrown down
> by God, and the way into his presence opened."

This is a classic example of traditional harmonization whereby elements from all four gospels are combined without the slightest sense of incongruity. It raises basic hermeneutical issues. First, the controlling assumption is that the different gospel accounts can and should be combined, and the resulting sequence regarded as an historical sequence. Or, to put it another way, it is assumed that every detail of what each gospel says about the crucifixion is straightforwardly historical and so can be taken in isolation from its gospel context and put together with other details in an imagined historical reconstruction. Yet we have already seen that the differences between the crucifixion accounts of Mark and Luke are part of a consistent difference of presentation within each gospel as a whole. Moreover, the differences are hardly the sort of differences that would arise if each evangelist had merely made a different selection from the same range of historical data, for the whole ethos of each account is significantly different. This is in essence a basic point of historical method, that historians must first assess their sources in terms of their special interests and tendencies; and if they discover that the material has been influenced by concerns that are not straightforwardly historical, then they must make appropriate allowance for this when drawing historical conclusions from the material.

Secondly, the understanding of the crucifixion that emerges is not in fact that of any one of the evangelists, certainly not that of either Mark or Luke. Although much is made of the cry of dereliction that Mark records, we have already seen that for Mark the crucifixion is a desolation that is total and is not mitigated by either "a loud shout of victory" or a "tranquil, voluntary, confident self-commendation". On the contrary, it is clear that both such elements, if introduced into Mark's narrative, would significantly change it. Stott's account of the crucifixion is entirely composed of biblical elements, but as it stands it is an imaginative construct whose claim to being biblical is at least debatable.

The other book to be considered is Michael Green's *The Empty Cross of Jesus*.[17] Again, this is a helpful work with whose main thesis I have no argument. But for present purposes two points are particularly significant. First, when considering the evidence from the gospels as to why Jesus had to die, Green simply presents an amalgam of points abstracted from all four gospels. Thus the death of Jesus was, among other things, inevitable, voluntary, an identification with sinners, a sacrifice, a ransom, a victory, total darkness, and total vindication (pp. 32-41). In all this, no consideration is given as to how the death of Jesus is understood in any one gospel. The distinctive portrayal of each evangelist is apparently less significant than an amalgam portrayal.

Secondly, Green apparently assumes that all the various aspects of the death of Jesus that he lists are compatible with, and complementary to, each other.

---

[17] London: Hodder & Stoughton, 1984.

Presumably because he wishes to be eirenic in an area that is liable to sharp controversy, he simply lists his points and does not attempt to develop their deeper implications or interrelationships. He comments that "although each evangelist contributes his unique perspective, the overall picture is clear, and abundantly substantiated" (p.41). That there might be a genuine tension between the evangelists is nowhere hinted at. Indeed, it is interesting to see how the difference of portrayal between Mark and Luke is subtly blurred. When discussing Jesus in Mark, Green says, "That victory is completed through the cross and resurrection, where he suffers *with dignity,* where in dying he *wins over* his executioners, and where he is raised in power to go before his disciples into the Gentile mission" [my italics] (p 43). The words that I have put in italics are those aspects of the crucifixion that are not Marcan at all, but rather are characteristic of Luke.[18] Then, when discussing Luke, Green allows the common thesis that Luke "gives no explicit doctrine of the atonement", but then utilizes Acts 20:28 to make the point that "His shed blood constitutes *a ransom*" [my italics] (p 44), thereby interpreting Luke with a theological category that is not Lucan at all but Marcan (as already noted, "ransom" is strikingly absent from the Lucan parallel to Mk. 10:45).

A Critique of the Assumptions Underlying Harmonization

In these two books that we have briefly looked at it is clear that certain basic hermeneutical assumptions are being made, even though they are never explicitly spelt out. Both writers stand, to a greater or lesser extent, within the classic tradition of Augustine which tends to minimize the differences between the gospels and assume that such differences as there are should be regarded as straightforwardly complementary. The fundamental assumptions underlying this approach are twofold. First, there is the conviction of faith as to the truthfulness and trustworthiness of the gospels. As a Christian theologian I have no quarrel with this. Secondly, there is the assumption that the narrative statements of the gospels can always, unless there is clear evidence to the contrary,[19] be equated

---

[18] This is not to say that elements within Mark's narrative are not open to be read in this way. For example, Jesus' rejection of wine (15:23) and silence under abuse (15:32) could not unreasonably be described as dignified. The point is simply that it is Luke's portrayal (and John's) rather than Mark's that readily suggests "dignified" as an appropriate description for the behaviour of Jesus.

[19] The parables are the classic example of narrative which is recognized as non-historical, because parables are imaginative stories designed to make a point (or points). But where no such clear literary genre can be appealed to, evangelical writers are generally reluctant to allow the presence of imaginative, non-historical material; everything must be assumed to be historical unless there is clear evidence to the contrary. Such clear evidence is usually extremely hard to come by, given the relative paucity of extant comparative and corroborative material. The issue is usually one of discerning

with, or translated into, statements of historical fact. It is this second assumption, which imposes important restrictions on how the truth of the gospels (the first assumption) is to be understood, that I wish to question.

It is, of course, fundamental to the Christian faith that it is rooted in history. What makes Christianity distinctive is precisely its focus upon Jesus of Nazareth, the man of Galilee, as the key to understanding and knowing God. Without Jesus, or without a reliable knowledge of him, the Christian faith would lose its distinctive content. As a general principle, that is unexceptionable. Problems arise, however, when one tries to pinpoint the precise extent of this rootedness in history, especially if one attempts to claim more than that the gospels are *substantially* (a usefully imprecise but still meaningful term) rooted in history. In principle, it is usually only this substantial historicity that is argued for, as in the admirable recent study by R. T. France, *The Evidence for Jesus*[20] (eg, p.15). In practice, however, there is a clear tendency, as illustrated above, to claim, or at least presume, more than this. The basic reason for this appears to be an apologetic concern, as is well illustrated in John Wenham's *Easter Enigma*.[21] Wenham sets out to harmonize the resurrection stories explicitly against a background of scholars judging the stories to be "a jumble of contradicting statements" which "cannot all be true" (p.10). The motive - to uphold the truth of the gospel text - is admirable. But the crucial question is whether the defence has not too readily accepted the terms on which the criticism of the gospels was made, which itself begged the question, and so has fought on the wrong ground.

The basic point at issue, I would suggest, is the status of each of the four canonical gospels as a true and authoritative (divinely inspired) interpretation of Jesus. If anything has emerged clearly from modern study of the gospels, it is the recognition that none of the evangelists presents a straightforward historical account of Jesus, but that each presents a distinctive portrait in which the historical material is selected, moulded, developed and interpreted by the evangelist so as to present those particular aspects of the significance of Jesus that he wishes to convey. Thus, to put it crudely, each gospel consists *both* of certain sayings and doings of the historical Jesus *and* of the interpretation that has been put upon these by the evangelist.[22] Although it is perfectly possible

---

literary genre, which requires an experienced literary judgment, and which rarely yields the kind of knock-down argument sometimes sought.

[20] London: Hodder & Stoughton, 1986.

[21] Exeter: Paternoster, 1984.

[22] As it stands, this of course simplifies what in reality was probably a complex process of transmission and interpretation by the early Church. But I do not think that that need affect the present argument since (i) the same positive assessment can be made of the whole process as of the evangelist, and (ii) the evangelist was the arbiter and interpreter of the process and represents the level at which the tradition was recognized as authoritative by the whole Church.

and legitimate for the historian to distinguish between these two, and to try to separate the former from the latter, this is hardly a way of reading the text that should be normative generally within the Christian churches that seek to live by this material as the word of God. If a doctrine of the authority of scripture is to be meaningful, it must be primarily the gospels as we have them, and not some historical (and usually debatable) reconstruction that goes behind the text, that is authoritative for the community of faith. This means that to regard each gospel as inspired and authoritative entails according inspired and authoritative status to each gospel's interpretation of Jesus.

Yet it is just this which is called in question by harmonization.[23] One of the basic principles of traditional harmonization is well enunciated in a passing statement by John Wenham: "It would *contradict nothing explicitly said* by Luke if we were to infer that the preparation of the spices and ointments to which he refers [23:56, in the context of Friday evening] did in fact take place after their purchase on Saturday evening; *it would simply negate an impression*" [my italics] (p 68). Thus one who wished to harmonize the crucifixion narratives could argue that because Mark does not explicitly say that Jesus did not utter the word *tetelestai* in his final cry and then entrust himself to his Father (even though he gives the impression that Jesus' agony was unrelieved), and Luke does not explicitly say that Jesus did not utter a cry of dereliction (even though he gives the impression that the harmony between Jesus and his Father was unbroken), it is therefore legitimate (because it contradicts nothing explicitly said) to combine the two accounts in the way that Stott does. The questionable nature of this kind of argument becomes apparent if, in Wenham's quotation, we replace "impression" with "interpretation". For in both crucifixion narratives that we have considered it is clear that the impression of Jesus that is conveyed, whether as anguished and forsaken or as calm and trusting, is in fact integral to the whole theological interpretation of the crucifixion by each evangelist. To negate the impression means to deny the interpretation. And yet, as argued above, it is precisely as interpretations of Jesus that the gospels are authoritative for the Church. An harmonizing approach which makes a composite picture normative and authoritative implicitly denies that both Mark and Luke (and

---

[23] I am not here thinking of harmonization in the sense of the historian's customary practice of trying to piece together differing accounts of the same event, something which is always legitimate in principle. In the hands of the historian this is essentially an heuristic approach, ie, you try it out and see if the result is convincing, and if it is not you abandon it. Traditional biblical harmonization differs from this in that (i) it tends to assume that differing accounts *must* fit together (ie, the approach is procrustean rather than heuristic), and (ii) it discounts the significance of the moral and theological concerns which have influenced each evangelist's portrayal, on the assumption that these never need (rather than sometimes may and sometimes may not) be in conflict with a concern for historical accuracy.

Matthew and John) have truly interpreted the event, for it qualifies the account of each and offers an interpretation that in fact is to be found in neither. By contrast, an approach which takes both Mark and Luke seriously sees both as true and authoritative interpretations; each, however, does not exhaust the meaning of the crucifixion, and so another interpretation is also possible. Thus both interpretations are affirmed and held in creative tension with each other.

Having said all this, however, I would not in fact wish to deny *any* place to traditional harmonization in a Christian use of the gospels. This is because the gospels have an authoritative status as scripture for the Christian, which causes them constantly to be read, meditated upon, expounded and applied. This naturally gives rise to imaginative and devotional reflections that may be of great value and yet have limited relation to the intended meaning of the evangelist. Christian commentary over the last 2,000 years is full of such material, and it would be arrogant and parochial to deny its value. It is still perfectly reasonable (though rather unfashionable) to adopt the venerable tradition of devotional meditation on the "seven words from the cross", as in the fine recent work of Richard Holloway, *The Killing*.[24] What is vital, however, is that practitioners should be aware of what they are doing, so that they do not claim their exposition to be "What the text really means", but recognize it rather as a free association of appropriate devotional applications whose value is determined by general theological and pastoral considerations.

It is a failure to make this sort of distinction that unfortunately mars John Wenham's *Easter Enigma,* a work in the classic tradition of harmonization. Despite the author's apparent intentions to reconstruct history, the book is not a work of history (though some of its suggestions may be historically tenable) because it ignores basic principles of historical method. Nor is it a work of theology, for it does not explore the meaning of Easter. Rather, it is an excellent example of imaginative devotion constructing scenes which may be imaginatively helpful to many readers. As history its value is limited, but as devotion its value may be considerable, though I fear that this is not quite what the author intended.

Implications for Understanding the Gospels

What implications does the above critique of harmonization have for an evangelical understanding of the gospels? First, the understanding of the relationship between historicity and truth must be modified. It must be conceded that the evangelists present pictures of the crucifixion which are indeed in agreement on the basic historical facts but which otherwise are incompatible at a strictly historical level. From a strictly historical point of view I do not think it is possible with any confidence to say more about the crucifixion than was said at the outset of this paper. Given the nature and extent of the differences between

---

[24] *The Killing: Meditations on the Death of Christ,* (London: DLT, 1984).

Mark and Luke, differences which are added to yet further when Matthew and John are taken into account,[25] we simply cannot know what happened on the historical level on that Friday beyond the basic outline of events. Of course, few of the traditional harmonizations are impossible, and some (though hardly all) may be historically valid.[26] The point is simply that no historical reconstruction can command respect if it does not take seriously the distinctive nature of the gospels as historical sources. For to a greater or lesser extent each of the evangelists has constructed a scene which, to recall our earlier analogy, is the literary equivalent of artistic interpretations such as those of Grünewald or Fra Angelico. The historical facts are presented by means of a profound interpretative reflection in which strictly historical concerns are of less significance than the creation of a scene into which the evangelist puts those words, characters and actions that convey the true significance of the profound mystery of the cross as he understands it.

The argument that there is "unhistorical" material of this nature in the gospels is hardly novel, and yet it has been largely resisted by evangelicals as somehow subversive of the authority of scripture. Perhaps this is partly because the argument has often used implicitly pejorative language, such as "fabrication" or "invention", to refer to such material, and so has not unnaturally provoked denial rather than recognition that the basic point at issue was valid but expressed poorly or tendentiously.

---

[25] Matthew's account is basically similar to Mark's, though with the important addition of the episode in 27:51b-53, which represents Matthew's interpretation of the cross as both "earth-shaking" and "life-giving".

Most distinctive is John's account which cannot be discussed here. Suffice it to note the interesting point that it is only John's account which makes a specific claim to eyewitness testimony (19:35). It is also John's account which, alone of all the gospels, has a large number of details peculiar to it which are all historically realistic (ie, independently attested as authentic contemporary practice) - the condemned man carrying his own cross (19:17), the exact term *titulus* for the charge affixed to the cross (19:20), the titulus in three languages (19:20), the squad on execution duty consisting of four soldiers (19:23, cf. Ac. 12:4), the practice of breaking legs to hasten death (19:31-3), and, arguably, the flow of blood and water from the recently dead body of Jesus (19:34). Moreover, John's account is entirely lacking in supernatural phenomena such as occur in the synoptics - the darkness at noon and the tearing of the temple curtain - the sort of elements that (rightly or wrongly) are often taken as indicative of legendary development. If one simply compared the crucifixion accounts of John and Mark on their own, one might well draw the conclusion that John's account looks to be the more historically accurate, while Mark's represents a distinctive theological moulding and interpretation, probably of later date!

[26] It is Matthew's extra episode in 27:51b-53 that most clearly resists any credible historical harmonization with the other gospel accounts.

In addition to this difficulty with language, there are perhaps three further reasons why this argument might be resisted. First, there is the problem of distinguishing what is historical from what is not historical. Since both look the same and there may be no clear criteria to distinguish them, there may be a fear that one could be left in a quagmire of uncertainty with regard to everything in the gospels. If you concede in one place then you may have to concede everywhere. But such an "all or nothing" approach, though perhaps initially plausible, is in fact unrealistic. As already emphasized, the historicity of the crucifixion is not in question, and the substantial historicity of the gospels can, and should, be maintained. From the historical point of view one must simply do what one does with any other historical text that one judges to be substantially historically accurate - accept its account as historical unless there is good reason to do otherwise. As long as the overall assessment of the historical value of the document is correct, one will always be more right than wrong in treating its account as historically accurate, even though on any given instance one may have to allow a degree of historical uncertainty.

Secondly, some might argue that any historical uncertainty would mean uncertainty about the truth and reliability of the gospels. It is hard to emphasize sufficiently, however, how important it is not to beg the question of the relationship of truth to historicity or impose anachronistic criteria of truth on the biblical text. On the one hand, one has to beware of a certain tendency, that naturally arises in a culture where science is exalted, to denigrate theology as a significant category of reality and truth; ie, the assessment of a story, in whole or in part, as theological may carry the implication that the story is not really, that is as an objective matter of fact, true. Such reductionism should have no place in Christian thinking. On the other hand, it is ironic that in our modern world, which has seen such a flowering of fiction (in the technical literary sense of creative, imaginative and meaningful writing of a non-historical kind, not in the popular pejorative sense of untruth), and in which fiction (both on the page and on the screen) is widely regarded as the most effective contemporary means of communicating moral and religious values, some should refuse to recognize the presence of such fictional tendencies, to a greater or lesser extent, within scripture. Our neat modern categories of "history" and "fiction" had not in fact been formulated in the world of the evangelists, who move freely and easily between the two.

This leads to the third problem, that is the lack of an appropriate category with which to designate the content of the gospels. The not uncommon suggestion that they should be classified as theology *rather than* history, as though theology were somehow incompatible with history, should rightly be rejected as both confused and confusing. But how then should one classify the gospels? In modern terms they bear some resemblance to historical fiction of the serious, well-researched kind, where known history is reconstructed and retold imaginatively, or to the documentary drama, where known historical events are dramatized to make them more interesting and accessible to a non-specialist public. In both cases it becomes extremely difficult to draw a line between what is, and is not, "historical", for a new entity has been created in which the relationship between truth and historical accuracy is more often than not a difficult matter of *judgment* rather than a simple matter of fact. The weakness of the analogy is simply that while historical fiction and documentary dramas may have a moral and religious dimension, that dimension is usually of secondary importance, whereas in the gospels the moral and religious concern is predominant to such an extent that in any assessment of their truth the judgment must be as much moral and religious as historical.[27] Perhaps in the end one can do no better than classify the gospels as gospels and allow the understanding of what that means to be drawn inductively from the careful study of their contents. It may well be that "gospel truth" is still the profoundest kind of truth there is.

The second major conclusion to be drawn from the above discussion concerns the theological use of the gospels. First and foremost are the implications for understanding the cross of Christ. It is customary in evangelical theology, as for example in John Stott's book, to argue that while there are many different facets to the meaning of the cross, there is nonetheless one basic understanding which undergirds or overarches all others, that is substitutionary atonement. As Stott puts it, "We strongly reject, therefore, every explanation of the death of Christ which does not have at its centre the principle of 'satisfaction through substitution', indeed divine self-satisfaction through the divine self substitution" (p.159). This understanding comes primarily through a combination of certain gospel texts, especially the cry of dereliction in Mark, with certain passages in Paul.

The point that I wish to make, however, is that while such an interpretation may to some extent be true to Mark's portrayal of the cross, it is *not* true to Luke's interpretation. To this extent the common thesis that Luke "gives no explicit doctrine of the atonement" is indeed well-founded. The story of the penitent thief which appears to be at the heart of Luke's portrayal does not show Jesus doing anything different from what he had always done during his ministry. As far as can be deduced from Luke's portrayal, the difference that the cross makes is fourfold. First it shows how trust in God and compassion towards people can be maintained to the very end, even through injustice, suffering and death. Secondly, it shows how through this trust and compassion the powers of evil are overcome. Thirdly, it shows how this suffering trust and compassion constitutes the essence of Jesus' kingship/messiahship. Fourthly, it shows how this trust and compassion overcome both sin and death for the believer (so esp. 23:43). The strong emphasis in Acts upon the resurrection and vindication of Jesus, rather than his death as such, would tend to corroborate such a reading of

---

[27] This point becomes particularly clear in any assessment of the portrayal of Jesus in the apocryphal gospels.

the gospel. In terms of well-known doctrines of the cross, Luke's portrayal looks something like a mixture of Aulen's *Christus Victor* thesis, which sees the cross as a victory over sin, death and the devil, and Abelard's "moral influence" thesis, which stresses the moving and transforming effects of Christ's supreme demonstration of how life under God should be lived.

What Stott's argument for *one* supremely normative understanding of the death of Christ does in effect is to impose a hermeneutic of evangelical theology upon scripture in such a way as to silence at least one of the (divinely-inspired) evangelists, that is, Luke. To argue that Luke does not in fact have a distinctive understanding of the death of Christ must ultimately resort to special pleading, and make the text of Luke conform to a predetermined norm rather than genuinely speak for itself. Even if some material in Luke might fit with a theory of substitutionary atonement (eg, 22:20, though this is textually uncertain),[28] his portrayal taken as a whole does not. There is, I suggest, a real conflict between the authority of scripture and a hermeneutic of an evangelical doctrine of the atonement as outlined by Stott. If Luke is given due weight as an inspired and authoritative interpreter of Christ in his own right, then what must be abandoned is not substitutionary atonement as such, for that may still be a valid reading of the familiar texts, but rather the insistence that this is ultimately the only true interpretation of the cross. If the canonical gospels are all given their full authority, the conclusion that will follow is that there is no one definitive understanding of the cross of Christ. Rather it is constitutive of a biblically-based Christian theology that the meaning of the cross is so rich and so profound that no one understanding can do it full justice .

This argument for the validity of markedly different interpretations of the cross may seem to some to be sacrificing the theological unity of the New Testament, and abandoning the classic Reformation principle that one should not "so expound one place of Scripture, that it be repugnant to another". But the principle that is often now applied to Church unity, that unity does not mean uniformity, applies equally to scripture. Mark's portrayal and interpretation of the cross may stand in some tension with Luke's both at the historical level and at an abstract dogmatic level, but that need not entail any ultimate lack of unity or contradiction between them. For it is constitutive of theological truth, ie, the Christian understanding of God and the world, that it is in essence complex and paradoxical and can only be truly grasped within the context of the Church's living in faith and obedience. It may not be possible to produce any one formal doctrine of the cross that, without being unduly general, can at the same time embrace and do justice to both Mark and Luke (and other New Testament witnesses). But within the context of the life of the Church, where the attempt is made to live in conformity to the word of God in scripture, it can and should be

---

[28] The verse perhaps represents an assimilation of Luke's distinctive account of the Last Supper to what became the generally-held version of that event.

proclaimed that the witness of both Mark and Luke are true - the cross brings life in both ways and both patterns of faith can exist side by side. The relationship between these two patterns of faith should be mutual affirmation and a creative tension, in which each is open to hear from the other a scriptural witness to Christ and his death that may not be immediately congenial but which is nonetheless true and points to dimensions of reality to which otherwise one might remain closed.

In conclusion, the aim of this essay has been rather ambitiously to try to point towards some general principles about the use of the gospels on the basis of a study of two short passages. The thesis of the essay is that customary evangelical use of the gospels, particularly with reference to the all-important death of Christ, has in fact been less than truly biblical; it is all too easy to use the rhetoric of being "biblical", while in reality adopting a partial and selective reading of scripture in which the ultimate, and often unacknowledged, authority is the theological emphasis of a particular Christian tradition. The argument may appear subversive of certain cherished aspects of evangelical theology and biblical interpretation; but I hope that the criterion by which it will be judged will not be whether it is true to evangelical tradition but whether it is true to scripture.

STORY IN THE OLD TESTAMENT

Introduction

The great acts of salvation in the Bible, the Exodus and Sinai covenant in the Old Testament, and the life, death and resurrection of Jesus in the New Testament, have been the subject of intense study in modern times. Given their centrality to the Bible and to Christian faith that is hardly surprising, indeed it is clearly desirable.

One fact about these acts of salvation, which has always been noted but usually rather taken for granted, is that they are presented in narrative, or story, form.[1] In the Old Testament the Exodus and Sinai covenant are part of one great narrative, Genesis - 2 Kings, which stretches from creation to the fall of Jerusalem. It is natural that this narrative, often designated 'salvation-history', has been regarded as the main literary form in the Bible and the central means of revelation. Usually significance has been attached to this in two main ways. First, it has been argued that because the narrative is historical in appearance it is appropriate to study it in the way that other ancient historical narratives are studied. This has led to historical analyses both of the events recorded in the text and also of the sources, transmission and composition of the text itself. Secondly there have been numerous theological arguments about the importance of history as the sphere in which God truly acts and reveals himself.

One of the most interesting and significant developments in recent biblical study has been a growth in literary approaches to the biblical text. Instead of asking predominantly historical questions such as 'What sources did the writer have?' or 'Did this event actually take place?' a growing number of scholars are asking literary questions such as 'What does this story mean?' or 'How is it that the author achieves such a memorable and moving portrayal?' Such literary questions, while not entirely novel, have tended to be neglected previously;[2] yet they point to areas of enquiry that are clearly important for our understanding. In the Old Testament in particular, whose narratives down the ages have captured the imagination of artists, poets, and musicians as well as ordinary believers, a literary approach may offer some deliverance from the

---

[1] It should be noted that the use of the term 'story' is quite neutral with regard to whether or not any story in question is historical or not. Although in popular parlance 'story' may often mean a tale without real foundation, that is not the meaning in scholarly discussion where the term simply means a consecutive narrative text without prejudice to the nature of its content.

[2] In, for example, the important and influential work of M. Noth, one looks in vain for any such literary appreciation of the narrative texts he discusses.

predominance of an historical study that has all too often seemed impervious to the reasons why these ancient stories have actually mattered to people. As such a literary approach is much to be welcomed.

It should be noted at the outset, however, that talk of a 'literary approach' may be potentially misleading for at least two reasons. On the one hand, the term 'literary approach' is in fact an umbrella-term that covers a vast number of different, and often mutually conflicting, approaches, which it is impossible even briefly to describe here. Since helpful surveys are available elsewhere,[3] the present discussion will concentrate on just one area of literary study, that which has attached particular importance to the story form of so much of the Old Testament. On the other hand, one reason why many literary studies are illuminating is because they are simultaneously theological studies. Given the thoroughly theological nature of most Old Testament narratives, it is hardly surprising that an approach which concentrates on what the text is saying and the way it says it should throw light upon its theological perspectives and assumptions. This means not only that a literary interest in story will often overlap with a theological approach to the text, but also that a sensitive appreciation of the characteristic assumptions and paradoxes of theology will often be needed by the literary critic.

With these two qualifications in mind, this essay will concentrate on three areas of enquiry. First, the current debate about the importance of story for theology; secondly, the ways in which approaching the biblical text as story can prove illuminating; thirdly, the question of truth in relation to literary and historical approaches to the biblical text.

The importance of story for theology

On a general theological level, much has been made of the importance of story as a peculiarly appropriate vehicle for conveying theological truth.[4] The basic reason for attaching importance to theology in story form is the fact that a story is so widely accessible to young and old, to educated and uneducated alike. Everybody likes a good story; and stories linger in the mind long after other things are forgotten. To say this is, of course, not to say anything new but rather to state the obvious. Followers of Jesus, whose favoured means of

---

[3] For an excellent summary survey, see R. J. Coggins, "The Literary Approach to the Bible", *Exp.T* 96 (1984), pp.9-14. For a fuller discussion see J. Barton, *Reading the Old Testament: Method in Biblical Study* (London: DLT,1984). Barton relates newer methods of study to more traditional methods, gives particular attention to structuralism, and helpfully sets the whole debate against a wider background of modern literary criticism.

[4] See e.g. M. Goldberg, *Theology and Narrative: A Critical Introduction* (Nashville: Abingdon, 1982); J. Goldingay, "Interpreting Scripture (Pt. 2)", *Anvil* I (1984), pp. 261-270.

teaching was the parable, should find nothing surprising in the idea that stories are a particularly effective means of communicating theological truth.

Generally speaking, a recognition of the value of story can be a valuable corrective to the dominant tendency in western theology to abstract and to analyze. Since so much modern theology rapidly becomes technical and abstract, it is not surprising that in the current enthusiasm for story it has been suggested that some of the problematic debates of modern theology may owe some of their problems precisely to the exclusively abstract form of the debate. To recast some of the propositions of, say, Christology in narrative form might, it is proposed, help shed fresh light on old controversies.[5]

Much theology of story is essentially an attempt to reflect seriously upon the fact that the foundations of biblical faith are given in narrative form: what is the value and significance of this particular form of communication, rather than any other? Or, in other words, what is the relationship between the content of a passage and the form in which it is presented?[6] Once this is grasped, one can readily see both that story is essential to Christian theology, and that storytelling must only be a part of theologizing and cannot be the whole. For both Old Testament and New Testament contain much material that is not narrative; law, poetry, proverb, and prophetic oracle in the Old Testament, and theological letters and apocalypse in the New Testament. In the New Testament in particular this extra material provides the indispensable reflection on the story of Jesus that enables the construction of a coherent and rational faith around the story, and the effective application of its challenge to a wide variety of situations. Although, for example, Luke 18:9-14 provides a brilliant picture in just a few words of what justification by faith means (note the technical sense in which 'justified' is used in verse 14), there is still a need for Paul's systematic analysis of justification in Romans if there is to be a coherent doctrine.[7]

The fact that much non-narrative material is given in its own particular forms, and not in others, must be respected and its implications thought through no less so than with narrative. Because the normative content of Christian faith

---

[5] See A. Harvey, "Christian Propositions and Christian Stories" in A. Harvey (ed.), *God Incarnate: Story and Belief* (London: SPCK, 1981), pp. 1-13.

[6] As an illustration of the relationship between form and content, one might compare what is said about the worship of YHWH in his official sanctuary in Deuteronomy 12 and Psalm 84. Because Deuteronomy 12 is in a law code, part of the message conveyed is that worship is a duty; whereas in a song such as Psalm 84 the emphasis is upon worship as a delight.

[7] One may compare the comment of R. Lischer, "The effectiveness of Martin Luther King as a preacher and agent of social change lay not in his ability to tell a story but in his incisive analysis of the situation in America and his prophetic call to justice. In his style of oratory he did not desert the black tradition [sc. of biblical storytelling], but the content and structure of his sermons are not organized around Gospel narratives but gospel principles" ("The Limits of Story", *Interpretation* 38 (1984), p. 35).

in the Bible is given in a variety of different forms, it is reasonable to expect that Christian theologizing should likewise adopt a variety of forms. The fact that from time to time somewhat extravagant claims may be made for one particular form, such as story, shows little more than that the theological world, like most other departments of life, has its fads and its fashions.

Reading Old Testament narrative as story

Given the need to take seriously the story form of much of the Old Testament, that is to try to grasp more of the meaning and significance of the text through studying the relationship between content and form, the value of the undertaking emerges in a variety of ways.

First, an interest in story will alert the reader to elements in a text that are characteristic of a story - plot, foreshadowing, irony, echo, repetition, contrast, tension, resolution, etc; elements which are clearly present in many of the most famous and memorable Old Testament stories. Interest in story means that scholars direct their attention to the text as meaningful in itself and look for those elements that make a text coherent and interesting. This makes a welcome change from the older style of literary criticism, which was in fact source-criticism, when "the literary critic...approaches the text with, so to say, a dissecting knife in his hand, looks out particularly for breaks in continuity, or missing links in the train of thought".[8] There is naturally a certain tension between these different approaches to a text, which raises interesting questions of method.[9] For present purposes, the important point is the positive approach to the text which interest in story encourages. My own study of Exodus 32-34, *At The Mountain of God,* shows how a text considered a "hodgepodge" by traditional source criticism may in fact have a coherence and integrity previously unsuspected. David Clines' study of Esther, *The Esther Scroll,*[10] brilliantly illustrates not only how a text can be brought to life, but also how the weight of scholarly analysis need no longer give such priority to questions of literary growth and development, even though these are still given due space .

Secondly, there is the fact that some truths can best, or perhaps only, be conveyed in story form because of the importance of symbol and image in human understanding.[11] To assume, as is often done, that the content of any

---

[8] So K. Koch, *The Growth of the Biblical Tradition* (London: A. & C. Black, 1969), p.69.

[9] For a discussion, see my *At the Mountain of God: Story and Theology in Exodus 32-34,* JSOTS 22 (Sheffield: JSOT Press, 1983), ch. 1.

[10] *The Esther Scroll: The Story of the Story* JSOTS 30 (Sheffield: JSOT Press, 1984).

[11] I would like to add 'myth' also, but modern debate has so muddied the waters by using the term in a diversity of senses that clear and constructive use of the term becomes extremely difficult. See the useful discussion of the significance of myth in H. G. Reventlow, *Problems of Old Testament Theology in the Twentieth Century* (London: SCM, 1985), pp. 154-167.

story can be translated without loss into discursive analysis ("What this story means is that...") is to make an unacceptable separation of form and content. This is not to say that the medium is the message. It is to say that sometimes the message cannot be entirely separated from the medium. For example, stories such as the creation of woman (Gen. 2:18-25), the burning bush (Exod. 3:1-6), or Elijah's encounter with God at Horeb (I Kgs. 19:1-18) have a depth and appeal which depends in part upon their use of symbolism (e.g. rib, fire that does not destroy, "still, small voice"). It is not easy to expound the stories in abstract form ("What this story means is that...") without saying something very much less interesting and memorable than the story itself. This does not mean that one cannot comment intelligently upon the meaning of a story. It does mean that the interpreter's comments should never become a substitute for the story, and their purpose should be to send one back to the story with fresh insight so that it is the story itself, better understood, that one is left with as the vehicle of truth and meaning.[12]

Thirdly, a story may communicate through what it does not say as well as through what it does say. A meaningful silence can be an unparalleled means of creating atmosphere and interest. The story of the Ascension of Elijah (2 Kgs. 2:1-18) is a good example. Standard commentaries leave its memorable impact largely unexamined and unexplained.[13] It is the silence in the story, that which is left unsaid, which, I suggest, provides the key. First, everyone involved, Elijah, Elisha, and the sons of the prophets at both Bethel and Jericho, know that Elijah is to be taken away (verses 1-5); yet nothing is said about how they know. Secondly, why does Elijah try to put Elisha off three times (verses 2, 4, 6)? The story implies both that Elijah was right to try and that Elisha was right to resist; yet no explanation is given. Thirdly, why is Elijah sent in stages to Bethel, to Jericho, and to the Jordan? Did he know where he was going, or was it only revealed to him step by step? And if so, why? There is no explanation. Fourthly, why should Elijah have to cross the Jordan and re-enact one of the most symbolic moments in Israel's history, the crossing into the promised land under Joshua? Again, nothing is explained. Fifthly, why is Elijah taken up to heaven east of the Jordan, outside the promised land? Because he had failed? Because

---

[12] The symbolic appeal of the burning bush is well illustrated by the fact that the 7-branch candlestick (menorah), which was part of the tabernacle and temple furnishings, and which became the symbol of Judaism, is probably a stylized representation of the burning bush (see J. D. Levenson, *Sinai & Zion* [Minneapolis: Winston Press, 1985], p. 20).

[13] See, for example, J. Gray, *1 and 2 Kings* (London: SCM, 1977), pp. 472-7; G. H. Jones, *1 and 2 Kings,* vol. II (Grand Rapids & London: Eerdmans/MMS, 1984), pp. 381-88. Jones' treatment is considerably more helpful than that of Gray, but is still incomplete.

his own origins were from Gilead, east of Jordan? Because this is the same region where Moses died? Again, silence.

The result of leaving so much unexplained is at least twofold. First, a sense of background depth and mystery is conveyed which fascinates and involves the reader.[14] Secondly, the story remarkably conveys a sense of the invisible presence of God. The sense of divine purpose and guidance is almost overwhelming, yet God himself remains constantly as it were offstage (the only partial exception being in verse 11). God is strongly present, and yet remains hidden. It is through a masterful use of the possibilities of narrative presentation that the writer has conveyed these effects.

The fourth point, which is related to the previous point and yet distinct, is that a story can communicate through assumption and suggestion. For example, the story of Joseph (Gen. 37-50) is well-known as an illustration of the sovereignty of God, a point indeed brought out explicitly in the text (Gen. 45:5-8, 50:20). One primary way in which this is conveyed is through those things which the writer takes for granted, for thereby the reader, who naturally identifies with what is happening in the story, is likewise invited to take the same things for granted too. For example, God's right and power to send famine (41:25-32), to determine the future (41:32), and to allow his faithful servant to suffer in various ways (37:28, 39:20, 40:23) are simply assumed. They are not in any way allowed to be problems ("How could God do such a thing?"). Rather, the story takes it as self-evidently true that this is how God is and how he works. Those readers who imaginatively and sympathetically enter into the story will thereby absorb these same assumptions themselves. Such a means of communication can be a valuable counterpart to explicit declaration.

Fifthly, a story may deliberately leave something vital to its understanding unsaid. This means that readers are obliged to use their imagination and intelligence if they are to understand the story properly. On the one hand, this means that the meaning of the story, once so grasped, will be more deeply appropriated; on the other hand, this makes for a greater likelihood that the story will be only partially understood, or even misunderstood.

A notable example is Genesis 3. Historically, this has been of enormous importance in Christian theology; and indeed its context at the beginning of Genesis clearly indicates that it is of fundamental significance. Yet its exact meaning is a matter of considerable debate, precisely because the story is deliberately somewhat elusive and enigmatic. The central difficulty is that God's clear statement of a death penalty for transgressing his prohibition and eating from the tree of the knowledge of good and evil (Gen. 2:17) is apparently not fulfilled (3:6-7). The interpretation of such a fundamental discrepancy between

---

[14] See also the famous discussion of Genesis 22 in E. Auerbach, *Mimesis* (Princeton, 1953), ch. 1.

what God says and what he does will largely determine the readings of the story as a whole.[15]

The majority of modern commentators are agreed that God simply did not do what he had said,[16] and explain this as showing either a change of mind or else (more theologically) God's sovereign freedom even over what he himself has said. Coupled with this is usually a tendency to downplay the traditional Christian interpretation of the story as the archetypal story of human sin and divine judgment as being a misunderstanding of the nature of the story.

But what if the narrator expected his readers to take for granted that it was inconceivable that God should prove false in such a way, and that therefore the apparent incongruence between what God says and what happens is to provoke the reader into a deeper understanding of what is going on? On such an approach the threatened death is to be found in the man and woman hiding in fear from God (3:8-10) and in the shifting of blame (implying lack of love and trust) from man to woman to serpent (3:11-13). That is, death is reinterpreted in terms of something in the inner life of people, a fear and distrust which separates them from God and from their fellows (i.e. "spiritual death"). The writer is thus showing that the real consequence of disobedience to God lies not in being suddenly struck down, which might naturally be expected but clearly does not in fact happen in life generally, but in a process of inner fear and alienation which destroys the love and trust that matter most in life.

It is not possible to prove that this second interpretation rather than the first is correct, for by the very nature of the story proof is not a possible option. The test must ultimately be whether an interpretation rings true and makes more sense than any other. Whatever conclusion one does come to, it is clear that one can only come to it by thinking intelligently and imaginatively to resolve what the story leaves as such unresolved.

Sixthly, a story can provide a pattern or framework for understanding life and experience. For many, life and existence on the purely historical plane may appear random or chaotic, without purpose, meaning or dignity. A story can so arrange things that pattern and meaning can be seen. The biblical story purports to be a true story. This means that as readers recognize in it the patterns of how God works, they can then find pattern and meaning for their own life and experience of God.

For example, life for the Jews in exile and the diaspora when they were deprived of all those things that had previously been central to their faith and identity - land, temple, king - must easily have appeared hopeless and meaningless. Stories such as those of Daniel and Esther do more than just show how life under God can be a reality in such situations. The way the stories

---

[15] See my essay "Did the Serpent Get it Right?", elsewhere in this volume.

[16] See e.g. C. Westermann, *Genesis 1-11* (Minneapolis & London: Augsburg & SPCK, 1984), p.225.

show, both explicitly and implicitly, that God is in control and that what people do does matter makes the stories a powerful medium for creating trust in the wisdom of God and in the meaning and significance of life even in difficult circumstances.

Finally, a story can act as a mirror to help people see themselves more clearly. That is, people naturally identify with the central figure in a story. The central figure can therefore be portrayed in such a way as to represent some characteristic of the story's intended audience; and when the audience recognize what is desirable or undesirable in the story they can then be led to recognize the same feature in themselves.

The most famous example in the Old Testament is Nathan's parable to David (2 Sam. 12:1-7a). Presumably, had Nathan simply related straightforwardly to David what he had done (2 Sam. 11), David would have been unmoved. But through the use of a story to which David instinctively responds in moral and emotional involvement, Nathan prepares the way for the irresistible punchline "You are the man", which has the necessary effect on the king (12:13). Interestingly, a similar technique is used again on David by Joab and the woman of Tekoa, again with effect (2 Sam. 14).

It is in such a way that the book of Jonah is also probably to be understood.[17] The book probably dates from a time when Israel was inclined to be too inward-looking and to adopt a negative and judgmental attitude towards other nations who did not know God in the way they did. Jonah is therefore made to embody such attitudes in such a way as to show how foolish and unacceptable they are.

The story creates interest and involvement for the reader by the use of a drily humorous "larger than life" style of telling. The most unlikely prophet (he flees from YHWH, 1:3) is sent to the largest city imaginable (three days' journey in breadth, 3:3), which happens to be the capital of the Assyrians, notoriously the most fearsome of ancient Near Eastern peoples (cf. Isa. 10:5-14, Nah. 3). When he finally gets there, this unlikely prophet has only to start preaching and he has the greatest success imaginable - *everyone* repents (3:5-6), so much so that even animals have to join in (3:7-8). But how does Jonah react to this unparalleled success? Is he pleased? Is he grateful? Because God spares Nineveh (3:10), Jonah sulks (4:1-5) and complains to God that he is too merciful (4:2)! That mercy which God had shown to Israel (Ex. 34:6f) and which Israel celebrated in its worship (e.g. Ps. 103:8) should not be shown to pagan foreigners.

But what are pagan foreigners actually like? The first chapter of the book has already devoted considerable space to the pagan mariners who took Jonah

---

[17] On Jonah, see e.g. L. Allen, *The Books of Joel, Obadiah, Jonah and Micah* (Grand Rapids: Eerdmans, 1976), pp. 175ff; B. S. Childs, *Introduction to the Old Testament as Scripture* (London: SCM, 1979), pp. 417-27.

on board. They were seen to be caring and responsible people who, though not themselves Hebrews, were fully prepared to acknowledge and worship YHWH (1:14-16). The pagan sailors are more attractive figures than Jonah. As for the Assyrians, their wickedness is emphasized, yet even they were prepared, when challenged, to turn to God and repent.

The reader is now ready for the final section (4:6-11) in which God exposes how narrow and petty Jonah is and delivers the unanswerable punchline (4:10-11) in which God's care for all has to be assented to by the reader, for God's question can be answered in no other way. The story's subtle blend of humour and seriousness involves the reader in such a way that when Jonah's bigotry is condemned, so is the bigotry of the reader: "You are the man".

These seven points do not exhaust the significance of story, but illustrate some of the main ways in which it can illuminate the reading of the Old Testament text. In general, one may say that the value of reading biblical narrative as story lies in recognizing and appreciating material that appeals to the imaginative and intuitive side of the human mind, where symbolism, suggestion, stimulation and enjoyment may be of greater importance than argument, appeal and explicit proclamation. It is perhaps particularly important for evangelical Christians, whose theology has traditionally appealed largely to human reason and will, to remember that there are large areas of a person's mind and personality that are left untouched by such an appeal.[18] It is a strength of the Bible with its many stories that it recognizes the many different ways in which theological truth may be communicated. An approach to faith and life which bases itself upon the Bible should hardly do less.

Story, history and truth

In this final section it will be helpful briefly to consider the question of truth with regard to the stories of the Old Testament. In modern Old Testament study the dominant concern has always been largely historical. One assumption that has been central to this is that questions of history are important for theological truth. The revelation of God has been a revelation in history, and if one denies the historical content of the traditions of Israel one thereby denies the

---

[18] One may note in this context the problems and challenge that the charismatic movement has posed to much mainstream Christianity because of institutional Christianity's almost inherent suspicion of "enthusiasm". The charismatic appeal to the emotional side of human personality has found wide acceptance among many who rightly felt that emotional expression and involvement in worship had been unduly neglected or suppressed. There is then, of course, the danger of the pendulum swinging too far, with the emergence of a style of Christianity that is unhealthily based upon emotional experience to the neglect of rational thought and a discipline of the will. It is only when a right balance between reason, conscience, imagination and emotion is maintained that a truly biblical faith will be seen.

theological meaning attributed to the traditions, or at least one risks reducing theology to a kind of gnosticism.[19] How then does the current interest in story relate to this?

This question may be approached through noting the tendency evident in some recent literary studies not simply to be disinterested in historical questions,[20] but also to suggest that the literary character of the biblical text shows that only a minimal historical content is present anyway. Robert Alter for example, whose brilliant *The Art of Biblical Narrative*[21] is the most stimulating and suggestive of recent literary studies, suggests that "prose fiction" is the best general rubric for classifying biblical narrative. Alter does not intend "fiction" to be pejorative. It is simply that many of the literary features of biblical narrative show the material to be such that it does not fit within the category of historiography as we recognize it. Stories may be based on actual historical occurrences, but their presentation has been shaped by what Alter calls the "fictional imagination". Overall, however, Alter gives the impression that biblical narratives have relatively little to offer the historian.

Such a use of "fiction", which is not uncommon, clearly requires examination, if only for the reason that fiction is often held to be the opposite of fact and truth; and so to describe a biblical narrative as fictional may seem to be saying that it is untrue. Two preliminary points may usefully be made.

First, it is clearly important that "fiction" should be properly defined and not used ambiguously. Although fiction has the general and popular meaning of an untruth or fabrication, it also has the specific literary meaning of a work of imagination. In such imaginative writing appeal to historical fact may be quite irrelevant to the determination of its value or truth, which must be established or denied on other grounds. It is clearly in this latter sense that Alter is using the term.

Secondly, there is no intrinsic reason, generally speaking, why a narrative should not be both historically faithful and well told as a story. It is vital in this sort of discussion to avoid unnecessary polarization and creating a false "either-or" dichotomy, when it may be a matter of "both-and". Nonetheless the fact that narrative might in principle be both accurate history and effective literature does not mean that any given narrative actually is, still less that all Old Testament narratives are. There is a wide variety of Old Testament narratives which resist

---

[19] For a statement and discussion of this position, see G. J. Wenham, "History and the Old Testament" in C. Brown (ed.), *History, Criticism & Faith* (Leicester: IVP, 1976), pp.13-73.
[20] Not untypical is a statement such as "The question of historicity is not addressed in this book since it is outside the range of my present interests" in P. D. Miscall, *The Workings of Old Testament Narrative* (Philadelphia: Fortress Press, 1983), p.8.
[21] *The Art of Biblical Narrative* (London & Sydney: G. Allen & Unwin, 1981).

neat categorization in terms of literature and history.[22] In the story of the fall of Jerusalem (2 Kgs. 25) there is a maximum of history and a minimum of literary art or theological development, while in the story of the Flood (Gen. 6-9) the opposite is the case.[23] Patient analysis of each case on its merits rather than sweeping generalizations is what is needed.

Rather than trying to discuss in general which elements in a story are likely to be literary in origin and which are likely to be historical - a huge undertaking - it will be helpful to focus instead on an underlying issue, that is what constitutes truth in a narrative. For the categorization of biblical narrative as fiction even in the technical sense does seem to stand in a certain tension with the traditional emphasis upon the importance of historical content in biblical narrative, and so raises the question of the basis upon which their theological meaning rests.

The central problem, in my judgment, is to do with the relationship between truth and history. Despite the admitted importance of a certain fundamental historical facticity in the Old Testament, it may properly be asked whether sometimes the relationship of truth and historicity has not been conceived somewhat too narrowly, so that the truth of a narrative has been made to depend too exclusively upon the historicity of its content. Any narrow equation of truth with historicity would seem to owe more to the influence of the rather limited horizons of certain kinds of post-enlightenment rationalism than to the tenets of historic Christian theology. It is my impression, though I cannot justify it here,[24] that the rather narrow equation of truth with historicity was first made by certain rationalists who argued of certain Old Testament narratives, "This is not historical, and therefore it is not true". This not unnaturally provoked a response along the lines of "It is true (because of the conviction of faith), and therefore it must be historical". The great emphasis so often attached, especially in the English-speaking world, to questions of history sometimes gives the impression of being part of a tradition of apologetic defence of the Bible to such criticism. But the defence too readily accepted the terms in which the criticism was couched, rather than insisting that, important as history may be for the Old

---

[22] One may compare the comment of R. E. Friedman, "The contemporary analyst wants to categorize this [sc. biblical] corpus as history or literature; but it does not fit our categories, precisely because it is older than the formation of these categories" ("The Prophet and the Historian: The Acquisition of Historical Information from Literary Sources", in R. E. Friedman (ed.), *The Poet and the Historian,* Harvard Semitic Studies 26 (Chico, California: Scholars Press, 1983). p.4).

[23] For observations on the varying relationship of biblical narrative to history, see also J. Barr, "Story and History in Biblical Theology" in his *Explorations in Theology* 7 (London: SCM, 1980), p. 8 (reprinted from *Journal of Religion* 56 (1976), pp. 1-17).

[24] For an important study of some of the intellectual assumptions prevalent during the rise of modern biblical criticism, see H. Frei, *The Eclipse of Biblical Narrative* (NewHaven & London: Yale UP, 1974).

Testament, history is but one factor among several that must be weighed in a consideration of whether and in what sense a story may be true.

It is worth remembering that, prior to the rise of modern thought when the historicity of biblical stories was generally assumed and was rarely a point at issue, the significance of historicity played a small role in most Christian and Jewish use of the Old Testament. What made the Old Testament valuable, or what made it problematic, were moral, theological, and philosophical considerations. At the Reformation, although the "plain sense" of the text was given greater weight, historicity as such still had only limited significance. It is well known that Luther evaluated biblical books by the degree to which they bore witness to Christ - a strictly theological criterion. Luther no doubt did not deny the historicity of Esther, but that did not prevent him from considering the book worthless for the Christian on religious and moral grounds.[25]

If it be accepted that the narrow equation of truth with historicity is in fact a departure from historic Christian theology under the influence of rationalist criticism, then it is clear that it needs to be modified. To say this is not to deny the importance of history. It is simply to qualify its importance, and insist that other factors, theological, moral, philosophical and imaginative, be counted along with it.

The breadth of the concept of truth may perhaps be further appreciated through a consideration of the novels, songs, plays and films of our modern culture. What makes most works valuable and gives them their appeal (in their various ways) is surely more than anything else the extent to which they succeed in being true, that is true to life in the sense of acutely depicting and interpreting the human situation and engaging with fundamental values. The interest of, say, David Lean's film of Pasternak's *Doctor Zhivago* hardly lies in the accuracy of its portrayal of the history of the Russian Revolution; rather it is the struggle of a man for freedom, truth and dignity both against the force of political power and against the tensions within himself, both of which problems are acutely posed by the upheavals of the Russian Revolution.

By contrast, many explicitly Christian novels, songs, plays and films have had limited appeal less, I suggest, because of the unacceptability of a Christian perspective in itself, than because they have been seen as ultimately superficial; they have given answers too quickly without sufficiently probing the reality of God and of human life (something which is rarely true of biblical narrative). That is, in an important sense their truth has not been sufficiently true. What is probably the most widely read modern Christian writing, J. R. R. Tolkien's *The Lord of the Rings*[26] surely owes much of its appeal not just to the fact that it is

---

[25] Luther's comment is widely quoted in introductions to works on Esther. See e.g. J. Baldwin, *Esther* (Leicester: IVP, 1984), pp. 51f.

[26] For the interpretation of *The Lord of the Rings,* see esp. H. Carpenter (ed.), *The Letters of J. R. R. Tolkien* (London: George Allen & Unwin, 1981). Many of the letters

a good story well told, but because it also searchingly explores the fundamental ambiguities of power and death. Its Christian values of grace, mercy and hope which confront and overcome evil are clearly portrayed, yet in such a way that they enhance rather than trivialize the story's seriousness.

Two things, therefore, may be said in conclusion. First, in our modern culture we easily and naturally apply the concept of truth widely and flexibly. We recognize without difficulty when a writing is intended as a work of fiction,[27] that is a piece of imaginative writing, and judge it accordingly. We often find that serious fiction contains and conveys important truths. It is unnecessary and wrong when we turn to the Old Testament to abandon all such understanding and insist more narrowly that historicity is the indispensable precondition for truth. Of course, questions of historicity do matter in the Old Testament, and there is the difficulty that we are not part of the culture in which the Old Testament was written and so do not share the assumptions and conventions that would have been widely held then. This should make for a proper caution in assigning literary genres and in judging whether or not writings were intended to be historical or to be imaginative, or varying degrees of both. If an Old Testament writing is judged to be historical, or even partially historical, in intention, then its truth will indeed depend, in whole or in part, upon the historical reliability of its content, and the investigation and establishment of this is the proper concern of the interpreter. But if it be decided that, for example, Jonah is a parable-like composition, which tells an imaginative (and unhistorical) story in order to make a moral and theological point, then it should be seen that this neither detracts from the truth of the book, for its truth would be of the same sort as that in the parables of Jesus, nor does it imply that therefore history is unimportant for the Old Testament as a whole, for each writing must be judged according to its own characteristics.

Secondly, it is important again to be reminded that the truth for which the Old Testament has always been valued is not simply truth with regard to what happened in history, but truth with regard to its deep understanding of the paradoxical character of God and the paradoxical nature and situation of humanity. Readers constantly sense depth in Old Testament narratives, and this is usually an instinctive recognition of the way many stories transcend their original Israelite context and have a meaning and relevance for the human situation of all periods. Usually readers do not bother to ask how it is that the

---

are Tolkien's responses to friends and critics after the publication of *The Lord of the Rings*, and they are highly illuminating for Tolkien's own understanding of his work.

[27] This is not, of course, invariably true. For example, many a reader of C. S. Lewis' *Letters to Malcolm* will have supposed that they are part of a genuine correspondence without realizing that the correspondence was simply a literary form adopted by Lewis as a (for him) more appropriate (because less explicitly didactic) vehicle for a treatise on prayer.

stories achieve this effect, and there is little reason why the ordinary reader should. Nonetheless it is a legitimate question to ask, and the current literary interest in Old Testament narratives as story is a contribution towards the answer.

POLITICAL WELLBEING IN BIBLICAL PERSPECTIVE

I

The Bible is of fundamental importance for Christian faith. However, it is always easier to assert the authority and relevance of the Bible than it is to demonstrate and implement such authority and relevance in a principled and realistic way. In few areas of life are such difficulties more acute than those of politics. If, therefore, we wish to bring a biblical perspective to bear upon contemporary political issues it is necessary initially to address questions of method and approach; unless our argument has methodological and conceptual clarity, we are likely to end up simply with a more or less sophisticated form of bandying proof texts.

Perhaps the greatest problem in using the Bible is that of finding in it what you want to find. The basic reason for this is that almost all biblical material is permeated with strong moral and religious values, and in discussion of such values it is particularly difficult to achieve appropriate objectivity since the discussion will engage with the already-existing beliefs and values of the interpreter. The language of religion and morality, and indeed of politics, is ultimately self-involving. If one's mind is already made up, and there is little or no attempt to combine one's already-existing commitments with a self-critical openness, then all arguments, however impressive in appearance, will have their outcome more or less predetermined in advance, i.e. they will be largely or wholly circular. Anyone at all familiar with debates about the gospels' presentation of Jesus will know this phenomenon well. The danger for us is to suppose that any proper use of the Bible will necessarily reinforce the values of Western liberal democracy - albeit not uncritically, especially, no doubt, with regard to the New Right.

In order to try to avoid falling into this trap here, a little preliminary distancing may be in order. First, the term "politics" is not to be found in the Bible, nor is even the concept. Both term and concept are derived from classical Greek culture, in particular the work of Aristotle. The Bible has nothing remotely corresponding to Aristotle's discussion of the *polis* and the role of the person as citizen within the *polis.* Within the Old Testament Jerusalem assumes a role of central importance, but the kind of moral and religious things that are said about it (e.g. Isa. 1-5, Pss. 46, 48, Lamentations, Zech. 8) bear limited relation to political discourse in the Western, predominantly Greek-rooted, tradition.

Secondly, the political values of the modern Western world are not always to be found in the Bible. The most unreservedly positive modern values are expressed in certain buzz-words, notably "democracy" and "human rights". These are nowhere to be found in scripture (nor, for that matter, in any of the great Christian polities of the past, be it of Rome, Constantinople, or Geneva). By contrast, perhaps the most negative buzz-words in current political parlance are "racism" and "apartheid", but they are concepts which can be found in scripture. However debatable their hermeneutics, the Afrikaners genuinely attempted to structure their society according to Old Testament principles and were not entirely mistaken in perceiving that racial distinctiveness and separation are important Old Testament principles. In our approach to scripture, therefore, the maintenance of a proper historical perspective is necessary both so that the material may be understood and so that we may be enabled to begin to stand back a little from some of our own cultural assumptions which we may take a little too readily as self-evident truths.

If, however, we are to use the Bible for our concerns, we cannot simply distance ourselves from it but must also seek, having established the distance, to reappropriate it and to reintegrate its perspectives with our own; the Bible must be not just a strange voice but also a living voice. In order to do this in a responsible way we need to face a number of familiar perennial problems, the most important of which revolve around the problems of establishing precisely what it means, and what presuppositions are necessary, for the Bible to function as scripture, that is, as not simply a collection of ancient religious texts of considerable historical significance but as the authoritative word of God for the world today. Given the constraints of this essay, I must state my working assumptions rather baldly.

First and foremost, if biblical theology is to differentiate itself from a history of ancient Jewish and Christian religion and is to function as a living voice within a modern context, one must be clear and explicit that one's starting point is "faith seeking understanding", that is the Christian quest to understand God and humanity in the modern world. This means that the agenda is set initially by modern need, and that therefore one's biblical theology must be thoroughly and consistently hermeneutical. Perhaps the least misleading metaphor for this is that of "dialogue"; there must be constant dialogue between biblical text and modern reader, each being interpreted and reinterpreted in the light of the other.

Although this may appear simply to be a statement of the obvious, I do not think that its implications have yet been worked through by biblical theologians in more than a preliminary way. All too often debates about biblical theology work with a crude dichotomy between "historical" and "systematic" approaches to the text, as though one could simply choose between them, and with a fear that if one is overt about a starting-point within contemporary Christian faith then one cannot be a good exegete. Of course there is always a danger of reading things into the text in the light of Christian presuppositions. But the answer to this is not to abandon, or pretend to abandon, one's Christian starting-point, for the presupposition will become more distorting if unacknowledged. Rather, the Christian presupposition should be acknowledged with an appropriate critical self-awareness and allowed to set a context within which the biblical text may be approached expectantly. The meaning of the Bible is not simply its meaning in its ancient historical context, vital though that is; the Bible is a book whose meaning and significance transcends its original historical context and has the ability to sustain living communities of faith in every generation.

Unfortunately, the recognition of the hermeneutical nature of biblical interpretation brings problems of its own. In the contemporary context the chief problem, I suggest, is that of ideological suspicion, a suspicion from which nothing in the hermeneutical process, neither text nor interpreter, is exempt. The danger here is that the biblical witness and its contemporary appropriation can be silenced, or at least rendered impotent, on the grounds that they are suspect ideological projections. The important question becomes not simply "What does the text and its interpretation say?" but "Whose interest does the text and its interpretation serve?" Within contemporary biblical study there are many examples of such a suspicious approach, of which I select two.

On the one hand, for example, ideological suspicion of a sociopolitical kind has been applied to the phenomenon of kingship in the Old Testament. Although the Old Testament itself presents the kingship of the house of David in a consistently positive light (i.e. YHWH is king over the world and over Israel, but delegates his kingship to humanity, supremely in the house of David), a suspicious reading views it negatively as an ideological projection on the part of the beneficiaries of a hierarchical system of institutionalized privilege, injustice and oppression. In contrast to these static and stultifying Davidic traditions, however, stand the traditions of early, pre-monarchic Israel, which represent a dynamic, sociopolitical egalitarianism.[1] In effect, this is the familiar

---

[1] N. Gottwald, *The Tribes of Yahweh,* (London, SCM Press, 1980) set the agenda in this regard. A good example of how this has influenced some scholars to denigrate the Davidic traditions may be found in J. L. McKenzie, "The Sack of Israel" in H. Huffmon et al. (ed.), *The Quest for the Kingdom of God: Studies in Honor of George E. Mendenhall,* (Winona Lake: Eisenbrauns, 1983), pp. 25-34. Here we learn that "among other blessings of civilization which David and Solomon anticipated was the police state" and that with the establishment of the Davidic kingship "the liberator god had become the symbol and the patron of an oppressive oligarchy" (p. 33). McKenzie even concludes with the astonishing observation that "I now feel much more certain that Jesus never accepted the title of Messiah" (p. 34). [Are we to suppose that Jesus both anticipated and approved the work of Gottwald?].

phenomenon of a canon within the canon, whereby the values of one part of scripture function as a critical norm whereby to relativize or undercut the values of another part, though it is difficult to resist the impression that ultimately the determinative values, at least in this case, originate outside scripture altogether.

On the other hand, the suspicions of feminist thinking are even more radical in their potential. For they can threaten not to play off one part of scripture against another but to undercut the authority of the whole.[2] The beliefs and values that are either implicit or explicit in Old Testament and New Testament are many and various, but insofar as they presuppose patriarchy they are all entirely consistent. If patriarchy is the ideology of male oppression of female, then the whole biblical witness becomes suspect. Of course, various defence strategies are possible; a closer analysis of the term "patriarchy" and its necessary implications (e.g. the rejection of any facile and emotive equation of patriarchy with male chauvinism or oppression), and a more sophisticated analysis of religious language (e.g. the nature of analogical language about God) can still allow the Bible to function as scripture despite the feminist critique. Nonetheless, the radical implications of feminist suspicion are clear.

At the same time, socio-political and feminist suspicions have been directed equally against the modern biblical interpreter who in the last two centuries has characteristically been a white, middle-class male and who has usually either explicitly or implicitly supported the prevailing socio-political establishment. As such, much modern biblical interpretation is suspected of having a vested, albeit usually undeclared, interest in the propagation of values that should in fact be questioned. Black, Marxist, and feminist theologies represent the perspectives of those who do not benefit from being white, middle-class, or male. If, however, due weight is given to such perspectives, in what way is it still possible to speak meaningfully of objectivity or rationality in interpreting the Bible?

Effectively, therefore, fundamental questions about the nature and purpose of biblical study are back in the melting-pot. Modern historically oriented biblical criticism arose, at least in part, as an attempt to escape the restrictive dogmatic categories of Protestant scholasticism, but has itself run into

The most notable attempt to make positive theological use of Gottwald's work is in the recent work of W. Brueggemann. Nonetheless, Brueggemann still views the Davidic traditions with consistent suspicion and when he makes comments such as "...the royal-temple establishment, which in the ancient world is the rough equivalent of the military-industrial complex" *(Hope Within History,* [Atlanta, John Knox, 1987], p. 33), one may suspect that within the hermeneutical dialogue the voice of the modern context is overwhelming that of the ancient.

[2] See e.g. E. S. Fiorenza, *In Memory of Her,* (London: SCM Press, 1983); L. M. Russell (ed.), *Feminist Interpretation of the Bible,* (Philadelphia: Westminster Press, 1985). Among recent contributions, there is a useful discussion of problems of definition and method in C. Myers, *Discovering Eve: Ancient Israelite Women in Context,* (Oxford and New York: OUP, 1988), ch. 2.

difficulties for at least two reasons. On the one hand, it tends to restrict the Bible's function to that of ancient history, and leaves unclear on what basis (if any) the Bible can function as authoritative for today. On the other hand it may have an undeclared ideological interest in disqualifying from the realm of significant discourse certain agendas that differ from its own (i.e. as long as the Bible functions primarily as a history of ancient religion, it can provide little challenge to the modern world, or disturb the relatively comfortable position which the academic interpreter has usually enjoyed). Hence the renewed hermeneutical debate which in one way or other seeks both to allow the Bible to function as authoritative scripture today, and to take seriously the concerns of the modern world.

Unfortunately, the importance of the issues at stake means that the task will never be uncontroversial. Although the *odium theologicum* of pre-modern debate may have been apparently dispensed with for a while, it was never resolved but only submerged under a new dominant consensus. It has now revived and reappeared and, in new and predominantly ideological forms, is alive and well in our "post-modern" era. The hermeneutical considerations that promise to free the Bible from the antiquarian exile of ancient history threaten to imprison it within the dogmatic dungeons of new ideologies.

How then should we proceed? At the risk of appearing to trivialize the issues at stake, I would like to spell out three principles that should underlie our use of the Bible in Christian thought, including Christian political thought, today. First, it is indeed true that there is no neutral ground, no pure and uncontaminated vantage point from which one can decide about religious, moral, and political issues. We all have to stand somewhere, and there is no total objectivity. That is as true of the biblical writers as it is of Christians today. However, it is not a matter of all or nothing, and between the extremes of total objectivity and total lack of it there are many possible intermediate stages with varying degrees of objectivity. Commitment is not incompatible with critical reflection, and our goal should be *appropriate* objectivity; appropriate both to the nature of the subject matter and to the scope of critical concerns in both theory and praxis. Or, to put it differently, one should maintain the *relative* autonomy both of the biblical text (arising out of, yet transcending, its ancient context) and of the critical interpreter (indebted to, yet not blinkered by, his or her context of belief and practice). Moreover, the same problems equally affect the advocates of ideological suspicion. Neither any ideology nor any critique of ideology can be self-evidently correct, and there must always be space for genuinely critical questioning of whatever kind is appropriate (and criticism may be as much a matter of praxis as of theory).

Secondly, the presupposition for authoritative use of the Bible today, and the context within which the biblical theologian must stand, is the Church. It is not that this is a "pure" vantage point, uncontaminated by history, culture and diversity. Rather, it is only within the context of a community of faith, whose existence is defined by the attempt to live out the biblical witness to God and humanity, centred in Christ, and where biblical praxis and reflection are necessarily combined, that one can with integrity bring biblical concerns, and the claims of God in Christ, to bear upon the world at large. Neither the biblical writers nor modern biblical theologians can be seen as untainted by various ideological concerns, but they need not be the passive and uncritical mouthpieces of such concerns. Indeed, insofar as the biblical text bears consistent witness to qualities such as love, justice, peace, trust, mercy, forgiveness, and these are recognized as central to biblically-oriented faith, then insofar as those who preserved, wrote and edited the biblical traditions did not themselves always exemplify such qualities (a point about which for the most part we can only speculate, usually on the analogy of our conceptions of the communal life of faith today), and insofar as modern interpreters may fail to exemplify these qualities, this does not invalidate the qualities but rather means that the people in question stand under the judgement of the very values they espouse and propagate.

Generally speaking, modern insights related both to a sociology of knowledge and to ideological suspicion are valuable for the biblical theologian in that such insights force him or her to recover a dimension of theology that traditionally was of central importance but which has been obscured by many of the attempts in modern times by theologians to justify theology as an objective and rational discipline when measured by the yardstick of empirical science. This crucial dimension is the integral relation between epistemology and ethics - what we know and how we know it cannot be separated from our personal and communal life commitments. Only insofar as our use of the Bible regains this insight will the notion of biblical authority have any real meaning within the modern world.

Finally, with regard to the question of the key whereby one can comprehend and utilize the unity and diversity of scripture, the answer for the Christian must be that Jesus Christ is that key.[3] That is, it is those beliefs and values that cluster around the person of Jesus that provide Christians with their sharpest and deepest insights into the nature of God and humanity. If one is to bring authentically Christian value judgements to bear upon different parts of scripture, then it is necessary that those judgements should be derived from the

---

[3] My concern is with the portrayal of Jesus in the gospels as authoritative, not with an "historical Jesus" "untainted" by the tradition and interpretation of the Church. The attempt to distinguish between Jesus and the interpretation put upon him in the gospels is a legitimate undertaking that is entirely proper for the ancient historian but is of limited value for the Christian theologian. This is essentially because the historical quest does not do justice to the nature of the gospels as scripture, that is writings through whose medium the Church can bear witness to Jesus in a way that transcends his original historical context.

scriptural witness to Jesus. Otherwise there can be no agreed method of procedure, and one will be left with the clash of conflicting value systems with no possibility of adjudicating between them. To say this does not, of course, resolve problems of interpretation, but it does set the context within which they should be approached.

II

Further to these general principles about the use of the Bible, I would like also to make four preliminary points about attempting to bring a biblical perspective to bear on questions of political wellbeing before moving on to offer my main thesis. First, one cannot look to the Bible to support any particular political system as it simply does not address the question in our terms. It envisages a variety of different socio-political structures - wandering clan, theocratic community, independent monarchy, dependent subject state - and sees strengths and weaknesses in them all. Insofar as we can find a preference expressed, it is in the Old Testament and it is a preference for what we might, with the licence of anachronism, call constitutional monarchy. This is because there are two dominant traditions in the Old Testament. One is the Mosaic tradition of *torah*, that is authoritative law for the guidance of Israel's whole life. The other is the kingship of the house of David, which is the focus of YHWH's rule over Israel. How these two traditions interacted in the historical context of ancient Israel has been the subject of much debate, but need not be our concern here insofar as we seek to understand the Old Testament as a work in its own right, an interpretation of God and his people arising out of Israel's experience but acquiring a dynamic and integrity of its own. The classic expression of their interrelationship is the one place in the Pentateuch where the topic of kingship is addressed, i.e. Deut. 17.14-20. According to this, kingship is an entirely acceptable institution (in v.15 the Hebrew is emphatic, "you shall/may indeed set a king over you..."), but as it is liable to corruption the king must be diligent in writing, reading, learning and obeying *torah* to guide him. Similar concerns are expressed in two other passages which depict David's charge to, and prayer for, Solomon (I Kgs. 2.1-4; Ps. 72;[4] cf. I Chron. 28.9). These latter passages represent a kind of job description by Israel's greatest king to his greatest successor and thus function as a central statement about the nature of kingship.

---

[4] On any reckoning, Ps. 72 is a classic expression of the king's responsibility to bring justice and peace. As the psalter stands, however, Ps. 72 is probably meant by its editors to be taken as a prayer by David (see Ps. 72.20) for Solomon (the psalm heading, *lis^elomoh*, should probably be rendered "for Solomon", not "by/of Solomon" as in RSV).

Secondly, it is of limited value to look to the Bible for the content of a political agenda, even in the broadest terms. For one is likely to conclude that such content must be the priority of justice and peace, which are indeed central to biblical concerns (e.g. Deut. 16:18-20, Am. 5:21-4, Isa. 2:2-4, Ps. 72, Rom. 13:1-7, 1 Tim. 2:1-2). The trouble is that at that level of generality almost no one would disagree, for these are concerns common to all responsible humanity. The Bible may indeed provide nuances to understanding justice and peace that cannot to be found elsewhere, but the formulation of this will not be straightforward for two reasons.

On the one hand, much of the Old Testament language about justice and peace can be paralleled in literature from the other great cultures of the ancient Near East. Although it is not necessary for something in the Bible to be unique or distinctive in order to be true and authoritative, there remains a legitimate concern to understand the particular way in which Israel interpreted common human concerns in the light of her God; but this means that justice and peace cannot be discussed without reference to biblical faith as a whole.

On the other hand, one must do justice to the dynamics of reinterpretation present within scripture. Of particular significance is the tension between Old Testament and New Testament as to precisely what constitutes justice and peace and how they relate to the purposes of God. One way of focusing this is to ask in what sense Jesus is the fulfilment of the messianic language of the Old Testament, for example Ps. 72. Christians affirm that Jesus is the fulfilment, for he is the one through whom God's will flows and is enacted in complete harmony and integrity. Nonetheless, given the plain meaning of the language about justice and peace in the psalm, and the traditional Jewish question as to why, if Jesus is the redeemer, the world is still so unredeemed, one must recognize that a coherent biblical understanding of justice and peace (if such can be formulated at all) will be far from straightforward and is likely to involve a high degree of tension and paradox.

It is clear, therefore, that an affirmation of the importance within scripture of justice and peace is, as such, of limited help to political debate. Either one will use the terms with such generality that there will be little that is distinctive about the biblical witness, or one will make the terms more specific by engaging in an extensive task of biblical interpretation that will tend to acquire an agenda of its own and will not be easy to re-engage with a specifically political agenda.

Thirdly, the Bible is also of limited use for the debate as to the appropriate policies to achieve the ends of justice and peace. This is a debate which should indeed be informed by Christian beliefs and values, but no one party can ever claim all the moral high ground. It is an inescapable feature of life that there is always a conflict of priorities and valid concerns, and there are few self-evidently correct policies.

Generally speaking, many political debates revolve around the tension between the concern for order and for freedom under law and the concern for justice in the face of the evils that constantly blight human societies - concerns which tend, not always helpfully, to be categorized in terms of "Right" and "Left". The crucial point for our discussion is the recognition that both sets of concerns are affirmed within scripture; one might, for example, take Gen. 1, the picture of ordered creation, or Rom. 13:1-7, with its emphasis on obedience to authority, as representative of the former; equally, one could take Exod. 15, the victory song of those freed from oppression, or Mary's song, the Magnificat (Lk. 1:46-55), as representative of the latter. If both concerns are recognized as valid within scripture, then the Christian must recognize the validity of both. This means that it will always be ultimately futile for those of either Right or Left to claim that the Bible *really* supports their position to the exclusion of the other. A truly biblical perspective must recognize the validity in principle of concerns wider than can be expressed by any one party or programme. In practice, of course, a particular emphasis one way or the other may be appropriate, indeed mandatory; but it should not be accompanied by exclusivist theoretical claims. In short, the breadth of the Bible means that it can in principle support a diversity of policies. Whether one's stance be blue, red, green, or whatever, all have legitimate concerns and all may appropriately be supported by Christians in the light of scripture.

Fourthly, any use of the Bible with reference to politics is made more complex by the use that already has been made in recent years. It is difficult to appeal to certain central biblical categories, such as "exodus" or "kingdom" or "the poor", without either an implicit coded agenda or at least the likelihood of conveying possibly unintended overtones. This can of course be overcome by extensive and careful definition of the biblical meaning of these terms, and that is indeed an important task. However, for present purposes I hope it may be helpful to offer a fresh approach.

III

The thesis I wish to advance is that if the Bible is to have any cutting edge in the political sphere, it is better to apply it less to the content than to the style of politics, less to the what than to the how. This has the advantage of cutting across conventional political divisions, which are formed largely according to the content of one's commitments, and will apply equally to those of whatever political persuasion.

Given the premise that Christ is the key to scripture, my thesis is that the main contribution of scripture to a debate about political wellbeing is through the principle of self-denial. On the one hand, this features prominently in the teaching of Jesus. It is enunciated as a central principle in Jesus' major pronouncement about his own life and mission and the nature of Christian life according to the synoptic gospels (Mk. 8:27-9:1 and parallels), and a similar statement is made at the climax of Jesus' public ministry according to John (Jn.

12:20-36, esp. vv. 23-6). On the other hand, it is something that is lived out by Jesus, and its meaning is demonstrated in Gethsemane, Calvary, and the events of Easter day. Moreover, it is this that is focused on by Paul in his theology and praxis of the Christian life (e.g. Gal. 2:20, Rom. 6:1-11, II Cor. 4:7-18, 10:1-12:13, Phil. 2-3).

If, then self-denial is to be our central principle, what does it entail? First, self-denial is not self-denigration. Self-denial presupposes the dignity and value of human life, as classically set out in the Old Testament, and as always affirmed within Jewish tradition. Without an appreciation of this presupposition, self-denial can easily be twisted into something life-destroying rather than life-enhancing.

Secondly, self-denial entails the recognition that human growth and maturation is not a straightforward process. The idea that because people by nature have certain urges and desires it must therefore be right to promote human growth through the fulfilment of these urges and desires is, generally speaking, false. A central biblical theme, shared of course by the wise of most religions and cultures, is that discipline is necessary to human growth, both because of the inherent paradoxes of human nature and because of sin. True discipline is always conducted according to fundamental moral principles, principles which a person must learn and integrate within his or her personality if maturity is to be attained. This process of appropriating morality through discipline may run counter to many natural tendencies; but if it is hard, it is not therefore less necessary. (It is only the corruption of discipline into repression that is unacceptable).

Can one say, however, that Christian self-denial is more than moral self-discipline? One way of posing this question is to ask how Christian self-denial differs from the moral seriousness of other stances both religious and non-religious, (e.g. Stoicism, Islam, Rationalism). Although the Christian would wish to affirm much common ground with these other stances, a Christian stance will nonetheless be distinctive in so far as it centres on the biblical portrayal of Jesus, a portrayal from which four interrelated features emerge.

First, Christian self-denial affirms human autonomy only in conjunction with God and his purposes. On the one hand, self-denial entails the recognition that there is a dimension of reality that transcends the human, even though it is in and through the human realm that this transcendent reality will normally be encountered. On the other hand, the encounter with transcendent reality is understood in terms of trusting obedience to the will of a personal God: "Thy will be done".

Secondly, discernment of the divine will is not an easy or straightforward matter, but presupposes a wider context and tradition to enable such discernment. Even Jesus, with his supreme access to the will of God, must be seen against the wider context of Hebrew scripture and Jewish faith as indispensable presuppositions. Jesus went to the cross "according to the scriptures". For the Christian the Bible as holy scripture functions to provide a context of presuppositions and parameters within which the attempt to discern God's will for human life is made. Moreover, discernment is not simply a private or individual matter, but presupposes life within a community where the corporate attempt to live in obedience to God provides the necessary context for testing individual claims to discernment.

Thirdly, the appropriation of the divine will may make great moral and personal demands. The prayer "Thy will be done", as taught in the Lord's Prayer and demonstrated in Gethsemane (Matt. 6:10, 26:42), envisages no passivity or resignation before an irresistible or inscrutable divine will, but rather an active and possibly prolonged struggle to appropriate and embrace that divine will as the motivating factor within human life.

Fourthly, the Christian understands the fruit of self-denial to be life, life in all its fullness. This process, however, is not simply a theological metaphor for a personal psychological process (though it may certainly include that), but rather entails seeing the resultant life as a gift. This means, among other things, that the result is not to be seen as automatic or predictable. We cannot know what the results of our actions will be, and often they will not be what we anticipated or even desired. This means that God's sovereign freedom is respected and trusted, and the limits of prudential action are recognized.

Although, therefore, self-denial has much in common with self-discipline as generally understood, a Christocentric understanding binds human action to the will of God. Moreover, much material elsewhere in scripture is amenable to interpretation in the category of self-denial, even if it does not use such terminology itself. For example, the law of the king in Deut. 17:14-20, can readily be read as a requirement for the king to deny himself and actively seek to appropriate the will of God, as can the prayer of Ps. 72:1 that it is the justice of God which should be given to the human king.

How, then, might such an understanding apply more specifically to the sphere of politics? On one level it might seem that this may not make much difference in practice, not least since in politics compromise and the pursuit of the lesser evil tend to be the order of the day. On another level, however, it is the larger presuppositions about the nature of human life that constantly exercise a profound influence upon its conduct in every sphere, and a tradition of political discourse and life that took seriously the kind of understanding of self-denial just outlined would constantly exercise certain constraints and encourage certain possibilities which might not be found otherwise. I would like, therefore, briefly to consider self-denial in relation to two areas of political concern, one specific and the other abstract; language and power.

Language is a fundamental and distinctive characteristic of human life. Language is the means whereby both personal self-consciousness and inter-personal communication becomes focused and enhanced, and in various ways it can be a major constituent of communal and specifically political identity. The

Bible itself is a product of language, values language extremely highly,[5] and can only function legitimately when its various uses of language are taken seriously. I would like to comment briefly on three relevant dimensions of language: rhetoric, lying, and freedom of speech.

Rhetoric, the ability to influence others through use of language, has always been prominent in politics. It is consistently esteemed and held suspect for essentially the same reason, the ease with which it lends itself to manipulation and propaganda. In essence what makes rhetoric legitimate is a form of self-denial; a refusal to use language for self-serving ends, and a respect for the integrity and legitimate concerns of those addressed.

Lying is an accepted feature of modern political life. It involves both the straightforward telling of lies and the more sophisticated manipulation of elements of truth in a cynical or self-serving way to create what amounts to a lie.[6] Perhaps this has always been so. Nonetheless, while the conflicting pressures of political life will no doubt always constrain speakers on occasion to be somewhat economical in their use of truth,[7] there remains a great gulf between a responsible telling less than the whole truth and the cynical manipulation or denial of truth. The ready acceptance of lying constitutes a profound debasement of political life, more serious than the traditional temptation to debase currency (i.e., inflation), simply because language is even more fundamental to human communication and exchange than is money. Linguistic self-denial will always be needed if the value of language, and thus the possibility of genuine human intercourse, is to be maintained.

Freedom of speech poses complex moral issues, not least for journalists in modern democratic society with their twin role as prophetic critic and popular entertainer.[8] In general terms, freedom of speech is not simply a good in itself (Christianity has traditionally, and not altogether unreasonably, attached more weight to saying what is right than to saying what you like), but rather is important as a safeguard against abuse of political power. But if it is to function effectively in that capacity, then it must constantly be on guard against reproducing the very abuses that it criticizes. Again, self-denial must be an integral element within true freedom of speech.

---

[5] Speech is the supreme vehicle of God's communication with humanity in the Old Testament, and in the Johannine writings of the New Testament Jesus himself is *Logos*. Use of language features in two of the Ten Commandments, and is prominent in Wisdom Literature. Its moral implications are forcefully expressed in Matt 12:33-7.

[6] At the time of writing the most striking recent example has been the Chinese government's portrayal on Chinese media of the student protests in Tiananmen Square.

[7] A classic biblical example of "economy with truth" is YHWH's advice to Samuel (I Sam 16:1-5).

[8] Some of the harder issues to do with freedom of speech have been posed with unusual sharpness by the Salman Rushdie affair and the debate it has engendered.

My second area of concern, already touched on in my first, is that of power. For politics is intimately bound up with the pursuit and management of power. Power, as we all know, corrupts, and from the biblical point of view it corrupts precisely because it offers to those who wield, or seek to wield, it models of apparently fulfilling human life set free from the constraints of self-denial. Obviously the nature of power is an infinitely complex subject, and here I will just comment briefly on three areas: personal ambition, warfare, and non-violent resistance.

Personal ambition may be but one element in the question of political power, but it is an important element nonetheless, for struggles for personal power on the part of people with large, and often insecure, egos is a significant part of any political process, and can often have a major distorting impact. All the notable stories within the Bible about political malpractice and corruption - most famously the trial of Jesus, but also e.g. Naboth's vineyard or Ahab's disastrous campaign against the Syrians at Ramoth-Gilead (I Kgs. 21, 22) - are at heart stories about powerful people succumbing to ambition, greed or fear in pursuit of their political career. From a biblical perspective, it is only those political figures who practise self-denial in the pursuit of their political goals who will be truly deserving of praise.

Warfare is an area in which the need for prudential self-denial has long been recognized. Recognition of the strong tendency of warfare to debase and corrupt human life, coupled with the possibility of enemies replying in kind to whatever is inflicted on them, has always led to attempts to impose constraints on the conduct of warfare, be it the problematic "holy war" of the Old Testament, the Truce of God, or the Geneva Convention. Modern debates about limitations on types of weaponry (nuclear, chemical, biological) all presuppose the recognized need for some kind of self-denial.

A major challenge to the principle of corporate self-denial in the sphere of warfare is posed by the terrorist. Terrorism means an organization which proceeds covertly against its perceived enemies with many of the means and weapons of warfare but without the potential vulnerability represented by a geo-political identity and a formal declaration of war, as without these there is no clear or legitimate target against which to fight back. Terrorists are classic parasites on civilization, since they depend on their enemies to some extent maintaining the constraints which they have abandoned. Terrorists pose the constant temptation to abandon constraint and adopt their own means so as to defeat them (a task which states discreetly give to their secret services). The danger is to become like that which one fights against, for evil triumphs when it is imitated. In terms of our argument, the maintenance of self-denial is all-important if, in response to terrorism, a society is to be maintained which is worth maintaining.

Having said this, however, it must be emphasized that the problems of identifying terrorism may be acute. One person's terrorist may be another person's freedom fighter, the difference being one's attitude to the regime against which terrorism is directed. That which a state identifies as terrorism may well arise as a response to unjust and manipulative use of law by a government which remains impervious to criticism and reform through normal channels. This does not mean that one cannot validly identify and condemn terrorism, but to do so requires a high degree of self-critical awareness and openness to reform of abuse.

The phenomenon of terrorism leads into our third reflection on power, that is the development of the concept and practice of non-violent resistance, classically represented in modern times by Mahatma Gandhi and Martin Luther King. However problematic non-violent resistance may become, it represents a genuine attempt to implement self-denial within a contentious political context. It recognizes both the corrupting power of violence, and the fact that a non-violent policy may require great sacrifice on the part of its protagonists, both insights that are central to a Christological understanding. Non-violent resistance is a modern phenomenon, not least because it depends to a large extent on modern media of communication to appeal to public conscience and bring moral pressure to bear. As such it is distinct from the traditional Christian view of the high value of costly resistance to evil, even if in obscurity and with no apparent effect. Nonetheless, the technological dependence of non-violent resistance does not empty it of moral significance, but rather makes it a prime example of how biblical insights may at least to some extent be translated into a modern idiom and responsibly appropriated in a modern political context.

In sum, then, a society which from a biblical perspective enjoys political wellbeing will be marked less by an agreed goal of justice and peace - fundamental though that is - than by the way in which justice and peace are pursued. This pursuit will be characterized at heart by the practice of self-denial, as understood biblically and Christologically. This understanding will have much in common with self-discipline as understood in a variety of moral and religious traditions, even though it will necessarily part company in some of its fundamental values and presuppositions. In crucial spheres, such as the use of language and the exercise of power, the serious recognition of self-denial will set the whole political process in a distinctive light. Although much of what has been said applies primarily to those in positions of leadership, the principle of self-denial is applicable to everyone who wishes in some way to contribute to the good of society.[9]

In conclusion, two final points. First, I am conscious that I have dealt very generally and selectively with political issues, and have said little that engages

---

[9] In the light of our discussion, the Self-Denying Ordinance of 1644/45 deserves mention in a footnote. Whatever the political concerns that surrounded this, it may not be entirely without significance that the parliament that passed the Ordinance did so within a cultural context in which faithfulness to scripture was highly esteemed.

directly with the categories and concerns of current debates. However, if there is to be any real value in an exercise such as discussing political wellbeing from a biblical perspective, it must surely lie in enabling one to stand back from familiar debates precisely so that one may refocus one's attention more freshly on the elusive presuppositions and value judgements that underlie the structures and routines of daily life.

Finally, I am aware that I have so concentrated on what is fundamentally an issue of personal (though not private) morality, that it may appear that the complex and multi-faceted nature of political reality has been insufficiently appreciated. But although what has been said is not the only perspective on political wellbeing, it is, I maintain, a consistently biblical perspective. Despite the multi-faceted nature of its own witness, the Bible gives consistent prominence to the personal factor - often to the considerable annoyance of modern scholars who may be searching the biblical text for concerns to which the text is generally opaque. It is indeed the case that Christians have much to learn from other sources, such as the study of the socio-economic dimensions of life which Marx classically brought to the fore, and need to incorporate such perspectives within their overall understanding. However, insofar as Christians reverence scripture as their authoritative interpretation of God and human life, it will be the moral and relational dimensions of life to which ultimately they will give most prominence.

POSTSCRIPT

In this essay, which was originally delivered as an address to the British Society for Christian Ethics, I have tried to define the term "self-denial" in a broad way, as a convenient shorthand for the dynamics of human life as seen in Jesus, a way of life which, among other things, is the necessary response to the suspicion of undeclared self-interest as outlined in the first part of the paper. In the ensuing discussion, however, many people had great difficulty with such a usage, and consistently gave "self-denial" a narrower meaning with predominantly negative overtones.

To some extent this seems to be for historical and emotional reasons, and to some extent it seems to be because the term feels inappropriate for those whose selves have been denied and oppressed by others (those more sinned against than sinning, those "underliving" rather than "overliving"). Even in this latter case, however, the term need not be inappropriate, since however much such people need first and foremost to receive positive and practical affirmation, there still remains for them the struggle to grow through oppression without self-pity and without allowing what they have suffered to destroy their humanity, which will involve precisely the kind of dynamics that "self-denial" is meant to convey.

I do recognize, however, that "self-denial" may have such inescapably negative overtones for many people that it will be difficult for it to function usefully within current debate. Perhaps a combination of definition and demonstration may enable the term to be regained. Otherwise, it is a matter of urgency to find other terminology which can effectively convey the central biblical insights into human life.

"OLD TESTAMENT" AND "NEW TESTAMENT": THE PROPRIETY OF THE TERMS FOR CHRISTIAN THEOLOGY

In his recent article, "Combating Prejudices about the Bible and Judaism",[1] John Sawyer writes with feeling about the impropriety of the continued use of the terms "Old Testament" and "New Testament" by Christians. He sees the terms as "damaging at all levels", "invidious", "anti-Jewish", symbols of "rejection" and "oppression". They perpetuate "traditional Christian attitudes to the Jews which range from arrogance and a sense of superiority to hatred and violence". As such, the language is "theologically indefensible". If, like racist and sexist language, the terms could be expunged from our vocabulary, then that could be a first step towards heightening awareness of problems in Christian attitudes towards Jews and towards reforming practical attitudes.

Some Christians may perhaps doubt whether such conventional terms can really be so apparently problematic. Moreover, as a Christian scholar myself who has just finished writing a book with the doubly heinous title *The Old Testament of the Old Testament*,[2] I am, not surprisingly, unpersuaded as to John Sawyer's main thesis. It would be appropriate, therefore, to respond briefly to his paper and suggest that he has in fact misunderstood the central point at issue.

To begin with, however, several areas of agreement should be noted. First, there can be no question but that there is much in the history of Christian attitudes towards Jews which is a matter of deep shame and which calls for repentance in so far as it still continues today. Secondly, there is great Christian ignorance about Jews and Judaism, and a major work of education is needed to correct false stereotypes (this is, of course, mutual, and Jews need similar education about Christianity). Nothing that is said in the following argument should be taken to call these two fundamental needs into question.

A further area of agreement is the implicit pluralism in Sawyer's approach. That is, he recognizes that the terms "Old Testament" and "New Testament" are terms specifically of Christian theology. They are therefore not necessarily proper to be used when the Bible is studied without the concerns of Christian theology setting the agenda. Herein is encapsulated much of the confusion about method and goal in modern biblical criticism. For the predominant concern of the last two hundred years has been, to use Jowett's famous phrase, to read the Bible "like any other book", that is, according to the agenda of the ancient historian, who seeks to handle the biblical texts in the same way that any

---

[1] *Theology* XCV (1991), pp. 269-278.
[2] Minneapolis: Augsburg Fortress, 1992.

other ancient texts would be handled. Yet the theological terms "Old/New Testament" imply that the material is privileged, and authoritative for today, in a way that other ancient texts are not, and so ultimately is *not* to be read "like any other book". To put it briefly, *how* we read the Bible depends on *why* we read the Bible, and unless the pluralism of legitimate stances towards the text is recognized, there is likely to be confusion. So when Sawyer observes that the British "Society for Old Testament Study" is not concerned to study the material according to the agenda of Christian theology but according to the agenda of the ancient historian, he is quite right to say that the name is inappropriate. It was adopted for general cultural reasons, at a time when the heritage of Christian privileging of the text as Scripture was still generally accepted in the West. Now that this is no longer the case, some fundamental rethinking is required, as Sawyer indicates.[3]

Beyond here, however, we part company. Partly this is because some of Sawyer's points are one-sided and overstated. To say that "Everyday expressions like 'Old Testament ethics' and 'the God of the Old Testament' suggest cruelty and ruthless legalism" (p.269) is simply untrue; I use the terms frequently, and neither I nor my students understand them in remotely the way he suggests. Moreover, to say that the Hebrew Bible is "not the same thing at all" as the Old Testament (p.272), mainly because of well-known differences in the ordering of the material, greatly inflates a relatively trivial point. Also, Sawyer does not take sufficiently seriously his own implicit pluralism. For example, he sees the interest of von Rad and Noth in a "Hexateuch" or "Tetrateuch" as serving "almost as if to deny the literary validity of the traditional Jewish grouping of the first five books of the Bible" (p.272); yet von Rad and Noth were concerned to formulate historical hypotheses about the origins and growth of the material and were not at all engaging with the question of the function of the material within Judaism. Sawyer is not comparing like with like.

Since the terms "Old/New Testament" are theological terms, the nub of the argument is whether they are theologically justifiable. Sawyer recognizes that there is a "theological judgement to the effect that the content of the 'OT' belongs to a period of God's dealings with the world which has been in some way superseded by the coming of Jesus Christ in the 'NT'" (p.273). But although he accepts that "for Christians, the coming of Christ changes things", he nonetheless rejects the theological argument for three reasons. First, the first Christians rejected any notion that "Hebrew Scripture itself was superseded". Secondly, "the Church recognizes no distinction between Isaiah and the Gospels in terms of inspiration and authority" and the Church often draws theological insights from Hebrew Scripture. Thirdly, the "problem with the supersessionist argument for preserving the traditional distinction between two parts of Christian Scripture is that it invariably tends to be related to a crude and

---

[3] Debate on this issue is more advanced in the USA than it is in England.

insulting view of Judaism as the religion of one part and Christianity of the other" (pp. 273-4).

The first two points relate to the historic Christian stance of privileging Jewish Scripture as fully Christian Scripture. This is beside the point, for the privileged status of the material is not in question. Indeed, there is something a little odd about Sawyer's argument in appealing to what "the Church recognizes" about Scripture while at the same time arguing that the terms which the Church has always used for Scripture are inherently corrupt. The point is not whether the Hebrew Scriptures are fully Christian Scripture, but whether the terms "Old/New Testament" say something inherently derogatory. So Sawyer's main argument is his third one, for he wants at all costs to resist anything that suggests the downgrading of Judaism.

The real difficulty is that Sawyer does not examine in what sense "for Christians, the coming of Christ changes things", and he uses the notion of "supersession" as an unanalysed bogey word. Let me suggest, therefore, that with regard to Scripture one of the main differences that Christ makes is with regard to religious practice. For the simple fact is that the Old Testament, in particular its centrally authoritative first five books, is full of prescriptions about appropriate religious practice on the part of Israel. The commands, for example, to observe the Sabbath, circumcise children, and keep the Passover are all commands of God himself, given in perpetuity. Yet Christians sit light to them all. They may observe equivalents - Sunday (in varying degrees of observance), baptism, and Easter - but this is hardly what the Hebrew text envisages. On what grounds can Christians revere this material as inspired and authoritative, and yet disregard its clear and crucially important precepts? The answer has always been to appeal to the notion of two dispensations: crudely, what was appropriate then for them is not appropriate now for us, because the coming of Christ has changed things. Indeed, one of the most characteristic of Jewish religious practices, the observance of *kashrut* (dietary laws) is clearly related to the distinctive status of Israel over against other nations (Lev. 11:43-5, 20:22-6) and is explicitly repealed in the New Testament (Acts 10); given that the Church is for Jew and Gentile alike, it is simply not possible for Christians to retain practices that speak of the unique vocation of the Jews, no matter how much they have divine authority within Hebrew Scripture.

I suggest that a study of Christian use of the Old Testament will reveal a consistent tendency to appropriate religious *principles* from the material and to neglect religious *practices*. The principles are, for example, belief in one God, who is personal, moral and sovereign; the dignity of human life, made in the image of God; the primacy for human life of such qualities as love, trust, obedience, mercy, forgiveness, hope; the living of the life of faith in community; the primacy of prayer in maintaining the relationship between God and humanity. These principles of Hebrew Scripture are common to Christian and Jew alike. Of course, in so far as these shared principles are related to other particular principles (for the Jew, the primacy of Torah, both written and oral, for the Christian the primacy of Christ crucified and risen) and are moreover embodied in particular practices and particular communities, they acquire distinctive moulding and emphases, which can keep their practitioners apart. But the important point for present purposes is that Christians appropriate the Old Testament as Scripture in so far as it illuminates and promotes these basic qualities of the Christian life. Where it does not do so - one thinks of the famous problems of the imprecatory psalms or holy war - the material is either set aside on the dispensation principle, or subjected to sophisticated re-interpretation.

Christian use of Jewish Scripture has, therefore, a peculiar logic to it in that, generally speaking, it keeps the principles and rejects the practices. But without appeal to the notion of dispensation - the coming of Christ changes things - there is no answer to the criticism that if Christians regard the Jewish Scriptures as authoritative, then they should do what they say.

For Jews, by contrast, the situation is different. Of course, Judaism is not the same as the "religion of the Old Testament" and stands at a considerable remove from it. But to say, as Sawyer does, that Judaism supersedes the religion of the Old Testament just as much as Christianity does is misleading, for they differ from the religion of the Old Testament in importantly different ways. For Christians, the coming of Christ is a qualitatively new divine revelation that necessarily in some ways relativizes and supersedes what went before. For Jews, there is no qualitatively new divine revelation. The status of Mishnah, Talmud, Targum and Midrash is, in principle, that of commentary, expounding and applying what is given in Scripture, but in no way superseding it. Even if in practice within rabbinic Judaism Talmud looms more largely than Scripture, the point of principle remains that Talmud does not in any way relativize or supersede Scripture. For the Jew there is a basic continuity, where there is a basic discontinuity for Christians. That is why the clear precepts of Torah - Sabbath, circumcision, Passover, *kashrut* - are still observed by Jews. However much the observance is indebted to post-biblical tradition, the point is the recognition of an obligation in some way to conform to the biblical precepts in a way that is not shared by Christians. However much Jews may differ among themselves as to the most appropriate way in which to observe the precepts, there is a clear logic to the Jewish position that is different from the logic of a Christian position.

To sum up, both Christians and Jews seek (at least in theory) to live a life of faith under the one God. But whereas for Jews the central theological concept around which all revolves is that of Torah, for Christians the central concept is Christ. With regard to Jewish Scripture, where Torah holds primary position, the Jewish position is relatively straightforward and easy to comprehend. The Christian position, at least as regards Jewish Scripture, is much less straight-forward, and needs justification. The notion of two dispensations, which is embodied in the language of "Old Testament" and "New Testament", provides that justification.

The fear may still perhaps remain, however, that the language of "Old Testament" is somewhat downgrading to a Judaism that stands in greater continuity with it than Christianity does. This is where I hope that my new book, *The Old Testament of the Old Testament,* may shed some light. For although it has generally been thought previously that the notion of two dispensations, with the corresponding language of "Old/New Testament" is unparalleled, I argue that there is in fact a close parallel in the very heart of Jewish Scripture.

When God reveals himself to Moses at the burning bush as YHWH (Exod. 3, esp. 3:13-15), this constitutes a new beginning, relative to the patriarchal traditions, that is comparable to the new beginning in Jesus Christ. Note in particular the clear statement in Exodus 6:3 that God was not known to the patriarchs by the name YHWH, which he now makes known to Moses. This implies a qualitatively new revelation of God (and I argue that it was characteristic of all the pentateuchal writers, and was not merely an idiosyncracy of P - the uses of YHWH in Genesis simply reflect the retelling of the material from a Yahwistic perspective, given the conviction that YHWH the God of Israel is none other than the God of the patriarchs). Thus there is one God, who successively reveals himself in different ways - the same problem as that of Old and New Testaments.

This issue of a qualitatively new divine revelation can be looked at from the other side. That is, there is the well-known hermeneutical problem of how Christians are to appropriate the Old Testament as Scripture - it is the same God, but things are different. Precisely the same problem, I suggest, was faced by the writers of the Pentateuch, when they were confronted by the patriarchal traditions. And I think it can be shown that the specific moves made by Christians - to go for the principles, rather than the practices, and to use the models of promise and fulfilment and typology - were precisely those moves made by the writers of the Pentateuch to appropriate the patriarchal traditions for Mosaic Yahwism and Israel.

If these contentions, which I argue for in detail in my book, are correct, then at least two things follow. First, the Christian idea of treating Hebrew Scripture as an Old Testament is justified by analogy with what happens within those Hebrew Scriptures themselves. Secondly, because the phenomenon happens in the heart of Jewish Scripture, there is a possibility of understanding it in a way that need not offend Jewish sensibilities. For one can see that although patriarchal religion has many affinities with Canaanite religion, and Mosaic Yahwism is bitterly opposed to Canaanite religion, yet there is never any polemic against the patriarchs. On the contrary, they are revered as the ancestors of Israel, and patriarchal religious practices, although often forbidden to Israel, are respected as appropriate to their time and place. Moreover, if one stands back and looks at patriarchal religion and Mosaic Yahwism each as coherent religious systems, one can see much that is admirable in each. The openness and lack of exclusivity characteristic of the patriarchal world (the one God relates to Abimelech and Pharaoh as to Abraham and Joseph; and there is almost no sense of choosing one deity and renouncing others, as in such a fundamental statement of Yahwism as Exod. 20:2-3) is deeply attractive to an ecumenical age. The moral depth and intensity of Mosaic Yahwism likewise presents a quality of human life that commands respect. And yet the two systems are to some extent incompatible, and one cannot simply marry the strong points of each together as in each case they are part of a total system.

Perhaps the relationship between Christianity and Judaism can be illuminated by this comparison. For it is difficult, and perhaps ultimately meaningless, to argue about whether patriarchal religion is superior to Mosaic Yahwism or vice versa. Both are God-given systems, and each has its own integrity. But from the point of view of the adherents of Mosaic Yahwism, for them patriarchal religion is no longer a valid option. So too for Christians, the observance of Hebrew and Jewish religious practices is no longer a valid option; but that should not preclude respect for those for whom it is.

THE NATURE OF CHRISTIAN BIBLICAL THEOLOGY

An interest in a theology of the whole Bible, as opposed to separate theologies of the Old and New Testaments, is no longer quite as idiosyncratic as it might perhaps have appeared a few years ago. In Germany, for example, there has been since 1986 an annual publication of a *Jahrbuch für Biblische Theologie*, with many distinguished mainstream biblical scholars (predominantly German) contributing. In USA there are journals such as *Biblical Theology Bulletin* and *Horizons in Biblical Theology*, or a series of books under the general heading *Overtures to Biblical Theology*. Indeed, the fact that H. Graf Reventlow can write a major bibliographic survey entitled *Problems of Biblical Theology in the Twentieth Century*[1] may suggest that the question has never in fact been far from the scholarly agenda.

Nonetheless, such appearances may be deceptive. On the one hand, attempts to produce a biblical theology, as distinct from discussions of its theoretical possibility, are few and far between.[2] Indeed, for many scholars the task is simply an impossibility in the light of the enormous diversity of material within the Bible, material diverse in origin and purpose, in form and content. If scholars are doubtful whether it is valid to speak even of NT/OT theology, rather than theologies, what hope is there for a biblical theology? On the other hand, there is as yet little agreement among the different advocates of biblical theology as to precisely what it is that they are advocating - fundamental differences of method and approach remain. As Phyllis Trible puts it, "Biblical theologians, though coming from a circumscribed community, have never agreed on the definition, method, organization, subject matter, point of view, or purpose of their enterprise".[3] In short, there is still everything to play for. The situation is well stated by Reventlow, who writes: "A 'biblical theology' has yet to be written. The way towards it is not only one of high hopes; it is also beset by a good deal of scepticism. It will only prove viable if premature solutions are rejected and all perspectives are considered comprehensively and with the necessary methodological care. 'Biblical theology' is in the widest sense of the term an exegetical, hermeneutical and systematic discipline".[4]

---

[1] London: SCM, 1986. ET from German of 1983.

[2] For a list, see J. Reumann (ed.), *The Promise and Practice of Biblical Theology* (Minneapolis: Fortress, 1991), p.5.

[3] "Five Loaves and Two Fishes" in J. Reumann (ed.), *The Promise and Practice of Biblical Theology*, pp.51-70. The quotation is on p.53.

[4] *Problems of Biblical Theology*, p.vii.

The purpose of this essay is not to be comprehensive but rather to focus on certain basic principles which, I suggest, are necessary if one is to produce a biblical theology that is to be truly a part of Christian theology. Since the major problem facing a biblical theology is, in my judgment, the need to distinguish it from yet another historical account of the religious beliefs and practices of ancient Israel and the early Church, we must start by seeing why it is that the religion of Israel and the early Church has taken the place that theology once had.

In the first place, one must note a major ambiguity in the term "theology". On the one hand it is often used of a descriptive historical account of any set of religious beliefs and practices. In this sense a theology of the Bible is no different an undertaking in principle from a theology of Homer or of the Enuma Elish or of the Qur'an; the aim is to describe the religious content of the texts as accurately as possible. On the other hand, theology is a constructive discipline within Christian faith which draws on the fundamental resources of the faith and produces accounts of how things in the present situation ought to be. It is vital that these two senses be carefully distinguished and not merged together. The one is the task of the religious historian, and the other is the task of the theologian proper. For clarity, therefore, I will refer to the former as history of religious thought and practice and reserve the term theology for the latter.

An understanding of the present context of debate must go back at least to the 18th century, to the famous inaugural lecture of J. P. Gabler, *De justo discrimine theologiae biblicae et dogmaticae regundisque recte utriusque finibus* ("On the Proper Distinction Between Biblical and Dogmatic Theology and the Specific Objectives of Each").[5] Whether or not Gabler's address in its own context had the kind of impact that it has had on subsequent thought seems doubtful, but the important thing is that it has become conventional to look back to Gabler's lecture as the first clear formulation of an approach that subsequently became commonplace; though it should be noted that many of the main lines of Gabler's thought had already been anticipated in the previous century by Spinoza in his *Tractatus Theologico-Politicus*.[6] The essence of Gabler's approach was to draw a sharp distinction between what the Bible meant in its original historical context and what it came to mean in subsequent ecclesiastical dogma, a distinction that had generally been lost sight of in theological debate.

Gabler's crucial contribution was twofold. On the one hand, he injected the consciousness of an historian into the reading of the biblical text and this has become received wisdom in most subsequent biblical study. Indeed, despite all

---

[5] For text and discussion, see J. Sandys-Wunsch & L. Eldredge, "J. P. Gabler and the Distinction Between Biblical and Dogmatic Theology: Translation, Commentary and Discussion of His Originality", *SJT* 33 (1980), pp.133-58.

[6] For a convenient edition see *A Theologico-Political Treatise* (New York: Dover, 1951. ET from Latin by R. Elwes).

the controversy that now surrounds the paradigm of historical approaches to the Bible, there can be no going back on its basic insights - if only for the simple reason that the Bible was written in ancient languages, Hebrew, Aramaic and Greek, and the more we know of those languages, which inevitably means knowing something of their cultural contexts, the better we will understand the Bible.

On the other hand, Gabler made the recovery of an historically aware reading of the Bible antipathetic to the use and interpretation of the Bible by classic Christian theology, for he was working in the context of the Enlightenment with its strong reaction, for various reasons, against the dogmatic orthodoxies of the Church, and this mood affected all the various branches of biblical and theological study. As C. K. Barrett has noted, "It is not accidental that the study of biblical theology, and the use of that term, go back to about the same period as the origins of what we call the quest of the historical Jesus".[7] The polemic against ecclesiastical dogmatisms, with a corresponding severing of links, led in due course to a study of the Bible according to the agenda and priorities of the ancient historian, untrammelled - at least in principle - by dogmatic concerns.

Of course, it is well known that the practice did not always live up to the principle, a fact which has been particularly evident to scholars who have not shared the Christian, and specifically Protestant, assumptions of most biblical scholars over the last two centuries.[8] Indeed, the fact that the distinction between the biblical text and dogmatic theology could be made to look like an extension of the Reformation dichotomy between Bible and Church, made it easy for the new historical approach to seem a natural companion for Protestant theology. Nonetheless, the fact remains that in principle it was generally accepted that the historical study of the Bible should be carried out without reference to the later ecclesiastical dogmas that had been based upon the text.

This second contribution of Gabler leads, however, to one particular problem that was not foreseen by Gabler himself. This is, quite simply, Why should the Bible be privileged over any other ancient historical document, or be assumed to have some special value for today? In academic terms, why should the study of the Bible (outside explicitly Christian institutions) be privileged by departments wholly or partly devoted to its study, and not instead be relegated to a subsection within other departments - either departments of oriental studies or

---

[7] "What is New Testament Theology? Some Reflections" in D. Y. Hadidian (ed.), *Intergerini Parietis Septum (Eph. 2:14): Essays...Markus Barth* (Pittsburgh: Pickwick Press, 1981), pp.1-22. The quotation is on p.3.

[8] See, for example, the comments from a Jewish perspective of J. D. Levenson, "The Hebrew Bible, The Old Testament, and Historical Criticism" in R. E. Friedman & H. G. Williamson (ed.), *The Future of Biblical Studies: The Hebrew Scriptures* (Atlanta: Scholars, 1987), pp.19-59.

classics, for the historical study of the Bible in its own right, or departments of literature or fine arts, for the cultural impact of the Bible within Western civilization? Until quite recently this issue has not usually been posed very sharply, or at any rate commanded widespread attention. This has been largely for cultural reasons - in the West, the Bible has been integral to Western religion and culture and so is still widely perceived as somehow special; although another factor has been that most of those engaged in studying the Bible have been Christians whose concern has been to promote a better understanding and use of the Bible within the Church.

Nonetheless, the situation has been fundamentally odd. For on the one hand the rhetoric of academic biblical study has been largely devoted to promoting an historical understanding of the text distinct from its later ecclesiastical appropriation. On the other hand, most biblical scholars have devoted their energies first and foremost to interpreting those texts that are found within the canon (other ancient texts often being interesting primarily as a means to that end), and they have assumed that their findings should have relevance for Christians today. That is, they have been guided by an ecclesiastical decision about the texts, i.e. a canon that is authoritative, that their historically-oriented rhetoric excludes. So, for example, there is a recurrent and never satisfactorily resolved problem that affects all attempts to write works of "OT/NT Theology" - how should these be distinguished from purely descriptive accounts of ancient religious belief and practice? Such works have generally been written by scholars concerned to relate their biblical study to the life of the Church, and so there has been a persistent feeling that their work should not just be of a descriptive historical nature but should also be constructive and prescriptive for faith today; that is, it should be theology as well as religious history. But this contemporary relevance has all too often been simply assumed rather than argued for (though of course Barth and Bultmann, among others, engaged extensively with the issue). As, however, Western culture becomes more pluralistic, people increasingly are studying the Bible without Christian assumptions; either from a religious perspective that is not Christian (there is a great resurgence of Jewish biblical scholarship) or from a purely secular perspective (historical, literary, or cultural). This means that the question of why the Bible should be given theological privilege can no longer be assumed but becomes a pressing problem.

The situation may be summed up by saying that scholars have on the one hand sought to read the Bible like any other ancient text (recalling Jowett's famous plea in *Essays and Reviews* in 1860 that the Bible should be read "like any other book"), and yet on the other hand have retained the ecclesiastical dogma of the canon which gives a privileged status to the biblical texts and implies that they should not be read like any other ancient text. (Debates among Christians as to the precise extent of the canon should not detract from the basic issue that Christians agree that scripture has a canon). The unsatisfactory, and indeed schizophrenic, nature of this is sharply pointed out by H. Räisänen in his recent *Beyond New Testament Theology*.[9] Instead of limping between two opinions, a choice should be made. Either treat the Bible as scholars treat other ancient religious texts, but don't assume that it should have any more (or less) relevance or authority today than any other major historical, literary or philosophical work from antiquity. This is Räisänen's preferred option, and has an obvious attraction for many a modern reader. In this context one should note the extensive recent interest in the Bible as a classic, with the same power to transcend its original culture that all great works have. Or treat the Bible as Christian scripture, which means adopting an ecclesiastical perspective from the outset, and treating it as authoritative for today precisely because it has a status different from that of any other book. Räisänen disapproves of this as too limited and potentially sectarian an approach. But the pluralism of modern society in no way denies the validity of a particularist stance within a given community of faith, particularly when in Christian theology particularity is espoused with universal intent.

Fundamental assumptions about the nature and purpose of one's study tend to be embodied in nomenclature. For example, there is a well known debate about the respective nature of, and relationship between, theology and religious studies. From this point of view, it might perhaps clarify matters if those scholars who quite legitimately are interested in the biblical texts as historical documents without prejudice to the question of their special relevance for today abandoned the theological and privileged terms "Old Testament" and "New Testament" and used non-theological names for the material. Alternative descriptions might be e.g. "The extant religious texts of ancient Israel as collated within early Judaism" or "Certain religious texts relating to the breakaway movement within Tannaitic Judaism focussed on Jesus of Nazareth, as collated within early Christianity". Since, however, such descriptions are too cumbersome for everyday use, abbreviated forms such as "Ancient Israelite Texts" and "Early Christian Texts" would serve perfectly well.

This question of nomenclature may be taken further through reflection on the recent great resurgence of Jewish biblical scholarship. For Jews, of course, the Old Testament is not an Old Testament at all, for they do not have a New Testament. They call their scripture simply "Bible" or "Tanakh" and tend to approach it in ways subtly but profoundly different from those of Christians, through the perspectives of Rabbinic Judaism rather than those of Christianity. A different starting-point makes for a difference in handling of the text.[10]

---

[9] Philadelphia: Trinity Press International, 1990.

[10] See e.g. J. D. Levenson, "Why Jews Are Not Interested in Biblical Theology" in J. Neusner, B. A. Levine, E. S. Frerichs (ed.), *Judaic Perspectives on Ancient Israel* (Philadelphia: Fortress, 1987), pp.281-307.

In recent years, the major alternative to the historical paradigm for biblical study has generallly been considered to be a literary paradigm. There is a current growth industry of literary approaches to the Bible, which bring hermeneutical issues to the forefront and engage' with questions of how the Bible can speak to the reader today in ways analogous to other great literature. The basic model here is of the Bible as a classic. In terms of nomenclature, "The classic texts of Israel and early Christianity" might perhaps characterize the subject matter according to this trend. Certainly, in the hands of its better practitioners many highly illuminating readings of the text have been offered (predominantly, and in my judgment significantly, these better practitioners in the Old Testament have been Jewish scholars such as Robert Alter and Meir Sternberg,[11] who, among other things, are creating an agenda more congenial to Jewish concerns with their background of close and imaginative readings of the text in midrash than the conventional historical agenda of liberal Protestantism). Although many Christians have naturally welcomed the newer literary approaches to the Bible, not least as a chance to escape from such old bugbears as the documentary hypothesis and the synoptic problem and those awkward questions about what *really* happened, the welcome should from a theological perspective be somewhat qualified. For despite the hermeneutical interests of many literary practitioners, the light that they shed on the question of how the Bible should function as Christian scripture, rather than solely as a great classic, is often hardly more than that offered by practitioners of the traditional historical paradigm.

From a theological perspective, the most significant developments have probably been "committed" approaches to the text, notably on the part of liberationist and feminist theologians. Where conventional historical criticism has had little to say about how the biblical text functions as scripture and engages with the values, beliefs, and practical priorities of people today, liberationist and feminist theologians have, in their different ways, sought to meet the need. Although it is too soon to say what the long-term contribution of such perspectives will be, particularly given their predominant nature as sectional protest movements, at the very least they should surely serve to remind the wider community of Christian biblical scholars that there are major areas of fundamental concern that their work is leaving untouched.

Perhaps the major difficulty here is that one of the great attractions of studying the Bible according to the agenda of the ancient historian was that it enabled scholars to escape from hoary old theological disputes and find a new common ground on which scholars of different persuasions could engage in fruitful discourse without being subject to *odium theologicum*. Yet this major

[11] See R. Alter, *The Art of Biblical Narrative* (London & Sydney: George Allen & Unwin, 1981); M. Sternberg, *The Poetics of Biblical Narrative* (Bloomington: Indiana UP, 1985).

strength is precisely the major weakness, for scholarship achieves safety only at the expense of removing the Bible from pressing contemporary concerns about which people feel strongly, which is precisely where the Bible has traditionally functioned, and where most Christians today still want it to function. Into this vacuum modern ideological concerns have now moved, and it is not difficult to see that the old *odium theologicum* is in fact alive and well, albeit in the mutant form of *odium ideologicum*. Those who value the relative calmness of historical debate may well regret the renewal of so much potentially acrimonious contemporary debate about the Bible. But insofar as one is concerned that the Bible should function authoritatively today such debates are inevitable. What matters is that controversial values and priorities should be neither ignored nor swallowed wholesale but rather be subjected to appropriate critical scrutiny.

To sum up. Basic questions about the presuppositions of biblical study are back in the melting-pot. This is particularly because of the breakdown of what one might call the post-Enlightenment liberal consensus, a breakdown which has been accompanied by a rise of cultural plurality within the Western world. Such plurality can help us see more clearly the fundamental principle - which has always been there but has often been obscured from view - that *how* we read the Bible depends on our particular stance and *why* we read the Bible. There is more than one perspective from which one may legitimately be interested in the material and each perspective will set its own agenda of questions and priorities in reading the text. A fundamental problem with the familiar historian's agenda has been the all-too-frequent imperialistic assumption that it is the only legitimate approach. Of course no responsible interpretation will abandon the insights to be gained from historical study; yet to accept such insights does not entail acceptance of the overall agenda and priorities of the historian. On the one hand this means that one must accept a legitimate plurality of readings of the biblical text. On the other hand, this means that a reading according to the agenda and priorities of the Christian Church has a validity which is ultimately the validity of the Christian Church itself. And this should hardly be surprising, since it is the continuing vitality of the Christian Church that preserves the presupposition that the Bible may be approached with expectations about its significance for readers today which no other book has. In cultures where the Christian Church is marginal, assumptions about the significance of the Bible are correspondingly minimal; and space given to its academic study follows in proportion.

If one accepts the validity of academic biblical study according to the agenda of the Christian Church, then the basic objection to doing theology of the Bible as a whole, rather than separately of the Old Testament and New Testament, disappears. For the increasing academic separation of Old Testament from New Testament is ultimately the consequence of the acceptance of a "Gablerian" agenda of historical study in conscious opposition to so-called ecclesiastical dogma of which the canon is a prime example. The basic problem of a "Gablerian" agenda is that quite simply it threw out the baby with the bathwater; or, to put it differently, it was hermeneutically naif. Of course it was legitimate for rationalism and pietism to react against the prevailing scholasticism of ecclesiastical biblical interpretation, which too easily isolated texts from their literary and historical contexts and attributed meanings that were overly indebted to the contexts of postbiblical theological debate. But from a theological point of view, all this means is that the Church was using its distinctive perspective on scripture badly, not that it was wrong to use its distinctive perspective at all. It remains appropriate, indeed necessary, that the Bible as a whole should be interpreted from the perspective of Christian faith. As J. D. Levenson has succinctly put it, "Practicing Jews and Christians will differ from uncompromising historicists, however, in affirming the meaningfulness and interpretive relevance of larger contexts that homogenize the literatures of different periods to one degree or another. Just as text has more than one context, and biblical studies more than one method, so Scripture has more than one sense, as the medievals knew and Tyndale, Spinoza, Jowett, and most other moderns have forgotten".[12]

What, then, might a biblical theology composed according to the agenda of the Christian Church look like? Clearly it will utilize appropriate historical insights, but it will eschew the agenda of the ancient historian as such. Rather, it will be concerned to interpret the text in ways that are as far as possible of common concern to all the various branches of the Christian Church in their great diversity.

If one starts by focussing on the actual use of the Bible within many Christian churches, at least three areas of concern emerge. First, there is the public reading and exposition of the Bible in the context of worship, where the primary concern is to preach and teach from scripture. The object of this is on the one hand to mould the general worldview and understanding of the worshipper and on the other hand to give general practical guidance to enable greater faithfulness in daily living. Secondly, there is the devotional reading of scripture in private, where the concern is the personal appropriation of biblical insights for everyday life - the classic form of which is the monastic *lectio divina*, but which exists in numerous other contemporary forms, aided by lectionaries, study guides, and daily Bible reading notes. Thirdly, there is the constant struggle of the Church to appropriate the ethical insights of scripture, so as to work out what it means to live as a truly Christian community in the complex context of the modern world.

---

[12] "Theological Consensus or Historicist Evasion? Jews and Christians in Biblical Studies" in R. Brooks & J. J. Collins (ed.), *Hebrew Bible or Old Testament? Studying the Bible in Judaism and Christianity* (Notre Dame: University of Notre Dame Press, 1990), pp.109-45. The quotation is on p.143.

In all these contexts, the Bible is used in the service of what might broadly be categorized as Christian spirituality, that is how one should live life under God both communally and individually. To focus on spirituality in this way should not of course be seen as anything particularly novel, for in a sense it is simply to restate the content of the classic New Testament statement about the function of scripture, that it is "profitable for teaching, for reproof, for correction, and for training in righteousness, that the man of God may be complete, equipped for every good work" (2 Tim. 3:16-17).

I suggest, therefore, that the primary and explicit purpose of a biblical theology should be to relate the Bible to the needs and concerns of the spirituality of the Christian Church, that is it should inform the corporate and individual living of the life of faith. If this is what the Church uses the Bible for, then this is what its biblical theologians should be doing to help them. Biblical theologians will of course presuppose the work of theologians active in other areas who use scripture in their own way there. For if the contemporary Christian life of faith is to be meaningful it must be undergirded by appropriate historical, systematic, philosophical and ethical explorations and formulations. But the demarcation between biblical and other theologians is *not*, as so often supposed, that the biblical theologian produces the raw material of a historical analysis of Israelite and early Christian belief and practice, which the systematician then transmutes into real theology. Rather, the biblical theologian works theologically with the text in the area of the dynamics of the life of faith, while other theologians work in their own areas and so make their own different contributions to the total edifice of Christian theology. And of course it should go without saying that these different divisions of theological labour need to work in mutual dialogue with each other.

With regard to a biblical theology of the life of faith, it should also be said that however much the theologian should stand within the particular context of the community of faith, this particularity should in no way serve as an excuse for insularity or for defensiveness. That is to say, the biblical theologian should be open to dialogue with other modern critical disciplines outside Christian theology, and be willing and able to incorporate relevant insights from them as seems appropriate. Generally speaking, the two most significant areas seem to me to be the social sciences, for insights into the communal nature of human belonging and believing, and psychology, for insights into the nature and development of the human mind. Such interdisciplinarity may well make one ask "Who is sufficient for these things?"; but the simple point remains that if one is to produce an account of the nature of the spiritual life that both does justice to its normative formulations in scripture and that is appropriate to the modern context, then one cannot simply take refuge in the great riches of past Christian tradition, but one must work through and critically appropriate other relevant areas of modern human understanding. Just as the Bible seemed at one time to be dissolved into a mass of historical fragments and to lose its significance for contemporary faith, yet is now beginning to reemerge from its historical dissection with a depth and potential in some ways greater than it had before, so too a Christian understanding of the life of faith may expect to emerge from the critical dissolution of sociological and psychological analysis with renewed vigour.   What one is looking for is a second naivete, an understanding which has gone through and survived the fires of criticism and which, although it stands in continuity with traditional Christian affirmations, knows that the second naivete is not to be confused with the first naivete of pre-critical simplicity.

If biblical theologians thus seek to interpret scripture so as to bring it to bear upon Christian spirituality, how should they go about this? Among the many things that could be said, a few preliminary points will have to suffice for the present. Generally speaking, the biblical theologian will be willing to follow the lead of the biblical writers in continuity with the classic stance of the Church.   The basic issues at stake here are metaphysical and theological questions about the nature of truth and reality. Although it is always potentially risky to generalize in this way, two examples may perhaps help clarify the point.

First, there is the acceptance of monotheism as a postulate. Most modern biblical study of monotheism has been devoted to a history of monotheism as a religious concept in ancient Israel, i.e. when did Israel's religion become monotheistic and how did the development relate to its historical context?[13] Options usually range from Moses to Second Isaiah and the trauma of the Exile, with a general preference for the latter. In the New Testament monotheism is already accepted as a postulate, though of course the development of Christology in relation to monotheism poses interesting issues of its own. What has at any rate become clear historically is the great diversity of religious belief and practice in ancient Israel and that for much of biblical history it is doubtful how far monotheism was a generally accepted concept. But how does this historical insight relate to the clear portrayal of the Bible taken as a whole that there is in fact only one God, however imperfectly this may often have been grasped. As J. A. Sanders puts it, "I am satisfied that the canon as a whole, of whichever Jewish or Christian believing community, pursues ultimately the 'Integrity of Reality', that is, the ontological and ethical oneness of God"; though he goes on to sound the cautionary historical note, "I do not believe that the vast majority of people or their leaders in either ancient Israel or Judah managed to monotheize very well".[14]

---

[13] See e.g. D. L. Petersen, "Israel and Monotheism: The Unfinished Agenda" in G. M. Tucker, D. L. Petersen, R. R. Wilson (ed.), *Canon, Theology, and Old Testament Interpretation: Essays in Honor of Brevard S. Childs* (Philadelphia: Fortress, 1988), pp.92-107.

[14] "Canon as Shape and Function" in J. Reumann (ed.), *The Promise and Practice of Biblical Theology*, pp.87-97. The quotation is on p.92-93.

One of the most interesting illustrations of this issue within the Bible is Exod. 6:2-3, "And God said to Moses, 'I am YHWH. I appeared to Abraham, to Isaac, and to Jacob as El Shaddai, and by my name YHWH I did not make myself known to them'". This epitomizes the point that Israel's religion and its knowledge of God as YHWH first came about through Moses, and that patriarchal religion in its ethos and practice was distinct from Mosaic Yahwism (and I have argued elsewhere that this represents the point of view of all pentateuchal writers, and is not just the peculiarity of P).[15] Now in terms of religious history it is not at all clear how the religion of the patriarchs themselves, insofar as it can be discerned, relates to the religion of Israel, not least with reference to what sort of deity they believed in; but the historian is likely to agree with Exod. 6:3 that the patriarchs did not believe in YHWH. Nonetheless it is the clear understanding of the writers of the Pentateuch that the deity of the patriarchs is in fact none other than YHWH who is the one God who revealed himself also as El Shaddai; and the writers make this point clear through the freedom with which they tell the patriarchal stories, especially that of Abraham, in terms of YHWH. What for the religious historian is a mass of varying beliefs and practices of uncertain historical relationship is for the biblical theologian, following the theological understanding of the writers of the Pentateuch, one God revealing himself in different ways. And the same considerations of course apply to the theologian's adoption of the New Testament conviction that it is none other than the God of Abraham and the God of Moses who is also the God and Father of Our Lord Jesus Christ.

As yet, relatively little work has been done on the monotheistic nature of the biblical canon as a whole, especially in the critical area of the Old Testament. But not only is there the kind of monotheistic interpretation of Israel's early traditions that we have just noted, but there is also the fact that the canon is prefaced by the unambiguously monotheistic stories of creation and the unmaking and remaking of creation in the flood which show clearly that the whole world without exception is beholden to the one God who is the sole supreme power. The effect of the placement of these stories of creation and flood at the outset of the Old Testament is that they form a kind of lens through which the rest of the Old Testament is read. They therefore encourage a more monotheistic reading of passages which in their original historical context might have had a slightly different sense. For example, the famous requirement of the first commandment "You shall have no other gods before me" (Exod. 20:3) could in its historical context allow that there are indeed other gods but that Israel is not to choose them. In a canonical context, however, the natural tendency is to deny that other gods have any reality beside the one God and therefore to interpret the reference to other gods as either referring to inferior

---

[15] See my *The Old Testament of the Old Testament* (Overtures to Biblical Theology; Minneapolis: Fortress, 1991), esp. ch.2.

spiritual beings or else as essentially *ad hominem*, that is to reject what other
peoples choose to regard as their gods, whether or not they have any ultimate
reality.   Whatever the vagaries of historical Israelite religion, the mature
interpretation that is put upon Israel's many traditions is that in fact there is only
one God and therefore everything is to be rethought and reread in this light.
And this is a process to which Israel's traditions lend themselves without
difficulty, because they were already tending in this direction.

It is here, incidentally, that one finds the basic key to the question of unity
and diversity.   Acceptance of the premise of monotheism means that the whole
biblical witness is to one God.   Whatever the diversity of witness to this one
God, it is the acceptance that it is one God - i.e. the adoption of the basic stance
of Christian or Jewish or Islamic faith - that makes it meaningful to subsume
biblical diversity under an overarching unity and provides a justification for
speaking of theo*logy* rather than theo*logies*.   The historian of ancient religion
necessarily can only produce theologies, in the sense of descriptive accounts of
diverse beliefs about the divine.   The biblical theologian can produce theology, a
constructive and prescriptive account of the diverse self-revelation of the one
God.

Given the premise of monotheism - indeed ethical monotheism, as classic
tradition has rightly interpreted it - the task of the biblical theologian is to
explore what it means to live life with the understanding of one God as the
ultimate reality.   Because of its traditional philosophical appeal, monotheism
has perhaps tended to be too easily taken for granted.   For it is, after all, hardly a
self-evident way of understanding a world in which evil and suffering are
rampant, and there is always a temptation to dilute monotheism by so promoting
the status of other spiritual beings - angels or the devil - that one is left with a
dualism or pluralism of ultimate powers.   It is vital therefore to probe those
biblical passages that most explore the nature of monotheism.   First, there is the
story of creation in Gen. 1 which sees the whole world as the work of the one
God and the object of his delight (for "good" in Gen. 1 is more an aesthetic than
a moral judgment).   Secondly, there is the story of the Flood in Gen. 6-9 which
by telling of the unmaking and remaking of creation explores the way in which
ultimately the very existence of human life, including human sinfulness, exists
by the mercy of the one God.   Thirdly, there is the book of Job which starkly
explores the nature of suffering in relation to the one God.   Fourthly, there are
the psalms of lament in which people effectively appeal to God against God;
here the practical implications of monotheism are keenly felt.   Fifthly, there are
the monotheistic exhortations of Isa. 40-55, which encourage practical
confidence in the one sovereign God and pour scorn and ridicule on all
alternatives.   The task of theologians is so to probe these passages that they can
spell out the kind of metaphysical framework within which the life of faith is to
be lived, a metaphysical framework whose primary interest lies not in itself as

such but in its practical implications for the kind of attitudes that are appropriate to humans who live in such a context.

A second example of the way in which the biblical theologian has to handle basic issues of truth and reality may be seen in the concept of election, as classically expressed in the words of Jesus in the Johannine portrayal, "You did not choose me, but I chose you" (Jn. 15:16). It would hardly be controversial to claim that an understanding of the dynamics of election as divine initiative and human response (whether or not mediated through Christ) is consistent throughout both Old and New Testaments, and indeed that the concept of election is as fundamental to biblical theology as is monotheism. Yet the concept is a subtle one that raises important issues of method and assessment.

One major issue revolves around the fact that election is a far from self-evident interpretation of life. Indeed, generally speaking, a common feature of life, whether that of groups or of individuals, is that the process at work appears to be the opposite of the principle of election. That is to say, the common pattern is that people, for whatever reasons, appear to be choosing God. It is only subsequently that the process comes to be understood as a response rather than an initiative. But if one has come to see that what at the time looked like an initiative was in fact a response, then how does one tell the story? If, as is entirely appropriate, one retells it in the light of one's mature understanding, it is likely to be a significantly different story from what one might have told at the time. This change of perspective points to an important difference between the religious historian and the theologian. In terms of the religious historian's agenda, the imposition of a later perspective upon an earlier risks being an obfuscation. The historian will insist on maintaining the two separate stories, both how it was at the time and how it came to be seen later, with a methodological inability to allow the fusion of the two stories into one story. Yet from the theologians's perspective, it is only the fusion of the two stories into one story that tells what *really* happened.

In terms of biblical narrative, it is clear that it is consistently presented with a fusion of perspectives, so that the reader may see what was really going on. For example, whatever the patriarchs themselves may have thought at the time, they were in reality being chosen by YHWH to be the forerunners of Israel.

What we see in the case of election we often see elsewhere. It is a common feature of human life under God that what God is doing or what is really happening may not always be apparent at the time but only afterwards. Even the historian who is concerned as far as possible to reconstruct how things were at the time needs the benefit of hindsight to be able to distinguish the wood from the trees. How much more so the theologian whose concern is to interpret what is happening in categories that do not have the same empirical quality as those of the historian. Biblical narratives in both Old and New Testament are written with the benefit of reflection after the event to make their meaning clear. There is the constant danger that the historian's desire to distinguish between event and interpretation risks removing from the biblical story precisely those elements that were deliberately designed to make it significant in the first place. In John's Gospel, for example, the historian may reasonably doubt the likelihood as to whether Jesus actually uttered the words "I am the bread of life" and "I am the light of the world" (Jn. 6:35, 8:12). But for the theologian the question of truth resides not in whether or not Jesus said the words or in exploring the self-consciousness of the historical Jesus but in whether or not one accepts that Jesus is as fundamental to life as bread and light. And that is a question that cannot be resolved except by the test of living the Christian life of faith.

It is here that the much-debated issue of interpreting the final form of the text becomes relevant. This is not some kind of dogmatic principle, but rather has two straightforward justifications. On the one hand, interest in the final form of the text attempts to do justice to the fact that the biblical narratives have extensive theological interpretation built into them precisely to make their content intelligible and accessible to their readers. It is natural, therefore, that the theologian who is concerned to follow the lead of the biblical writers will feel doubtful about the helpfulness of penetrating to earlier forms of the tradition, however much it may be allowed that this is a perfectly valid and legitimate undertaking for the historian. On the other hand, it is the final form of the text that is encountered by the Church in general in its reading of scripture. If this is the form in which the text is encountered, this is the form in which questions about its meaning and truth will primarily be raised. Of course, the theologian will often consider it appropriate to explain dimensions of the text in terms of its possible prehistory. But the object of this should be to illuminate, rather than undercut, the nature of the text in its canonical form.

How then might a biblical theology be structured? The first issue must be that of the relationship between the testaments, or, in other words, the position of Christology. Here at least two basic points may be made. First, there is a sense in which a theology of the whole canon relativizes or diffuses Christology. It is not Christ as such but rather God who is the primary unifying category. However much one may legitimately interpret the Old Testament christologically, any theology which gives proper weight to the Old Testament as a valid witness to God in its own right must recognize that christological interpretation represents a particular kind of rereading the material that is not the only valid way. Alternatively, christological interpretation becomes diffused in the sense that one primarily looks for those elements that in some way are compatible with or tend towards the New Testament portrayal of Christ. Nonetheless, Christ must remain the ultimate norm for any Christian biblical theology.

Secondly, the basic mode by which the New Testament utilizes the Old Testament is to appropriate most of its religious principles and interpret them christologically and to reject many of its religious practices. In place of these rejected religious practices are substituted alternative Christian religious practices as appropriate (esp. baptism and Lord's Supper in place of circumcision and passover). Thus, for example, belief in one sovereign moral God is retained from the Old Testament as is belief in the dignity of humanity made in the image of God and the sinfulness of humanity which generally fails to live up to its vocation. Fundamental religious attitudes such as justice, mercy, forgiveness, love, hope are continued, together with such basic religious practices as prayer, fasting and almsgiving. But whereas in the Old Testament these practices are centred in the sacrifical worship of the Temple, in the New Testament they are centred in the non-sacrificial worship that is focussed in Christ.

An analogy to this can be found in the Old Testament itself, in what I have called The Old Testament of the Old Testament. When God reveals himself to Moses at the burning bush as YHWH, this constitutes a new beginning relative to the patriarchal traditions that is analogous to the new beginning in Christ. Or, to put the same point differently, the Yahwistic writers of the Pentateuch were faced with the same hermeneutical problems arising out of the patriarchal narratives as Christians have been faced with arising out of the Old Testament. Each time there is a sense that it is the same God but that things are different and therefore appropriate moves must be made to overcome this difference. Again, the religious practices of the patriarchs were widely ignored but their religious principles were largely adopted. Abraham in particular was seen as a model for the faith of Israel.

It is this continuity of religious principle across different dispensations that gives rise to what is often misleadingly called "timeless truths". The point is that such things as love, justice, mercy and prayer are so religiously fundamental that they are able to be embodied in a variety of ways and to transcend any particular embodiment. This is why biblical theology should focus on spirituality, because it is the dynamics of life under God that is the most constant factor running throughout the biblical material.

What further considerations might be appropriate for structuring a biblical theology? I suggest that its basic structure should revolve around the language and concepts of personality and personal relationships. For it is perhaps the deepest and most persistent emphasis of the Bible, and of the Jewish and Christian faiths that relate to it, that God is personal, that humanity in the image of God is personal, and that the relationship between God and humanity is best understood by analogy with personal relationships. Of course, the terms "person" and "personality" are concepts that need careful conceptual analysis if they are to have a cutting edge; but that they are, when defined and used carefully, indispensable to biblical and Christian theology is hardly in doubt. Thus the three basic concepts that will structure a biblical theology will be a personal God, human life that is endowed with personality, and the relationships between God and humanity.

Further, it is a fundamental principle that the relationship between God and humanity is always one of divine initiative and human response. Although there is indeed an important biblical emphasis on God's responsiveness to humanity, to upright human action and to prayer, the context in which people can in some way make a difference to God is always a context that is created by God in the first place. Although the obvious biblical category for expressing this is election, perhaps the most basic way of expressing it is, in John's famous words, "God is love" (1 Jn. 4:8,16). Love, of course, is a term so widely used and misused that, like person, it needs careful analysis and definition; but again, carefully used, it is indispensable to biblical and Christian faith. It has always been at the heart of the Christian faith that God is love. This is an apt characterization of the biblical message, not just because of the explicit statement of John, or even because this is the precise tenor of the most extended description of the character of God in the whole Bible, a description significantly set on the lips of God himself (Exod. 34:6-7), but because it is the consistent thrust of all the biblical material that God reaches out to humanity for their good. It is this initiative of God that then sets the context for appropriate human response, both to God and to one another; again, in John's words, "We love (or, Let us love), because he first loved us" (1 Jn. 4:19).

There are several advantages in taking "God is love" and "We love, because he first loved us" as an interpretative key to biblical theology. First, it characterizes something that is as constant as anything is throughout scripture, despite the many forms that it takes. Secondly, such a formulation represents common ground between the major Christian bodies (and to some extent between Christians and Jews). Although, for example, Protestants tend to depict the heart of biblical spirituality in terms of the primacy of faith, it is clear that the dynamics represented by faith - the trusting response of humanity to the initiative of God - is equally represented by the language of love. Thirdly, the primacy of love offers a possible resolution to some of the difficulties posed by the necessarily Christological focus of Christian faith. Certainly for Christians the love of God and our resultant love for one another is given definitive content by Christ in his incarnation, death and resurrection (as classically stated again by John - 1 Jn. 4:9-12). But although for Christians this Christological content is primary, it still remains possible to give content to the love of God without such Christological content, for this is what is entailed by taking the witness of the Old Testament seriously. This is where a Christological reading of the Old Testament needs to be leavened by an historical awareness, to the effect that the Christological reading is a rereading of the text in the light of Christ that introduces a perspective that was not originally there. A biblical theology should both give primacy to the particularity and finality of Christ as the supreme manifestation of the love of God and recognize that the love of God may yet intrinsically have a content that need not be Christological.

One final point will suffice to round off this exploratory prolegomenon to a biblical theology. This is that the arrangement of material should probably in general be topical. This is common in treatments of the Old Testament but unusual in the New where the tendency is to opt for the message of particular writers. The reason for this is that the concerns of spirituality most naturally fall into topics. Some of these topics will be already familiar, most obviously those that structure the life of faith, such as God, humanity, Christology, election and covenant. But other topics should enable one to discern aspects of the text that are sometimes overlooked, for example, the dynamics of repentance or of waiting on God or of prayer, or the relatively neglected theme of spiritual discernment which includes not only the well-known topic of true and false prophecy in both Old and New Testaments but also the recurrent biblical theme of people's constant inability to see what God is doing even when it is before their very eyes.

Ultimately, however, the proof of the pudding is in the eating. The vital task is not just to discuss the possibility of biblical theology but actually to do it in a way that is exegetically rigorous and hermeneutically enterprising. If this prolegomenon is found to be basically on the right lines, it will give some idea of the kind of biblical theology that I hope may emerge in due course.

South Florida Studies in the History of Judaism

240001	Lectures on Judaism in the Academy and in the Humanities	Neusner
240002	Lectures on Judaism in the History of Religion	Neusner
240003	Self-Fulfilling Prophecy: Exile and Return in the History of Judaism	Neusner
240004	The Canonical History of Ideas: The Place of the So-called Tannaite Midrashim, Mekhilta Attributed to R. Ishmael, Sifra, Sifré to Numbers, and Sifré to Deuteronomy	Neusner
240005	Ancient Judaism: Debates and Disputes	Neusner
240006	The Hasmoneans and Their Supporters: From Mattathias to the Death of John Hyrcanus I	Sievers
240007	Approaches to Ancient Judaism: New Series Volume One	Neusner
240008	Judaism in the Matrix of Christianity	Neusner
240009	Tradition as Selectivity: Scripture, Mishnah, Tosefta, and Midrash in the Talmud of Babylonia	Neusner
240010	The Tosefta: Translated from the Hebrew: Sixth Division Tohorot	Neusner
240011	In the Margins of the Midrash: Sifre Ha'azinu Texts, Commentaries and Reflections	Basser
240012	Language as Taxonomy: The Rules for Using Hebrew and Aramaic in the Babylonia Talmud	Neusner
240013	The Rules of Composition of the Talmud of Babylonia: The Cogency of the Bavli's Composite	Neusner
240014	Understanding the Rabbinic Mind: Essays on the Hermeneutic of Max Kadushin	Ochs
240015	Essays in Jewish Historiography	Rapoport-Albert
240016	The Golden Calf and the Origins of the Jewish Controversy	Bori/Ward
240017	Approaches to Ancient Judaism: New Series Volume Two	Neusner
240018	The Bavli That Might Have Been: The Tosefta's Theory of Mishnah Commentary Compared With the Bavli's	Neusner
240019	The Formation of Judaism: In Retrospect and Prospect	Neusner
240020	Judaism in Society: The Evidence of the Yerushalmi, Toward the Natural History of a Religion	Neusner
240021	The Enchantments of Judaism: Rites of Transformation from Birth Through Death	Neusner
240023	The City of God in Judaism and Other Comparative and Methodological Studies	Neusner
240024	The Bavli's One Voice: Types and Forms of Analytical Discourse and their Fixed Order of Appearance	Neusner
240025	The Dura-Europos Synagogue: A Re-evaluation (1932-1992)	Gutmann
240026	Precedent and Judicial Discretion: The Case of Joseph ibn Lev	Morell
240028	Israel: Its Life and Culture Volume I	Pedersen
240029	Israel: Its Life and Culture Volume II	Pedersen
240030	The Bavli's One Statement: The Metapropositional Program of Babylonian Talmud Tractate Zebahim Chapters One and Five	Neusner
240031	The Oral Torah: The Sacred Books of Judaism: An Introduction: Second Printing	Neusner